ANGLICANS
AND
ORTHODOX

For the peace of the whole world; for the stability of the holy churches of God, and for the union of all, let us pray to the Lord.

In memory of the late Canon William Davidson Cooper (1904–1978), priest and historiographer of the Scottish Episcopal Church who entrusted to the present writer (when a student of no status or repute) the cause of the Scottish Nonjurors and their aspiration to Orthodox Communion. This work is a belated honouring of that trust.

ANGLICANS
AND
ORTHODOX

Unity and Subversion 1559–1725

Judith Pinnington

GRACEWING

First published in 2003

Gracewing
2 Southern Avenue
Leominster
Herefordshire
HR6 0QF

ISBN 0 85244 577 6

Typesetting by Action Publishing Technology Ltd, Gloucester GL1 5SR

Printed in England by
Antony Rowe Ltd, Eastbourne BN23 6QT

CONTENTS

ACKNOWLEDGEMENTS

The first seed of this book was sown by Metropolitan Seraphim of the British Orthodox Church with a view to a series of informative articles in the *Glastonbury Bulletin*, but over almost ten years the project has grown far beyond the original idea of a mere chronicle. Right 'up to the wire', as it were, it has gone through major modifications of perspective.

There has been no overall advice except latterly from Professor David Melling, who read the penultimate draft carefully and critically, and from others, from time to time, veiled advice not to proceed at all! One might say that the book has been prepared largely in academic and ecclesial isolation. It suffers from that isolation in many respects, but working at a great distance from other writing in the field has perhaps encouraged a certain 'objectivity' in the author which has made possible reflections of a kind which closer contact with other specialists might have made difficult.

Since 2000, Chapter 3 has benefited from some wise comments by Dr George Bebawi, the Academic Director of the Institute for Orthodox Christian Studies in Cambridge. Chapter 1 should have benefited more than it has from exchanges with Professor Patrick Collinson, Dr Richard Rex and Dr Anthony Milton. Chapter 4 has been illuminated by conversations about John Covel with Mrs Michelle Courtney, Librarian of Christ College, Cambridge, and with Archimandrite Efrem Lash.

Thanks must be extended for the groundwork help offered

by Mr Stephen Gregory and Miss Georgette Stavrou, former librarians of the late and much lamented Sion College Library which made possible the maximum use of the library's seventeenth-century books in a very limited amount of time. Thanks must also be extended to the staff of the Public Record Office, the British Library and the Bodleian Library for making the briefest of visits extremely rewarding. It has more recently been a great pleasure to be able to browse at will in the Dimitri Obolensky collection in the Library of the Institute for Orthodox Christian Studies.

Friends and acquaintances at Cambridge who are much more competent in information technology than the author have repeatedly helped to move log-jams. In this regard special mention must be made of Professor David Frost, Ruary Grantham and Jenny Bailey. David Frost also read the pre-Cambridge draft with enthusiasm and commended it to Gracewing Publishing.

The book is abjectly indebted to the personnel of Gracewing for tolerance towards repeated mishaps in the production of a text since that fateful day of 11 September 2001 when the first face-to-face discussions about publication took place in the knowledge of what had happened to the World Trade Center a mere two and a half hours earlier. That event has inevitably hung over the whole transaction during the intervening year. Mercifully Tom Longford has not overtly had misgivings about an interest which he showed in such a heightened atmosphere.

Gratitude also needs to be expressed for the support shown by Archbishop Rowan Williams and Bishop Kallistos. One way or another, Bishop Kallistos has been a constant presence in the life of the author since undergraduate days at Oxford, while Archbishop Williams has been a steady support in the wilderness time of the last twenty years through a shared membership of the Jubilee Group. It is flattering to enjoy the advocacy of two such distinguished figures at the end of a not nearly so distinguished academic career.

On a more personal note, I owe more than I can say to my friend and companion in faith, Revd Liz Wells, for mingling with mine her painful pilgrimage from the rancour of Christian division to true *koinonia* in Christ. Our starting points were so different, but we recognize in each other the same dereliction and need for healing.

Finally thanks are due for the tolerance and understanding of colleagues on Cambridge City Council for easing duties at critical points in the preparation of the final text.

Cover Illustrations

Front cover
18th-century copper engraving of Gloucester Hall, Oxford.

Back cover
Inscribed tablet in the Cathedral of Aghia Sophia, Bayswater, commemorating the foundation of St Mary's Church, Crown St, Soho in 1677.

(*Photograph: London Metropolitan Archives*)

The inscription reads:
In the year of Salvation 1677, this Temple was erected for the Nation of the Greeks, the Most Serene Charles II, being King, and the Royal Prince Lord James being Commander of the Forces, the Right Reverend Lord Henry Compton being Bishop, at the expense of the above and other Bishops and Nobles, and with the concurrence of our Humility of Samos, Joseph Georgirenes, from the Island of Melos.

PREFACE

If this is in any sense a strange or unusual book it must be
largely due to its author's hybrid background – engaged in
Orthodox Tradition, committed to a lifelong study of Anglicanism and grounded in the modern history discipline chrono-
logically before becoming involved in theology. A former
departmental chairman in a graduate ecumenical programme
once said he preferred his church historians to have been first
grounded in 'secular' history. The wisdom of this view has
been born out by decades of subsequent work in the field.
'History', writes the Dominican scholar Father Christian
Duquoc, 'represents a principle of reality which is too rarely
respected ... The Church is inseparable from its history.' He
detects 'official and traditional reticence' about how history
affects our perception of scripture, sacraments and councils,
among much else. History has both a positive and a negative
role in our consciousness, even when it comes to our church
commitment. It 'creates' institutions and, as Duquoc says, the
institution 'prevents the contingent trace from being swallowed up in forgetfulness or death'. Yet at the same time any
group, including Christian believers, 'tends to hold in its
memory that which glorifies it'; turning history into a particular 'celebration'. There is an IRA history, a Palestine Liber-
ation Movement history, an Israeli history, a Serbian history,
an Albanian history, a Japanese, German, French and Russian
history – and yes, a Welsh, Scottish and English history. The
'needs of memory', says Duquoc, 'nourish a Manichaeism of

individuals and events'. Memory thereafter takes on an apologetic form: it 'separates itself from effective history'. If one is true to 'scientific' history, even in one's exposition of a religious tradition, one will find that it 'speaks of what is lost' and lends plausibility to our 'inability to incorporate the freedom of the kingdom in the system of social relationship', thereby helping us – if we but let it – to avoid creating 'false celebratory narratives of our Christian history' which ignore the harsh uncertain realities of all history'.[1]

For these reasons, this book makes no attempt to surround the seventeenth-century Orthodox Church with a cloak of untouchability, for although to the eyes of faith it may be eucharistically centred for all eternity in the life of the Trinity and the Communion of Saints, it is also a creature and victim of time. It is necessary for this book to have any value that the reader should see the seventeenth-century Orthodox Church through the eyes and perceptions of those Anglicans who then encountered it.

That quintessential Anglican scholar Eric Mascall once referred with characteristic understatement to the 'non-theological factors' in Christian disunity. There are some who would deny that there can ever be such a thing as a non-theological factor in such disunity because everything making for it must come down to a question of sin and sin is, by definition, theological. Such a view might usefully be contemplated by those modern 'professional' ecumenists who function as if Christian division was simply a consequence of semantic misunderstanding to be politely discussed and 'ironed-out'. But any serious church historian will know that encounters between very different Christian traditions, especially those at two stages removed from one another, have always been fraught with social and cultural difficulties which are often quite beyond people's ability to handle or even conceptualize. Sometimes an anthropologist can see this more clearly than either a theologian or a historian. This book seeks to explore just such an encounter. It may look quite different now from the way it looked three centuries ago. If we fail to come to terms with the difference, then we are always going to fall into hidden elephant-traps in our most sincere search for unity.

A brief historical overview is necessary for the sake of those readers to whom it was never taught at school or university. The Eastern and Western parts of the Christian Church gradually fell apart between the so-called Photian schism in the ninth century and the excommunication of Michael Caerularios, Patriarch of Constantinople, by Cardinal Humbert in 1054. In succeeding years Eastern Christians were alienated from the 'West' still further by the sacrilegious sacking of Constantinople by the 'Frankish' forces of the Fourth Crusade in 1204, aided and abetted by the avaricious mercantile state of Venice, and the temporary replacement of the Byzantine Emperor and Patriarch by Latin nominees. After the restoration of the Byzantine Emperor in 1261, the Byzantine Empire was increasingly under pressure from the expansionist Turks. With some understandable distaste, it sought military assistance from the West, using its church hierarchy through two 'reunion' councils, that of Lyons in 1274 and that of Florence (Ferrara) in 1438–45 to weight the balance in its favour. It did not work. The Western princes wanted too much as a price for their military aid and the theological compromises made by some of the Greek bishops were forcefully repudiated 'at home'. The Turks pressed on relentlessly and captured Constantinople in 1453, turning the great Cathedral of Holy Wisdom into a mosque. The more perceptive in the West belatedly grieved: the composer Guillaume Dufay wrote a motet bewailing the fall of Byzantium. Others concentrated their attention on 'salvaging' Greek manuscripts for their own intellectual adornment and soon forgot calls to crusade to recover the city of Constantine. In any case, western Europe in the fifteenth century was on a rollercoaster to intellectual and social fragmentation. The Fifth Lateran Council of 1512–17 failed to stem the drift to chaos. The Augustinian Martin Luther was in Rome during the Council but turned aside in dismay to follow a different path. The West was split by the Reformation. England, which at various times might have remained with the Latin Church, eventually – for reasons of continental influence and dynastic accident – adopted a mediating role, repudiating Rome, recognizing the sovereign as 'supreme governor' of the Church, retaining much of its medieval structure but incorporating in a not very systematic way many continental Reformed attitudes. This hybrid Church, calling itself from the start 'Catholic and Reformed', maintained an uneasy unity through the reigns of Elizabeth I, James I and Charles I, through the channels of Crown and Parliament and the episcopal courts and visitational procedures. Some bishops adhered, more or less, to the Calvinist positions brought back by the 'Marian Exiles' after the collapse of the papal restoration under Queen Mary: others attempted to treat the Geneva and Frankfurt positions as open questions to be debated in the context of the long traditions of the Fathers and the Schoolmen. Richard Cheney, Elizabeth's Bishop of Gloucester, sustained lengthy theological debates with the 'Puritans' on this basis, regarding himself as standing firmly in Catholic tradition. By the end of Elizabeth's reign, while the delicate balance was still maintained, a clear Anglican-Catholic tradition could be seen to emerge in Overall, Field, Andrewes, Crackenthorpe, and Bancroft among others, and by the reign of Charles I a now consolidated tradition stood off against an increasingly militant Puritan movement, with some of its members, notably Bishop Richard Montague of Chichester, even willing to negotiate with the irenic Franciscan Christopher Davenport in an effort to reconcile the Thirty-Nine Articles with the decrees of the Council of Trent.[2]

It was these 'Caroline Divines' who rediscovered the Greek Fathers and indeed, with the help of new editions coming off the continental presses, became more expert in them than were most of the modern Greeks. This discovery had a marked impact on their way of looking at Reformation issues and when the outcome of the Civil War led to the collapse of the Church of England in any way they could recognize it and virtually disenfranchised them as church leaders, it led to an increasing interest in coming to closer quarters with the Eastern Church. We see that process starting during the Interregnum with Bishop Cosin's contacts in Paris and then after the Restoration of Charles II we see the interest transplanting itself to Constantinople and issuing in the main substance of this book.

In Chapters 1 and 5 there will be references to *Scottish* bishops. Here is a further complication of an intricacy far too great for this humble preface to sustain. In 1560 the Church in Scotland was forcibly reformed according to the Genevan model. A few bishops were left in possession of their 'temporalities' for several years, but the government of the Church became prebyteral. In the 1590s James VI determined to restore the episcopate and the new wave of bishops included at least one High Churchman who, as the reader of Chapter 1 will see, was as knowledgeable of the Greek Fathers as any of the English Carolines. But they differed from their English counterparts in having few of their mind among the lower clergy and laity. In 1638 the Covenanters against 'English' ecclesiastical policy (notably the imposition of the 1637 Prayer Book) swept the bishops aside and so the situation remained until the Restoration of the monarchy in 1660, after which episcopacy was reinstated. During the Restoration period Scottish society polarized on religion as never before. While the Presbyterian 'covenanter' element persisted and at one stage was a threat to royal government in Scotland, for the first time since the Reformation a solid body of clergy and laity espoused what might be anachronistically called 'Anglican' views. This meant that when, following the Revolution of 1688-9, the Scottish Parliament dispossessed the bishops yet again, they had enough grassroots support to maintain ecclesial life on a voluntary basis. They aligned themselves with those English bishops who, while having withstood James II's efforts to enfranchise Roman Catholics and Protestant Dissenters, refused to renounce their oaths to him at the Revolution in favour of William and Mary and took a small number of clergy and laity into 'NonJury'. Together we find Scottish and English NonJuring bishops and divines negotiating with the Greek Patriarchs and the Russian Holy Synod in Chapter 5.

Historical circumstances and shifts in mental climate frustrated all these efforts to re-establish links with the Christian

East and it was left to the Victorian period, in the light of the Oxford Movement, to pick up the threads again. From the 1870s onwards, some Anglicans began to think that they had the measure of 'Eastern Orthodoxy'. They imagined not only once again that they might have some affinity to it but also that their tradition had a favoured position with the Orthodox. How often since then has one heard ordinary Anglicans confidently say that *of course* the Orthodox recognize their orders! In the generation before 1870, the generation which saw Britain at war with Orthodox Russia in the Crimea, a handful of English churchmen had striven to build bridges. Of these, John Mason Neale, the great hymnographer, was the most outstanding for his theological acumen, empathy and skill in communication. Plagued by chronic ill-health throughout his short life, he was not able to spend time in Orthodox lands: sickness prevented him from accompanying Bishop Alexander Penrose Forbes of Brechin to Russia as his chaplain. Despite this handicap, his achievement was immense, not only in his translation of Greek hymns for Anglican use but also in his great scholarly project on the history of the Eastern Patriarchates, which he never lived to complete. Before Neale, chaplains and consuls in the 'near' and 'middle' East had sent home reports of variable value, and there were travellers' tales, like those of Thackeray and Kinglake, part romantic, part salacious. But there was nothing that could be called normal relations with the Orthodox nor any sound basis for understanding that could be accessed by the theologically literate reader.[3]

Direct Anglican contact with the Orthodox took institutional form with the founding of the Eastern Churches Association in the 1860s. An account of the visit of Henry Parry Liddon and Charles Dodgson (the begetter of Alice) to Russia in 1867 was published.[4] There followed in 1869 and 1870 a tightly chaperoned visit to England by Archbishop Lycurgos of the Cyclades and senior Anglicans participated in the Bonn Reunion Conferences alongside Orthodox, especially that of 1874 of which Liddon, Bishop Christopher Wordsworth of Lincoln and Bishop William Rollinson Whittingham of Maryland were the most senior. Without question the *intellectual* catalyst for all this activity was Neale's published work, but that alone could not have the urgency which built up over a short period of time. It required also a public event and the most powerful public event to serve that purpose was the Crimean War. R. F. Littledale in his preface to a little book on the Eastern Churches, published in 1870 in the wake of Archbishop Lycurgos's visit, wrote:

> Several attempts had been made at an earlier period to attract the attention of Englishmen to the venerable Orthodox Communion, but the labours of Rycaut, Covel and King[5] had no practical issue and were unknown beyond a very narrow circle of scholars, as proved to be the case, even in our own day, with the still more learned toils of Dr Neale. It was impossible, however, for thoughtful men to find themselves engaged in a war in defence of the Crescent against the Cross, without meditating on such a singular inversion of the old Crusading spirit, and desiring to Know somewhat more of that unfamiliar type of Christianity with which they were being brought face to face. Ever since that time a lively interest in all which concerns the religious usages of the Christian East has been roused amongst us and has been fostered by the graceful and brilliant, if not accurate and profound, work of Dean Stanley.[6]

When the main text of this book had been completed but publication delayed by unavoidable circumstances over many years, the writer had an experience which all scholarly writers fear may happen when publication of their work is deferred – the discovery of a newly published book which appears to plough the same furrow. The book in question is Father Arthur Middleton's *Fathers and Anglicans: the Limits of Orthodoxy* (Gracewing, Leominster, 2001). This work by a senior parish priest in County Durham had also probably been long in gestation. One might guess that its origin might be found in the Anglo-Orthodox Society and its journal *Anglo-Orthodoxy*. Both the Society and its journal are now history,

replaced in historical evolution by *Pilgrimage to Orthodoxy*
and more latterly by the British Deanery of the Antiochian
Orthodox Church. When Father Middleton started his work
his aim must have been in some sense to save Anglicanism for
Orthodoxy, albeit a *western* Orthodoxy. It is no longer clear
whether such an aim is even a remote possibility if one under-
stands Anglicanism in its current institutional form. World
Anglicanism seems to be in a very fissiparous state. In his
book he undoubtedly establishes a historic tradition of Anglicanism which is 'Orthodox' in some very fundamental sense.
But perhaps the only hope for that tradition is now as a
remnant – the fate of the NonJurors once they had lost their
footing in the constitutional settlement of the Church of
England after the Revolution of 1688. What would happen if
the Church of England was finally disestablished it is difficult
to say, but it is *prima facie* unlikely that many more clergy,
let alone congregations, would look to world Orthodoxy than
have already done so in recent years. Even the NonJurors,
with all their fresh patristic learning, had only tiny communities in back-street oratories.

The Middleton book fortunately does not duplicate the one
now being offered, although it covers a good deal of the same
ground as that covered by Chapter 1. It is essentially a study
of Anglican theological *method*, whereas the present book is a
study of *resources* and *mindset*. There is a common perspective linking the two books – a vision of incarnational ecclesiology, which must find room for the 'patristic mind'. It is
encouraging that an Anglican and an Orthodox can meet on
that ground even in these disorienting times. Father Middleton's discussion has a leisurely pace, unconfined as it is by
historical narrative and perspective, especially by the sordid
mess of ecclesiastical politics. As a result his vision is more
crystalline than the reader will find in the present book, which
tends more to the volcanic! Each major figure treated by
Father Middleton has a chapter or a major part of a chapter to
himself, so that it is easy for the reader to obtain a thumbnail
sketch. What he does *not* attempt to do, except in the final
section, is to give a feel for the unstable ground on which

these theological giants stood in their search for spiritual coherence. That is essentially the territory of this book.

In addition to *Fathers and Anglicans*, there is one other volume, yet to appear (the estimated time is Spring 2003), which readers concerned with the issues might profitably consult when it becomes available through the academic publisher Peter Lang AG. This is a set of papers delivered at a conference held in Worcester College Oxford between 30 August and 2 September 2001 under the general title *Anglicanism and Orthodoxy 300 Years after the 'Greek College' in Oxford*. Some of the papers deal with issues not dealt with here except in passing, such as that of Professor Brown Patterson on 'James VI & I, Archbishop George Abbot and the Greek Orthodox Church', that of Dr Colin Davey on 'Metropanes Kritopoulos and his Studies at Balliol College from 1617 to 1622' and that of Professor John Barron on 'Archbishop Joseph Georgirenes and the Pre-history of the Greek College'. Even those papers which do overlap with what is found here – those by Dr Charles Miller on Thomas Smith and by Archimandrite Efrem Lash on John Covel – are useful in their own right for a different perspective and (in the case of Father Efrem's paper) some additional background material on the origins the Arnauld/Claude controversy. A paper by Bishop Kallistos of Diokleia on the clandestine conversion to Orthodoxy of the Fifth Earl of Guilford at the end of the eighteenth century throws a penetrating light on the loss of sensitivity to Orthodoxy among the British 'establishment' during the period between the efforts of the NonJurors to enter into communion and J. M. Neale work in the 1850s and 60s. Papers by Father Donald Allchin, Father Gregory Woolfenden, Canon Chad Coussmaker, Professor William Green and Father John Jillions update Anglican-Orthodox contacts to the point of the setting up of an Institute for Orthodox Christian Studies at Cambridge in 1999. Professor Green's paper on the Anglican-Orthodox Theological Commission was as enlightening as his informal comments on its future were unsettling. Anglicans concerned with the future dialogue should consider coming forward with material support for the Institute, because its economic future is still by no means assured at the moment of writing.

The dedicatee of this book, the late Canon W. D. Cooper, who died many years ago after a lifetime of study of the old 'Pisky' tradition in Scotland, would not have recognized his beloved Scottish Episcopal Church had he survived into the 1990s, although he began to see the writing on the wall in the early 1960s. Likely he would have searched in vain for the living trinitarian pattern which had guided his life as it had guided the life of John Skinner the Elder in the eighteenth century. It would have been like looking for a programme on a computer whose systems have been corrupted. Hopefully, however, this small book, together with Father Middleton's volume and the forthcoming set of conference papers, may to some degree vindicate the trust he placed in those who came after him and be recorded in the Book of Life.

One last-minute comment is made necessary by the extended editorial process. Bishop Kallistos offered some important suggestions and corrections but at a very late stage in the proof corrections where regretfully not all of them could be accommodated without disrupting the text. Those points which could be accommodated have been; the rest will be gratefully borne in mind in any future writing.

Judith Pinnington
Cambridge
Commemoration of the Hieromartyr Cyprian
Bishop of Carthage and St Aidan, Bishop
of Lindisfarne, 31 August 2002

Notes

1. Christian Duquoc, OP, *Provisional Churches, An Essay in Ecumenical Ecclesiology* (London, 1986), pp. 24, 27, 30-1, 33.
2. Cf. John Berchmans Dockery, OFM, *Christopher Davenport, Friar and Diplomat* (London, 1960).
3. The most recent biography of Neale is that by Michael Chandler, *The Life and Work of John Mason Neale, 1818-1866* (Leominster, 1995). See also Leon Litvak, *John Mason Neale and the Quest for Sobornost* (London, 1994). This contains a literary analysis of Neale's work on Greek hymns.

4. See Michael Chandler, *The Life and Work of Henry Parry Liddon (1829-1890)* (Leominster, 2000), pp. 32-4, 145-6, 149.

5. John Glen King, Anglican chaplain to the St Petersburg embassy in the 1760s, published the first English translation of the Slavonic service books, prefaced by a very long introduction. There is a list of subscribers appended to the book which could be used to research the range of interest in the subject at the time. An article on King is in preparation.

6. *The Holy Eastern Church: A Popular Outline of its History, Doctrine, Liturgies and Vestments, By a Priest of the English Church. The Preface by the Rev. Dr Littledale* (London, 1870, 2nd edn. 1873), pp. vi-xi. The reference is to the work of Arthur Penrhyn Stanley, Regius Professor of History at Oxford, later Dean of Westminster, *Lectures on the History of the Eastern Church* (London, 1861). As a 'Broad' Churchman, Stanley was not well-equipped to access a patristically-based community. He called the Orthodox a 'petrified Church'.

FOREWORD

by The Most Revd and Right Honourable
Dr Rowan Williams, Archbishop of Canterbury

There have been studies before now of the history of relations between Anglicans and Orthodox; but I cannot think of any that have shown quite as much patient exploration in so wide a variety of original sources. This is the monument of decades of scholarship and reflection. We meet here a succession of well-meaning but rather puzzled Westerners, trying to make sense of Levantine churches which have every claim to be the kind of primitive non-papal paradise they could approve of, yet which look remarkably different from what a Western reformed historian would have imagined. There is a good deal of entertainment to be had from these pages in the misfire of perception and interpretation so typical of these encounters.

But the serious and deeply original point that emerges is to do with what is needed to understand both a contemporary Christian community that does things differently from us, and the reality of church life in the past in *its* difference from us. Dr Pinnington rightly pinpoints the dwindling vocabulary available to late seventeenth-century Anglicans for thinking about the given objectivity of the work of grace in a sacramental body. For many Anglicans of this era, as a thinner and drier view of reason began to dominate, the significance of the Church of the Fathers became more a polemical construct than a living community in which people had experienced the transforming power of the triune God through prayer and sacrament. In other words, there is a limit to the success of any Church history or doctrinal history that ignores the question of how humanity is transfigured in Christ; and when we know that, we also have more resources for understanding some of the variety in contemporary Christian experience and expression.

In the seventeenth and early eighteenth centuries, the encounter was often between Anglicans whose vision was distorted by both cultural snobbery and a cerebral, text-bound theology, deprived among other things of monastic anchorage, and Orthodox who, as harassed and undereducated minorities, had no way of articulating their own heritage in a way that pointed to the active transformation of persons by grace. Dr Pinnington rightly leaves us with some very searching questions about the proper language and register for ecumenical discussion, and the need for realism all round as to the histories of advantage and disadvantage that mould how we read the experience of others. At the heart of this book is an eloquent call to be aware of the full reality of the Church as mystery and gift. It is a delight and a challenge to read.

+ Rowan Cantuar:

INTRODUCTION

by the Right Revd Bishop Kallistos of Diokleia

Reading the work of Dr Pinnington, I called to mind a pamphlet that came into my hands some fifty years ago, written by Michael Ramsey, later Archbishop of Canterbury, and entitled 'The Church of England and the Eastern Orthodox Church: why their unity is important'. As Archbishop Michael indicates, Anglicans have long had the sense of a 'special relationship' with the Orthodox. He recalls the petition in the *Preces Privatae* of the seventeenth-century Bishop Lancelot Andrewes, in which he prays 'for the whole Church, Eastern, Western, our own'. 'In recovering the ideal of non-papal Catholicity', says Archbishop Michael, the Church of England 'looked instinctively to a Catholicism which embraces both East and West. Rome, Luther, Calvin could not do this. The Anglican divines could and did.'

It is Dr Pinnington's aim to explore more fully the implications of this 'special relationship'. Focussing upon the seventeenth century, she shows in fascinating detail how widespread at this time was the Anglican interest in Eastern Orthodoxy. Allowing proper scope to non-theological factors, she seeks to contextualize her chosen witnesses, noting how they each had their own personal agenda. The story is recounted here from the Anglican standpoint; another book could, and I hope will some day, be written viewing the encounter through seventeenth-century Orthodox eyes. Dr Pinnington has presented us with a work of original scholarship on a theme of major significance. I am grateful for the many things which this work has taught me. It deserves to be read by anyone seriously concerned with Christian unity.

It was unfortunate that during the seventeenth century, when so many Anglicans were sincerely seeking to learn more about Orthodoxy, the Orthodox themselves were singularly ill-placed to respond to Western overtures. Dr Pinnington speaks rightly of the tragic 'brokenness' of the Christian East at this time, suffering as it was under Turkish domination. If in the pages that follow the Orthodox seem often to speak with an uncertain voice, we should not forget the severe difficulties which they had to face. Yet the Turkish era was not simply a period of 'brokenness' for Eastern Orthodoxy but equally a time of hidden glory. In the words of one who figures prominently in this book, the English consul at Smyrna, Paul Rycaut, 'The stable perseverance in these our days of the Greek Church . . . notwithstanding the Oppression and Contempt put upon it by the *Turk* . . . is a Confirmation no less convincing than the Miracles and Power which attended its first beginnings. For indeed it is admirable to see and consider with what Constancy, Resolution and Simplicity, ignorant and poor men keep their faith.'

The story told in this book ends on a note of failure, with the collapse of the negotiations between the Orthodox Patriarchs and the Anglican Nonjurors in the early eighteenth century. Have the doctrinal discussions of the twentieth century been any more successful? Obviously there is much less mutual ignorance; personal contacts are today incomparably easier than they were three hundred years ago. But even so, organic unity seems still a long way off. The high point in Anglican–Orthodox *rapprochement* came during the 1920s and 1930s, especially at the Bucharest conference in 1935. By contrast, the official Joint Doctrinal Discussions, inaugurated at Oxford in 1973 and still in progress, have proved a disappointment to both sides. The participants have produced two agreed statements, at Moscow in 1976 and at Dublin in 1984. These are full of valuable insights, but have had virtually no impact upon the daily life of Christians in either church community. Is that not the problem with almost all 'official' ecumenism? Its deliberations seem to take place *in vacuo*.

Sadly, due to the emergence within Anglicanism of an ever-increasing liberalism, in both doctrinal and moral questions – due also to the unhappy growth within Orthodoxy of a harsh and intransigent integrism – the two sides are markedly further apart today than they were sixty years ago, or for that matter in the seventeenth century. Yet surely this does not mean that we should grow fainthearted in our eirenic efforts. As Arcbishop Michael reminds us, in the pamphlet from which I have already quoted, 'Nothing in the world matters more than the fulfilment of the prayer of our Lord "that they may all be one".' He is right to speak of prayer. Discussions between theological experts, so Dr Pinnington insists in her epilogue, are never sufficient. What is needed far more is a prophetic vision, a sense of eschatological urgency. There can be no progress without repentance – without *metanoia*, in the full sense of a change of mind and heart – and without a continually renewed openness to the Holy Spirit. Visible unity will come about only through a miracle from God. It is our task, however, to prepare ourselves for that miracle.

Even if the twentieth-century Anglican–Orthodox dialogue has not brought about reunion, it has none the less fostered countless friendships on a personal level, and this is vitally important. Such personal friendships were less common in the seventeenth century but they were not unknown, as can be seen for example in the career of Patriarch Metrophanes Kritopoulos, so vividly recorded by Dr Colin Davey. From such ecumenical friendships the future reintegration of Christendom may gradually develop. As Cardinal Suenens has emphasized, in order to unite we much first love one another, and in order to love one another we must first get to know one another.

May Dr Pinnington's book contribute to this reciprocal knowledge and this shared love.

Kallistos Ware
Bishop of Diokleia

'Despite all our technical progress, our basic ignorance still remains. We do not understand our own nature, our own inner capacity to become, by God's grace, Christ's Body upon the earth ... Social structures do not exist apart from the human spirit. The harm of structures and systems comes from the destructive actions human beings commit through them.'

Emilianos Timiadis, Metropolitan of Sylivria. Representative of the Ecumenical Patriarch to the World Council of Churches, 1959–1984, *Towards Authentic Christian Spirituality* (Brookline Mass., 1998), pp. 105, 119.

'... the world we live in is a world in which we do not have clear paths open before us: we are not able normally to decide on a simple course of action and carry it through without opposition, or the need for adjustment and adaptation ... We are still refusing to look at certain other human beings in the trust that we shall see in them Christ's image. And it is that failure to look which cuts us off from certain specific human embodiments of grace, and so from the fullness of our own hope and salvation.'

Rowan Williams, Archbishop of Wales; Archbishop of Canterbury from 2002, *The Truce of God* (London, 1983), pp. 25–26, 41.

'If this report – since there is such a frequent mention of sources – should at times be felt to be "fluid", we beg the reader's forgiveness: it has been unavoidable. To speak of "sources" and "fluidity" is to preclude all possibility of composition, so perhaps we should instead introduce the concept of "bringing together", of "conduction", a concept that should be clear to anyone who as a child (or even as an adult) has ever played in, beside or with puddles, draining them, linking them by channels, emptying, diverting and rerouting them until the entire available puddlewater potential is brought together in a collective channel to be diverted on to a different level or perhaps even duly rerouted in orderly fashion into the gutter or drain provided by the local authorities. The sole object here, therefore, is to effect a kind of drainage. Clearly a due process of order. So whenever this account appears to be in a fluid state in which differences in and adjustments to level play a part, we ask the reader's indulgence, since there will always be stoppages, blockages, siltings, unsuccessful attempts at conduction, and sources "that can never come together", not to mention subterranean streams, and so on, and so on.'

Heinrich Böll, *The Lost Honour of Katharina Blum Or How Violence Develops and Where it can Lead*, Tr. Leila Vennewitz (London, 1975), p. 8.

PROLOGUE

GREEK ARCHBISHOP AND SAXON PASSION BEARER

Pascal in one of his *Pensées* said: 'The last thing one discovers in composing a work is what to put first.' The chance discovery in a bookshop window display in Magdalene Street, Cambridge, of a book on Edward Aetheling, the forgotten son of King Edmund Ironside, made the original Chapter 1 seem a tame beginning for a work which aspires to being more than a simple narrative. Hence this afterthought of a Prologue.

Nowhere has the record of Britain been more distorted than in its ecclesiastical history and its underlying dynamic. The broad pragmatic categories of 'western' and 'eastern' Christianity which barely pass muster on a wider canvas are, in the case of Britain, and especially the 'English Church', deeply damaging to reality. It is easy to assign Christian life in that sector over many centuries to 'the West'. And, indeed, by force of immediate pressures from the continent of Europe, the English Church, in both its unreformed and reformed states, makes layers of sense as a 'western' entity. Its canon law clearly belonged to a western pattern of canon law moulded by concepts of Roman jurisprudence; its reformed Articles bear a family resemblance to those in Germany and Switzerland; its unreformed Liturgy is identifiable as belonging to a post-Gregorian 'Roman' family of Liturgies, with regional, in particular 'Sarum', variations. But the spirituality of the medieval English Church, to be found quintessentially in Julian of Norwich and Richard Rolle, differs markedly from trends in western Europe and finds echoes in 'eastern' hesychasm.

Therefore it is not unduly odd to see around the English Church a shadow or penumbra of something that is not simply 'western' and which may indeed be fairly described as 'Byzantine'. That shadow has been shorter or longer depending on immediate circumstances. Consciously perceived 'eastern' affinities may have been relatively shortlived compared with the periods of nescience. Nevertheless they left their traces and demand both due honour and a sort of reconciliation. This is surely part of what the search for wholeness in the Christian ecumene is all about.

The first extensive period of 'Orthodox shadow' was the seventh to eleventh centuries, the consolidation period of Anglo-Saxon culture. Awareness of the Greek Fathers was fostered by the appointment of Theodore of Tarsus as Archbishop of Canterbury in 668. Although probably educated in Athens, Theodore was living at Rome when he was recommended to Pope Vitalian as a possible Archbishop of Canterbury. Under him the monasteries of SS Peter and Paul and St Augustine at Canterbury became centres of Greek learning, and Bede writes in his *Ecclesiastical History* of many scholars who were as 'well versed in the Greek and Latin tongues as in their own'. This, it has to be remembered, was a time when the Church in Rome was still in its initial phase; its worship was a mixture of Greek and Latin, and as the researches and recorded reconstructions of the musicologist Marcel Perès have shown the resultant mix was more Byzantine than Roman as we have come to know it from a slightly later period. Theodore brought with him numerous Greek manuscripts which formed the core of the library of St Augustine's monastery.

There was considerable coming and going between the Byzantine empire per se and Anglo-Saxon England after Theodore's day. There is a record, even, of a Greek bishop at the court of King Edgar. Many of the less exalted Greek visitors were refugees from the Iconoclast conflict. These brought with them ikons which had a profound effect on Saxon sensibilities.

Signs of that effect are still to be found at Winchester. Professor Donald Nicol has written that during the late Saxon period Constantinople 'acquired a mystical significance for the English', so much so that King Edward the Confessor sent envoys to the Emperor to enquire concerning the meaning of a dream that he had had concerning the Seven Sleepers of Ephesus.

In the last years of Saxon England there is evidence of a diminution on the number of scholars skilled in construing Greek, but there was no diminution of Byzantine awareness, an awareness which is reflected in the large number of English people making the pilgrimage to Jerusalem via Constantinople.[1]

Edward the Confessor stood on the cusp of irreversible change, not merely in dynasty but also in ecclesiastical orientation. Although he was married to a Norman and had a markedly Norman court, he had no intention at first – perhaps never – to see a Norman takeover after his childless death. Whatever the truth or falsity of the rumours that he sent Earl Harold to the court of Duke William to do a deal, before that he had had every intention of being succeeded by a Saxon kinsman and indeed made extraordinary efforts to ensure it. The successor he had in mind was Prince Edward, known as the Aetheling, and Edward had been brought up at Kiev as a model Byzantine.

Prince Edward, as a child of but a few weeks, together with his elder brother Edmund (also an infant), was carried away to Baltic lands by a self-sacrificing Danish noble who feared that his master Canute would seal the Danish conquest of England after the death of the children's father, King Edmund Ironside, by 'eliminating' them also in the age-old fashion of teutonic *kingship*.

In due course the royal children arrived in Kiev where they were warmly received by their distant uncle, Yaroslav the Wise. Yaroslav and his Metropolitan Theopemptos educated them in Byzantine ways. The children had arrived in Kiev at a time of immense religious and cultural development, when many monasteries – including the famous Monastery of the

Caves – were founded and the city was fast becoming a 'city of beauty and culture', an image of Constantinople, complete with its Hagia Sophia cathedral. Like Constantinople, it claimed a tenuous foundation by St Andrew and, at the hands of the Prince and his Metropolitan, the people received a legal code claiming to be based, like the Constitution of Justinian, in 'grace and truth' and to be a salve for sin. In due course, with Yaroslav's blessing, Edward was married to the ducal kinswoman, Agatha of Friesland, and fathered the future St Margaret of Scotland, the wife of Malcolm II.

Yaroslav had it in mind that the brothers should play a part in his grand design of a Northern-Eastern alliance in the face of the Normans and the residual elements of the Frankish empire. This had clearly anti-papal implications. In 1054, Yaroslav strongly resisted the blandishments of the triumphalist Cardinal Humbert. In sending the English princes to Hungary in order to assist the exiled sons of St Stephen to regain the Magyar throne for Christianity, he was aware of Venetian and Roman infiltration on the other side. Several Latin bishops were executed. The elder Edmund died – seemingly in battle – but Edward survived and his presence in Hungary became known to the Confessor who sent for him to become heir presumptive to the English throne.

Edward arrived on the south coast late in 1057 but immediately fell victim to a conspiracy, presumably in some way involving Godwin and Harold of Wessex. There is a bafflingly laconic reference to his murder in the Anglo-Saxon Chronicle. With it Yaroslav's grand design began to fall apart. Its prospects depended not only upon Edward Aetheling's accession but also upon the continued unity of the Rus. Yaroslav had consciously gone against the fissiparous traditions of Nordic society which generally ended in the partition of kingdoms among quarrelsome sons. He aspired to a true sense of imperium; he may even have called himself 'Ruler of the North' and used the Byzantine imperial formula 'to accomplish unaccomplished things'. In that sense it became him to construct vast international alliances. But unlike the Bulgar rulers he avoided claiming the imperial title, preferring to 'enjoy full membership in the pan-European family of Christian princes, marrying his children to the kings and princes of Norway, France, Hungary, Poland and Germany'.

As Edward Aetheling was returning to his birthplace out of a sense of duty, Yaroslav was dying and in dying perpetuating the appanage or 'udely' system of his ancestors, with Kiev the patrimony of an elder son whose brothers were disinclined to recognize the suzerainty of Kiev, as he himself had done from the Novgorod of his youth. Whether Edward the Exile could have held the alliances together, we shall never know. That he would have resisted the growth of Roman imperium is virtually certain in the light of his Hungarian experiences. The record of his military exploits in Hungary, although fragmentary, shows that he was certainly no weakling.

After Harold's encounter with William of Normandy and his subsequent overthrow by the invading Normans, nothing was left of the grand design or of any real hope of England's continuance in the Byzantine sphere, although a shadow of a shadow persisted in Edward Aetheling's daughter. As Queen of Scotland, Margaret patronized the semi-Coptic Culdee hermits of Lochleven and encouraged her sons Ethelred and Edgar to do likewise. Her principles of spiritual renewal, as suggested by the so-called *Douai Chronicle* of the seventeenth- century priest William Lewis Leslie remind one not a little of the project of Duke Yaroslav. There are differences among historians over her real influence on the Scottish Church; it is unlikely to have been significant on structures but her devout ascesis and her feeding of the poor left an abiding impression and assured her canonization in the Western Church. Her cultus spread to Spain and the Low Countries, but she transcended all western traditions. In this she pulled against her husband who overthrew Macbeth's Celtic order and became an ardent Romanizer.[2]

Notes

1. E. Schwartz (ed.), *Acta conciliorum oecumenicorum* (Berlin, 1927), p. 48; J-M Sansterre, *Les moines Grecs et orientaux à Rome au époque byzantine et carolingienne* (Brussels, 1980), pp. 93, 117–119; Deno J. Genakoplos, *Byzantine East and Latin*

West. Two Worlds of Christendom in Middle Ages and Renaissance (Oxford, 1966), p. 42; John Meyendorff, *Imperial Unity and Christian Division. The Church 450–680* (Crestwood, NY, 1989), pp. 76, 296, 308, 320–1, 365–73. There is a slight essay on Theodore in Andrew Phillips, *Orthodox Christianity and the English Tradition* (Hockwold-cum-Wilton, 1995), pp. 305–16 and an academic symposium, *Archbishop Theodore*, edited by Michael Lapidge with contributions, among others, by Sebastian Brock and Henry Chadwick (Cambridge, 1995). Theodore is known to have brought with him to Canterbury a collection of Greek manuscripts, which formed the basis of the libraries of both foundation monasteries.

For the Byzantine influence in Roman ecclesiastical chant, see Egon Wellesz, *Eastern Elements in Western Chant* (Oxford, 1947). See also Michel Huglo, 'Relations et influences reciproques entre musique de l'Orient grec et musique occidentale', in *The Proceedings of the XIII international Congress of Byzantine Studies*, Oxford, 1966 (London and Oxford, 1967), pp. 267–80, and the recording by Ensemble Organum, prepared by Marcel Perès, under the title *Chants de L'Église de Rome. Périod byzantine* (Harmonia Mundi, Paris, 1986). Charlemagne ordered Byzantine hymns to be translated into Latin to be used at his court. For Vitalian's misgivings about Theodore's Byzantinism, see Paul the Deacon, *Historia Langobardorum*, English translation by W. D. Foulke (Philadelphia, 1907), 5.30. For Byzantine influences on the Anglo-Saxon Church, see C. J. Godfrey, *The Church in Anglo-Saxon England* (Cambridge, 1962), pp. 369–70, 375. It may be noted in passing that the coronation rite used by King Edgar and his Saxon successors was distinctly Byzantine (as was that of Charlemagne). For the wider significance of this, see Michael McCormick, *Eternal Victory. Triumphal Rulership in late antiquity, Byzantium and the early Medieval West* (Cambridge, 1986), especially pp. 363–6. See also Judith Herrin, *The Formation of Christendom* (Oxford, 1987), pp. 454–7. William Maskell, *Monumenta ritualia* (London, 1882) contains the texts and the phil-Orthodox W. J. Wickham Legg has a study in *Missale Westmonasteriense and Three Coronation Orders*. There is also a study of the English Coronation rite by P. E. Schramm. For Edward the Confessor's Byzantine contacts, see Frank Barlow (ed.), *The Life of King Edward who rests at Westminster, attributed to a monk of St Bertin* (London, 1962), especially pp. 67–71. For Anglo-Saxon pilgrimages see E. Joranson, 'The Great German Pilgrimage of 1064–1065' in *The Crusade and Other Historical Essays Presented to D. C. Munro* (New York, 1928), pp. 3–43. For Donald Nicol's comment in context,

see his paper 'Byzantium and England' in his collection, *Studies in Late Byzantine History and Prosopography* (London, 1986).
2. For Edward Aetheling in Kiev and Hungary, see Gabriel Ronay, *The Lost King of England. The East European Adventure of Edward the Exile* (London, 1989), pp. 40, 53, 56, 61–63, 65, 66, 83–88, 117ff, and 125–42 passim; John Fennell, *A History of the Russian Church to 1448* (London, 1995), pp. 12, 20, 39, 43, 55, 68. For Hilarion's sermon see Ludolf Muller, *Der Metropolitan Ilarion Lobrede auf Vladimir den Heilgen und Glaubersbekenntnis* (Wiesbaden, 1962). See also Dmitri Obolensky, *The Byzantine Inheritance of Eastern Europe*, VIII (London, 1982), p. 64. For Hagia Sophia Cathedral see Anzej Poppe, *The Rise of Christian Russia*, IV (London, 1982) pp. 27–28, 31–32, 39–59; V, 10. For Yaroslav's motivation, see John Meyendorff, *Byzantium and the Rise of Russia. A Study of Byzantino-Russian Relations in the Fourteenth Century* (Crestwood, 1989), p. 15; Ihor Sevcenko, *Byzantium and the Slavs in Letters and Culture* (Cambridge, Mass. and Naples, 1991, pp. 164, 415, 573. For Margaret of Scotland, see Alan J. Wilson, *St Margaret Queen of Scotland* (Edinburgh, 1993), pp. 71–72, 79–80, 89–93 and Turgot's 'Life of Margaret' in W. Metcalfe (ed.), *Ancient Lives of Scottish Saints* (Felinfach, 1895, reprinted 1998), Part 2, pp. 297, 301, 306–7, 309, 313.

For the Great Schism, the best account in English is still that by Steven Runciman, *The Eastern Schism. A Study of the Papacy and the Eastern Churches during the 11th and 12th Centuries* (Oxford, 1955).

Note on the Aetheling and Devotion to SS Boris and Gleb

Edward's willingness to set all his immediate concerns and advantages aside in order to return to England, a country of which he had no direct knowledge, suggests a massive sense of duty. One must assume that the Confessor's envoys warned him of the dangers to anyone claiming to be heir. The refusal of Princes Boris and Gleb to defend themselves against an assault on their lives by their own brothers was immediately seen as an act of Christian obedience. Although they were not formally canonized as 'Passion Bearers' until 1072, it is clear from the insertion of a liturgical panegyric into the Primary Russian Chronicle under the year 1015 that their cult already existed when the two Saxon brothers arrived in Kiev. It may therefore be assumed that Edward was influenced by the martyrs' example or at least could not stand mentally aside from it. See Obolensky, op. cit., VIII, p. 66.

CHAPTER ONE

REALITY TWO STAGES REMOVED: IN SEARCH OF THE FATHERS

When John Mason Neale began his sadly incomplete and part-posthumously published *History of the Holy Eastern Church* in the 1840s[1] his object was to further by scrupulous historical scholarship the cause of reconciliation between the western and eastern parts of 'Catholic Christendom' by bringing into prominence 'the vast heritage of Divine Truth which all hold in common'.[2] He set himself to this task on a rebound from the ultramontane Catholicism of Montalembert whom he met while convalescing on Madeira and whose attitudes to Anglicanism he found repellent.

George Williams, introducing the readers to the final and posthumous volume, saw the state of Anglican Orthodox scholarship as being that of a 'death-like lethargy'. Neale himself in his volume of general introduction described the work as 'the first attempt to present a systematic view ...'[3]

Neale was obviously dissatisfied with all previous Anglican writing on the subject. Leon Litvack in his recent study of Neale's ecumenical pilgrimage suggests that the reason for this was a feeling that previous writers lacked a fundamental empathy for the processes of Orthodox life. It would therefore be useful to explore the pre-Neale mind-set since it has never yet been systematically attempted.

After the Norman Conquest only a few Englishmen who worked abroad like Adelard of Bath and John of Salisbury had any direct experience of the Greek Church, and then mostly with Greeks in southern Italy. The great Byzantinist Donald

Nicol found no increase in English interest in Eastern Christianity as a result of the 'Frankish' conquest of Constantinople in 1204. Only a handful of English scholars was still bothering to learn Greek, for even the most basic of purposes, and the few travellers who brought back Greek manuscripts were not usually Greek scholars themselves. It was the Franciscans who tended to be the exception to the rule, probably because of Francis' own interest in the Middle East. Both Robert Grosseteste and Roger Bacon took Greek studies seriously. Indeed the first major post-Conquest scholar of Greek was Robert Grosseteste, Bishop of Lincoln from 1235 to 1254. His knowledge was primarily of the classical and patristic authors. Significantly, he did not get a chance to learn Greek until he was over sixty years old, for want of grammars and lexicons. He learned it not at Oxford, where he taught, but during his busy ministry at Lincoln. Kathryn D. Hill has made a close study of what can be known of his working methods and contacts.[4] She finds that he knew one 'Nicolas Grecus', a magister who served in his household at Lincoln, and that he met several Greeks from southern Italy who visited Oxford during his time there. One of his theological assistants, John of Basingstoke, moved to Athens and was taught there by a mysterious woman theologian, Constantia. The biggest product of Grosseteste's Greek learning was the translation into Latin of the works of St John Damascene. John had not previously been known in the West outside Italy and even there he was not translated until the twelfth century. Grosseteste also translated into Latin the Pseudo-Dionysius and the apocryphal *Testament of the Twelve Patriarchs*. The *Testament* spread throughout Europe.

At this stage very little was known of Orthodox liturgy in the West. The Latin delegates at the Union Council of Florence (1438–45) confessed their innocence of it. This ignorance was at its most profound in England where the 'Cretan' influence noticed by scholars in certain parts of Western Europe is scarcely to be found. Such Cretans as there were in England at this time were probably merchants to a man.[5]

The visits of two Greek scholars in the late fifteenth century

– Joannes Argyropoulos and Andronicus Callistus – left no abiding impression on English Greek scholarship.[6] Indeed, we have a depressing account involving Henry VIII and Sir Thomas More at Oxford which shows just how much Greek studies were denigrated during the early years of the following century. Some dismissive remarks made by a university lecturer in a sermon at Mass so disturbed the King that he immediately ordered a debate between the preacher and More. More spoke first and so eloquently on the importance of Greek studies that the lecturer gave up in confusion, but not before he had revealed profound ignorance in his embarrassment, by suggesting that Greek derived from Hebrew. Knowing the strength of opposition to Greek in the University, More wrote a formal letter of remonstrance.[7] The situation at Cambridge was a little better. Erasmus lectured there in Greek on St Jerome while he was translating St Basil's commentary on Isaiah and was succeeded by another continental Grecian, Johann Siberch of Cologne.[8] Bishop John Fisher of Rochester possessed a copy of the Liturgy of St John Chrysostom, given to him by Erasmus, and troubled to make a Latin translation of it. Briefly in the 1550s John Cheke, as Lady Margaret Reader, lectured on St John Chrysostom and Maximus the Confessor.

The medieval pattern of contact via Italy continued into the sixteenth century. William Grocyn (?1449–1519), for instance, studied with Demetrios Chalcondylas at Florence. Only William Lily can be found to have studied in Greece itself.[9]

This, then, was the situation when the Ecclesia Anglicana became the Church of England, a transformation which was essentially a phenomenon internal to the Western Church and its medieval theological tradition and flavoured by local social and economic trends which bore no relation to Byzantine Orthodoxy, now under the Turks.

Naive Anglo-Catholics of the nineteenth and twentieth centuries have striven to read more Eastern influence into the Tudor liturgies (for largely polemical reasons) than can really be demonstrated. It is true that Cranmer and Gardiner locked

themselves in controversy over the eucharistic doctrine of
Hilary, Cyril of Alexandria and Gregory of Nyssa; both men
were prisoners of the western tradition deriving from Augustine's realist-symbolism and the controversy did not help
Cranmer in a particularly Orthodox direction.[10] Cranmer's
commonplace books reveal a significant but patchy annotation
of the Greek Fathers, chiefly facilitated by the Italian humanist Protestant Peter Martyr Vermigli. A list of citations was
printed in the Parker Society series in 1846 and it suggests,
among other things, a certain aversion to the Cappadocian
Fathers. Latin citations were more substantial in the notebooks
than Greek and many of the Greek, although interesting, are
idiosyncratic – Eusebius of Emesa, Hesychius of Jerusalem,
Theodoret of Cyrrhus. Even more significantly, he seems to
have relied little on the new continental editions, so most of
his notes must have come from pre-print scholastic sources.
Thirdly, most of his Greek citations had to do with the
eucharistic controversy with Rome, possibly thanks to the
pioneer catenas of target texts compiled by Hermann Bodius.
C. W. Dugmore and Arthur Middleton have shown that within
the constraints of anti-Roman polemic, Cranmer used quotations from Gregory of Nyssa and Cyril of Alexandria in a way
which would have pleased the Orthodox. C. W. Dugmore
believed that as early as 1544 Cranmer was studying the
Liturgy of St John Chrysostom alongside the Mozarabic
Liturgy. Cranmer's reading notes certainly suggest that he
possessed a great many patristic liturgical texts at that time,
including Erasmus's edition of St John Chrysostom; a copy of
Chrysostom's commentary on the Pauline Epistles, again from
the same time, bears the Archbishop's autograph. But a more
recent scholar than Dugmore, G. J. Cuming, has suggested
that Cranmer had only the Latin version of John Chrysostom
published in Venice in 1528. Although by 1545 all the Byzantine service books were available in the West in one form or
another and Constantine Palaeocappa sold several copies of
the Liturgy of St James to prominent people including the
King, their use at best seems to have been polemical, against
Rome.[11]

The English Litany of 1544 shows some sign of Eastern wording, including its final prayer; but the only solid influence from Greek in any of the liturgical revisions done between 1544 and 1549 seems to have been a little quotation from St Basil.[12] In any case, the verbal similarities are generally such that they could just as easily have been drawn from the Roman, Sarum or York liturgies, with all of which Cranmer was equally familiar. Indeed, some phrases attributed by enthusiasts to Greek influence could even have come via Luther, Bucer, Peter Martyr or John à Lasco.[13] The 1549 prayer 'for the whole state of Christes churche' is a case in point. The very positioning of it and other prayers alleged to be Greek-influenced belies any idea of a real understanding of Orthodox worship.[14] Needless to say, anything that might have been gained from the East in the 1549 Prayer Book was lost in the 1552 revision, and so the normative 1559 Book, based as it was on 1552, was denuded of Orthodox phraseology. (The prayer of St John Chrysostom now familiar in Evening Prayer – 'Almighty God, who hast given us grace at this time . . .' – was excluded until the Carolines restored it in 1662.)

This does not detract from the undoubted study which went on between 1552 and 1559. John Jewel, Elizabeth's first Bishop of Salisbury and a 'Geneva Exile', had already read Nicolas Cabasilas's commentary on the Liturgy and by the time of his famous Paul's Cross sermon in 1560 had bought and read Guillaume Morel's edition of the Liturgy of St James as it came off the press in that year. We may assume that the resonances of such reading were passed on in encouragement to others to read, but Jewel's own Greek quotations in his controversy with the Roman, Harding, seem like convenience quotations to make a polemical point rather than part of his mental furniture. Matthew Parker, Elizabeth's first Archbishop of Canterbury, made his own collection of texts – in many ways as interesting as Cranmer's – and it included a set of Anglo-Saxon manuscripts presumably acquired to show that the pre-Norman Church, like the Greek, did not teach transubstantiation.[15] Only towards the conclusion of Elizabeth's reign is there some evidence of solid Greek liturgical reading in Thomas Bilson and Richard Field. Archbishop Michael Ramsey discerns the major difference between the sixteenth and seventeenth divines:

> Whereas the Edwardian and Elizabethan divines had been interested in the Fathers chiefly as a means of proving what had or had not been the primitive doctrine and practice, the Caroline divines went farther in using the thought and piety of the Fathers within the structure of their own theological exposition.

He goes on to say that the Carolines, freed from the shackles of Reformation disputes, were liberated into patristic incarnationalism and that it was this that led them to 'reach out to Eastern Christendom'.[16]

The big boost to understanding came with Lancelot Andrewes and of him we shall speak later. Meanwhile other types of Greek contact were beginning to emerge. For some reason which is not at all clear, George Abbot, James I's Calvinist Archbishop of Canterbury, wrote to Cyril Lucaris, the Patriarch of Constantinople, asking him to send four Greek students to study theology in England. He is hardly likely to have picked up at that stage the idea to be fostered by Sir Thomas Roe, the English ambassador to the Porte, that Cyril himself was a closet Calvinist. The request is more likely to have been connected with the appearance in England of a Greek refugee from the Turkish galleys, Christophoros Angelos. Angelos published a tract in Oxford bewailing how his Church was 'destitute of all perfection and knowledge' on account of 'the Great Turke' (or rather on account of some of the Sultan's wicked magistrates by which the Church suffered much misery). Angelos had been sent to Trinity College Cambridge by Bishop John Overall of Norwich, of whose eucharistic theology we shall have something to say later. Overall was a leading patristics scholar of his day. Unhappily, the young man developed asthma in the damp climate of Cambridge and had to move to Balliol College Oxford where he made many contacts. He announced that there were no settled schools for Greeks in which the Christian faith could be taught and that Christian teachers had to keep on the move with their students for their own safety. Angelos was believed because he brought with him letters of commendation from three Greek bishops. The comments of Angelos on the poverty of formal teaching for Greek Christians may have misled English scholars into not expecting contemporary Greek theology to be worthy of their attention. Patriarch Jeremias II did in fact instruct his bishops at a Synod of 1593 to establish a school in every diocese and Patriarch Cyril Lucaris tried to establish a tertiary academy at Constantinople in 1624 after the pattern of the school he attended at Padua. He put in charge of it the best man he had: Theophilus Korydaleos. It probably never achieved what either he or Korydaleos intended for it, largely because of Lucaris's own overthrow and murder, although it survived in some shadowy form until the late eighteenth century. At best it produced a small intellectual elite for the Turkish civil administration rather than outstanding theologians. In his conversations with the Lutheran divines Jeremias had the rare advantage of the services of Theodore Zygomales, who was not only deeply versed in Greek theological tradition but also understood western intellectual trends. But this proved to be an exceptional situation whose value rapidly devalued. William McNeill had noted that while the 'Greek manner' in the visual arts survived under the Turks and impacted Western art in the person of El Greco, in literature it survived largely in catechetical writing in only a few monasteries.[17]

Patriarch Cyril does not seem to have sent four poor students, but he did send a noted scholar from Athos, Metrophanes Critopoulos, who settled at Balliol College Oxford where Christophoros Angelos had also studied. Critopoulos quickly made himself unpopular, ostensibly because he sided with Abbot's numerous enemies at Court. He was back in Constantinople by 1631, but thereafter rose through Cyril's patronage to become Metropolitan of Memphis and Patriarch of Alexandria. (In a short time he turned against his doomed patron, a not uncommon occurrence in the seventeenth-century Greek Church).[18] Nathaniel Canopius also studied at Balliol and with some success. According to the gossip Anthony à Wood, he introduced the habit of coffee-drinking to Oxford and (no connection, one may hope) was made a minor canon of Christ Church by Bishop Laud. But he was later to suffer at the hands of the Puritans during the Great Rebellion because of his association with Laud. Sir Steven Runciman wickedly suggests that it may also have had something to do with his fondness for singing the *Akathiston* on all possible occasions! He too returned to the East and became Archbishop of Smyrna.[19]

Despite such distinguished visitors, Runciman can find no evidence of any effort to enlighten Anglicans on the beliefs and practices of Orthodox. On this the visitors (perhaps wisely, since it was a time of Puritan politics and grassroots anti-popery) kept a low profile. Runciman suggests that the new commercial contacts in this period were probably more important than the intellectual in creating possibilities for understanding, bringing as they did at least a few choice Englishmen into direct contact with Orthodox life for the first time.[20]

The merchants of the Levant (=Turkey) Company had little interest in matters theological, but those who were drawn to Greek lands in their wake sometimes did, especially the chaplains to ambassadorial and consular staff. Indeed, even some of the ambassadors and consuls were sometimes no mean scholars. Runciman singles out Sir Thomas Roe, Sir Peter Wych and Sir Paul Rycaut in this regard. Of Sir Paul Rycaut we shall have much to say in a later chapter. Because of this high level patronage Edward Pocock laid down his later reputation as a leading orientalist by serving as chaplain at Aleppo from 1630 to 1638. Pocock was in Constantinople at the time of Cyril Lucaris' murder and was able to make a detailed report to William Laud.[21] In turn he paved the way for the later chaplains at Constantinople, Thomas Smith and John Covel, to whom it will be necessary to give detailed attention.

The information so conveyed must have been confined to a

small circle. The books touching on the modern Greeks which sold in any numbers were lamentable. Edward Brerewood's encyclopedic *Enquiry into Languages* (1614) was very muddled on the Greeks although not especially hostile, while Robert Burton's *Anatomy of Melancholy* (1621) dismissed the Greek Church as 'semi-Christian'. This was largely because of its invocation of saints, but not all contemporaries made such a stark judgement. Sir Thomas Browne in his minutely erudite *Religio Medici* of 1635–42 had a more Olympian tolerance towards Rome and Orthodoxy alike:

> We have reformed from them, not against them; for (omitting those Improperations and Terms of Scurrility betwixt us, which only difference our Affections, and not our Cause,) there is between us one common Name and Appellation, one Faith and necessary body of Principles common to us both; and therefore I am not scrupulous to converse and live with them, to enter their Churches in defect of ours, and either pray with them, or for them. .... Holy-water and Crucifix (dangerous to the common people,) deceive not my judgment, nor abuse my devotion at all. I am, I confess, naturally inclined to that which misguided Zeal terms Superstition. My common conversation I do acknowledge austere, my behaviour full of rigour, sometimes not without morosity; yet at my Devotion I love to use the civility of my knee, my hat and hand, with all those outward and sensible motions which may express or promote my invisible Devotion I should violate my own arm rather than a Church, nor willingly deface the name of Saint or Martyr. I cannot laugh at, but rather pity; the fruitless journeys of Pilgrims, or contemn the miserable condition of Fryars; for though misplaced in Circumstances, there is something in it of Devotion. I could never hear the Ave Mary Bell without an elevation, or think it a sufficient warrant, because they erred in one circumstance, for me to err in all, that is, in silence and dumb contempt.[22]

In Chapter 4 we shall have cause to encounter a fellow-spirit with Brown in the person of the Revd Dr John Covel of Christ's College, Cambridge, another natural scientist and would-be benevolent phenomenologist.

More discerningly, William Forbes, Bishop of Edinburgh, knew Patriarch Jeremias's reply to the Wittenberg theologians of 15 May 1576 and quotes Jeremias precisely and without condemnation as saying that invocation 'truly and properly befits God alone' but is paid to the saints 'by accident, so to speak . . . from a certain grace and privilege'.[23]

The need for a detailed knowledge of the Fathers was put by Samuel Ward, Master of Sidney Sussex College Cambridge, in a remark to the young John Bramhall, who later came to favour dropping the *Filioque* on the ground 'who dare say that the fruits of the primitive Fathers was insufficient?' Ward said that it was not possible that 'the present controversies of the Church should be rightly determined or reconciled without a deep insight into the doctrine of the primitive fathers and a competent skill in school theology [i.e. the theology of the Schoolmen]. The first affordeth us a right pattern, and the second smootheth it over, and planeth away the knots'. By the 1620s and 30s it had become possible to gain a grasp of the Greek Fathers at considerable speed. This was demonstrated by John Pearson, later Bishop of Chester, who had made great headway before even he had left school.[24] At this stage Charles I issued injunctions requiring the Universities to teach the Fathers.

Textual patristic influence on the Caroline divines was considerable but its effect on their spiritual thinking was very diffused and probably not very conscious, if only because filtered through and merged with the western *devotio moderna*. Even the most palpably Orthodox in spirit, Jeremy Taylor, never referred to his sources when writing about mystical union and theosis.[25] It is unlikely that they read any commentary on the Liturgy apart from Nicolas Cabasilas. Although they knew many really obscure modern Roman works like Tomas Manrique's *Censura in Glossas Juri-Canonici* (Cologne, 1572), Isidore Mosconius' *De Majestate Ecclesia Militantis* (Venice, 1602), Abraham Bzovius' *De Pontifice*

Romano (Cologne, 1619), Celsus Mancini's *De Juribus Principatuum* (Rome, 1596) and Stanislaus Orichovicz, they appear to have known no comparable Greek works. For instance they seemed to be unaware of John Nathaniel's *Commentary on the Liturgy of St John Chrysostom* published in Venice in 1574 (admittedly little more than a catena of quotations from Cabasilas, Symeon of Thessalonika and Germanos of Constantinople) nor did they appear to know the fairly recent works of Manuel of Corinth (d.1551), Pachomius of Rhus (d. *c.*1553), Meletius Pigas (d.1601), Damaskonos Studites Metropolitan of Naupactos, Maximos Margunios (d.1601), Gabriel Severos (d.1616), Joannes Kartanos, Maximos Peloponnesios or Theophilos Korydaleos. It is surprising that no one used Gabriel Severos, who spent most of his life in Venice defending Orthodoxy against Rome, or Zacharias Skordylios who answered in detail the charges of Cardinal Guise against the Orthodox or Maximus Peloponnesios who wrote against Rome on the Eucharist. Admittedly much of this late sixteenth and seventeenth century work was not what might be termed (in George Maloney's expression) 'original theology' but it did form a concerted and consistent rebuttal of Rome and – again in Maloney's view as a sympathetic Jesuit scholar – served its purpose of a holding action against Rome and Protestantism.[26]

Whatever *was* used tended to be grist to the Anti-Roman case and in the heat of controversy the subtleties tended to be lost. Nowhere is this more obvious than in Richard Crakenthorpe (1567–1624), described by Anthony à Wood as 'a great canonist, and so familiar and exact in the Fathers, Councils and Schoolmen that none in his time scarce went before him'. However he was rightly described as 'foulmouthed' against the Papists, not least where Archbishop Marc-Antonio De Dominis was concerned. This is hardly surprising. De Dominis, Archbishop of Spalato (Split) in Dalmatia was a marvellous prize when he converted to the Church of England in 1617. When six years later he returned to Roman obedience after being Dean of Windsor and participating in several Anglican episcopal consecrations, it was mortifying to see how he proceeded to berate his foster-mother in print. Crakenthorpe's response, the posthumously published *Defensio Ecclesiae Anglicanae*, used an overwhelming array of both Latin and Greek Fathers like grapeshot and the Latin text splutters with venom.[27]

We get closer to the heart of things with Lancelot Andrewes, Bishop of Ely. Andrewes owned a copy of Morel's 1560 edition of the Liturgy of St James and also copies simultaneously published by Morel of the Liturgies of St Basil and St John Chrysostom.[28] It is clear that he also owned some Orthodox office books. Without question, these gave a character to his famous *Preces Privatae*, a handbook of private devotions written in Latin and later translated into English. F. E. Brightman assumed that the preponderant influence was that of the Liturgy of St James, but it would be difficult to prove because in his composition Andrewes seems to have absorbed much into his subconscious without the need for precise verbal quotation. This very fact of course makes him all the more impressive because it makes him appear deeply Orthodox 'in spirit'.[29]

In the early part of the seventeenth century the supply of Greek books seems to have almost dried up. Laud corresponded with Cyril Lucaris via James Ussher, Archbishop of Armagh, with a view to obtaining rare books. Ussher warned him that Greece had been 'so often gleaned' that there were only one or two places, like Mount Athos, where they could still be got.[30] Despite this, during the 30s, 40s and 50s Anglicans like Herbert Thorndike and William Nicholson did study not only the long-circulated texts of the Liturgies of St Basil and St James but also the less easily obtainable printed texts of the Maronite, Mozarabic and Ethiopian rites. Victor Scialach's Latin edition of the Maronite Liturgy was seen by a remarkably large number of Anglican scholars by the middle of the century.[31]

The disruption caused to Anglican life by the Interregnum of 1649–60, during which the bishops were deposed and the Prayer Book banned, while causing much grief and suffering, led to an opening up of Anglican theology. This is seen best in two theologians, John Cosin and Jeremy Taylor. Taylor's case is the more subtle of the two and will be deferred until later in this chapter. We shall first deal with that of Cosin.

Cosin, who became Bishop of Durham at the Restoration, was a disciple of Andrewes and Overall (he called Overall his 'lord and master'). He had a prodigious memory for patristic and liturgical quotations, which was conceded by the Presbyterian Richard Baxter who felt its force at the Savoy Conference yet in no way resented it even though it was to his discomforture. After the Restoration it was noted that he stood firm on 'the principles for which he had suffered'. That suffering involved an enforced sojourn in France during the Commonwealth and Protectorate. There he studied major contemporary Roman works on liturgy in far greater depth than any of his contemporaries, including George Calixtus' *De Sacrificio Christi* (Helstadt, 1644) and works by Randulf Fitzralph, the Roman Archbishop of Armagh, Alfonso a Castro, Miguel Medina, Suarez, Vasquez, Baronius, Bellarmine, Soto, Salmeron, Jansen, and Francesco Ferrara. Calixtus was particularly significant because he dealt with issues arising out of the East-West schism, which Cosin was able to marry up with the *Euchologion seu Rituale Graecorum* (Paris, 1647) of the Dominican Prior of Chios, Jacques Goar (1601–53). Cosin also read backwards in time through the Ratisbon Colloquium of 1541 to Cajetan and Gabriel Biel. He had by him always Aubert Le Mire's 1608 Antwerp edition of Eusebius' *Ecclesiastical History*. While in Paris, Cosin collected most of the Paris Bibliotheca edition of the Eastern liturgies and attempted, like Thorndike, a historico-textual comparison of liturgies, in which he detected numerous borrowings. But his study also convinced him that the Liturgy of St James was indeed substantially that which Cyril said was in use at Jerusalem and that the surviving texts of the Liturgy of St Mark corresponded to what was used at an early date in Alexandria. He even explored the transmission of St Mark into Ethiopia.

Not satisfied with mere textual study, Cosin closely read Nicolas Cabasilas' commentary for how the Liturgy of St John

Chrysostom had come to be used, and supplemented this reading by long conversations which he had at the Louvre with Metropolitan Cyril of Trebizond, a self-confessed disciple of Cyril Lucaris, in which they discussed the dogmatic basis of Orthodoxy. In these conversations Cyril hotly denied that the Church of Rome was 'the Mother and Mistress of the Greek Churches', and Cosin understood him also to say that transubstantiation and the invocation of saints were with the Greeks an 'Article of Faith', but Cosin may have misunderstood this last point. Cyril said that saints were prayed *for* 'in reference to their peaceable Rest, in the State of Death, and their Happy Resurrection to Eternall life'. He felt bitter about the murder of Lucaris, which he attributed to the rancour of the Jesuits who had never let him be. Cosin inferred from these discussions that Orthodox might be prepared to see the Anglican formularies as 'consonant to the orthodox and Catholic religion of the old Greek Fathers, with whom it was both his duty and mine, and all others' belonging to our Churches therein, to retain communion and unity together'. In an affidavit he testified that when Cyril of Trebizond visited him in his Paris apartments he insisted on seeing a copy of the Prayer Book and declared it to be sound. Cosin heard Cyril celebrate the Liturgy of St John Chrysostom in a private chapel at the Louvre before no less a person than Queen Henrietta Maria. (Her son James, Duke of York, scrupling at being seen to be present, observed from a private closet with the help of a crib provided by Cosin.) Cosin observed very closely, noting that at the Invitation none came forward for communion but the deacon.

All of Cosin's works, both before and after the Paris exile and including the sermons, were replete with patristic reference. A good example to take at random, because of its being compact, is his early sermon on the mission of the Church which he preached at the consecration of Francis White as Bishop of Carlisle in 1626.

Cosin was satisfied from his conversations with Metropolitan Cyril that the Council of Trent's 'new and additional articles of faith', i.e. purgatory, transubstantiation and universal primacy, were not in any way acceptable to the Greeks. He was assured that Greek prayers for the dead were solely for their 'peace, rest ... and happy resurrection'.

The unique advantage that Cosin possessed during his exile of becoming equally familiar with Roman and Orthodox ideas might be expected to show itself in his own theology. He was clearly able to use his comparative study of Orthodox and Roman ordination rites to some effect in his defence of Anglican orders, as a letter to Bishop Morley shows. He could equally throw light on the deficiencies of Anglican discipline from his comparison of Greek and Roman fasting rules. (See a letter to Mr Wood of Wadburgh.) His comparative study of the anaphoras of James, Clement, Basil and John Chrysostom led to a strong conviction about eucharistic sacrifice. He wished a specific reference to the 'unbloody sacrifice' to be inserted into the Prayer Book. If the Eucharist was the place where men and women were made 'sons of God' and partakers of the Divine Nature, this must be directly related in terms of identity with the Sacrifice of Calvary pleaded eternally in the Heavenlies. To be fair, the seed of this awareness is found in a sermon of 1632, but the direction of his thought can only have been strengthened by his liturgical studies. By the time of the Restoration, Cosin was convinced that the sacrificial nature of the Eucharist should be brought to the fore by placing the Oblation immediately after the Words of Institution. He recalled that his mentor, Bishop John Overall, had always made this alteration when celebrating. He tried to get it through Convocation together with a more explicit *epiclesis* but was blocked. He apparently felt bitter about it. In his *History of Popish Transubstantiation*, first published in Latin during his exile in 1657 and later issued in English in 1675, he expressed his sympathy with Ephrem the Syrian's analogy of the hypostatic and the eucharistic presence, seeing in both cases no confusion of natures but a retention of proper substance, so that the Crucified and Ascended Lord was wholly and objectively present through the Bread and Wine. He dismissed the 'corporal and oral' teaching of Rome as quite different from this. It had only become a controlling obsession at Trent; at the last contact with the Orthodox, the Council of

Florence, the matter had been 'undetermined'. He produced an impressive catena of both Western and Eastern patristic witness to back his assertion.

Cosin did not regard the Eastern heirs of the Fathers as inconsistent in rejecting purgatory but praying for the dead. 'What though their souls', he wrote, 'be in bliss already; they may have a greater degree of bliss by our prayers; and when their bodies come to be raised and joined to their souls again, they shall be sure of a better state; our prayers for them will not be in vain, were it but for that alone'.

Cosin's sojourn in Paris had one further advantage. It made him acutely aware of the precise 'political' character of papal policy in Greek lands, in collusion with Venice and the French, a matter which will figure largely in later chapters of this book. Although he used Goar's *Euchologium*, he did not trust it, nor its use by Roman controversialists and 'missionaries'. He knew the subversive activities of the Jesuits in the Mediterranean and the Balkans and his knowledge of that informed his account of the career of Archbishop Marc Antonio De Dominis after his departure from England and renunciation of Anglicanism. He may have drawn John Covel and Thomas Smith's attention to the Claude/Arnauld controversy over Orthodox eucharistic belief: it certainly made sharper his own work on transubstantiation.[32]

It was reported that at Cosin's death his papers fell into hands that did not take proper care of them. Many were 'strangely scattered about' and a considerable number were lost. One work that very nearly was lost in this way but survived was his treatise on transubstantiation.[33] This was to prove a spur to the thinking of Thomas Smith himself and Henry Dodwell, as we shall see in Chapter 3.

It will have been noticed by the reader that the Liturgy of St James seems to have had pride of place among Eastern liturgies with the Carolines, as indeed it was to continue to do with the English and Scottish Nonjurors in the eighteenth century. The Greek St James, in a late medieval *textus receptus*, was continually printed throughout the sixteenth and seventeenth centuries. It looks as if Jeremy Taylor, like Cosin, knew also the Syrian St James, either from manuscript sources or from the Latin translation of 1572. The frequency of its citation, however, was not due simply to its availability. There must have been more copies of St John Chrysostom in circulation. Taylor is on record as thinking St James the major witness to the spirit of 'primitive' worship. In his *Collection of Offices* of 1658 he drew very heavily on St James, especially for its anamnesis, epiclesis and acclamations. Among other Caroline divines to show an intimate knowledge of St James, G. J. Cuming cites Hamon L'Estrange (*Alliance of Divine Offices*, 1659) and Anthony Sparrow, Bishop of Norwich (*Rationale upon the Book of Common Prayer 1657*).[34]

The biggest deficit in even later Caroline knowledge of contemporary Orthodoxy was that they appear to have been completely ignorant of *Russian* Orthodoxy.[35] But for the average Englishman of that time, Orthodox lands and cultures, especially Muscovy, were (to adapt a saying of Neville Chamberlain) 'far away places of which we know nothing'! The idea of the Eastern Church or the Greek Church was for most generic, something to image over against Rome on the far side.

By the 1670s more detailed information on the actual working of the Orthodox system was beginning to become available in print from the pens of Thomas Smith and Sir Paul Rycaut, but only in relation to Greek lands. By then the Greeks themselves were being exposed to the workings of the Anglican system in London and Oxford in a form which previous scholarly visitors had not encountered and they did not like it. First-hand Anglican observation and Orthodox anguish will both be touched on in following chapters. Here in this introduction we must conclude with some reflections on how the Anglican norms of sacrament and tradition conditioned them for their entry into *terra incognita*.

Günter Thomann finds the concept of the Church in the Thirty-Nine Articles 'rather unsacramental', in spite of their reference to the spiritual power of the 'dominical' sacraments and the concession of 'a certain sacramental nature to Orders,

Penance &c'.[36] This is fair comment. It is true that a very early reformer, Robert Barnes (burnt at the stake in 1540), understood the development not only of the Roman ritual but also that of James, Basil and John Chrysostom and refused to be categorized as 'Lutheran', though happy enough to quote Bugenhagen. Dugmore argues that Barnes can best be categorized as 'anti-papal'.[37] The same might probably be said of Latimer. But the deeper the Reformers entered into a struggle to the death with Rome the less discerning they became about tradition and sacrament. The rejection of transubstantiation was emblematic. It was done with such vehemence that for a long time there was a dread vacuum at the heart of Anglican sacramental theology. Crakenthorpe was characteristically corrosive, High Churchman though he was, in his handling of transubstantiation in Chapters 48 and 74 of his *Defensio Ecclesiae Anglicanae* of 1625.

The 'judicious Hooker' had bequeathed a warning about the corrosiveness of eucharistic controversy which could have been better heeded. But perhaps by 1597 the intellectual canker had gone too far:

> I wish that men might give themselves to meditate with silence what we have by the sacrament, and less to dispute the manner how.

Hooker's reticence gave rise only to uncertainty among later scholars over whether he was a subjective 'receptionist' or an objective 'virtualist'! Despite one notorious passage, he does seem to be the true starting point of a long tradition of Anglican 'virtualism', intentionally or not, insofar as he started the habit of speaking of Christ in the Eucharist as 'mystically yet truly' working through *koinonia*, 'in grace and efficacy' transubstantiating us from 'death to life' through our 'concurrence'. Hooker's own worshipful attitude is unmistakeable:

> O my God, thou art true;
> O my soul, thou art happy.

But Hooker was also a scholar. In his systematic Neo-

Thomist way, he threw out seminal ideas on how liturgy and sacrament should be understood in relation to the life of the Trinity, with sacramental presence as the 'sequel of an infinite and incomprehensible substance' possessing 'force and efficacity' through the Spirit. This, he argued, was the means by which Christ has a 'mutual and inward hold' of us 'and we of him'; so that we may stand freely before God as redeemed and capable of true worship. He even uses a marvellously patristic image of joy at 'wading' in the Eucharist as in a sea.

J. E. Booty seems to suggest that Hooker's continuous experience of Prayer Book worship was determinative. Undoubtedly Andrewes was influenced by Hooker to expound the Eucharist in terms of the life of the Trinity, permeating the Eucharist as like a flood of life-giving water. Nicholas Lossky sees Andrewes' eucharistic theology as not so much a mental construct as an inward sense of union with God born of prayerful discipline – 'brought to the touch and taste of the perfect, awesome, life-giving and saving mysteries' by God reaching out to make us holy. The vocabulary is recognizably Orthodox, and is but just one example of how his *Preces Privatae* 'reassembled' the core of Orthodox experience without slavish imitation.

But there was a limitation in Hooker's normative influence – his fear of confronting ideas about the Eucharist as sacrifice. Andrewes was correspondingly reticent in his *Response to Bellarmine*, saying of 'commemorative sacrifice': 'if it be lawful so to speak ...'[38]

Richard Field (1561–1616), Dean of Gloucester, attempted a process of 'ravelling back' to an earlier sense before the Reformation trauma, seeing in the eucharistic elements the Body of Christ 'in mystery and exhibitive signification'. Field dared to say in face of the Puritans that the canon of the Roman Mass, like the anaphoras of all other ancient liturgies, contained 'nothing in it contrary to the rule of faith and the Profession of the Protestant Churches.'[39]

John Overall (1560–1619), Dean of St Paul's and Bishop successively of Coventry/Lichfield and Norwich, more cautiously but with similar intent, said in his *Catechism* of 1604 that the 'whole Christ' was 'indeed really present' in the Eucharist and 'really received' but not in a 'carnal, gross, earthly way by transubstantiation or consubstantiation, or any like fictions of human reason . . .'[40]

Andrewes was more exultant on the matter as befitted his Orthodox devotions. While none of the Fathers, he said, knew of any change in the *substance* of the elements, they all knew 'that the elements are changed' at the 'coming of the almighty power of the Word'. In much the same spirit, Bramhall deplored those who would 'anatomize mysteries': he simply believed in Presence. William Forbes, Bishop of Edinburgh, held that the 'Body and Blood' were 'really, actually, substantially present and taken'. He called both Bilson and Andrewes in aid to argue that God could indeed make one body penetrate another if He so willed, although logically no earthly body could be in different places at the same time. He daringly suggested that transubstantiation as a philosophical concept should not in itself be condemned as heretical, though it was 'not a point of faith' and had issued in much abuse.

Forbes had an advantage over many of his colleagues in having read a good deal of Greek writing of the previous three centuries and not only the Fathers. He cited Nicetas' *Thesaurus* (a copy of which he had seen in the Bodleian Library), in addition to Samonas of Gaza, Nicolas Cabasilas, Mark of Ephesus, Bessarion, and Patriarch Jeremias II. He cited Jeremias as saying to the Lutherans that the true Body is 'contained under the species'. He was also able to cite the Venetian Greeks' answer to Cardinal Guise in 1571 that the elements were 'so changed . . . that neither the bread nor the accidents remain' but excused this as a case of being carried away by a desire to ingratiate.

Forbes's ability to enter into the spiritual perception of the Orthodox in matters sacramental was matched by his ability to grasp the difference between Latin purgatory and the concept of the Just awaiting the resurrection in glory in 'hidden receptacles' as understood by the Greeks.[41]

Although Forbes's approach to the Orthodox is very

impressive, the most subtle (if largely intuitive) melding of Anglican and Orthodox thinking is to be found in Jeremy Taylor. The Roman Catholic Thomas Carroll says that Taylor reunites the 'commemorative, demonstrative and prophetic dimensions' of the eucharistic signs precisely as the Fathers knew them.[42]

The strongest patristic influence on Taylor in this regard was that of St Cyril of Alexandria from whom he derived the following understanding of the role of the Spirit in the eucharistic community:

> Whatsoever the Spirit can convey to the body of the Church, we may expect from this sacrament; for as the Spirit is the instrument of life and action, so the blood of Christ is the conveyance of his Spirit ... no words being apt and proportionate to signify this spiritual secret ... A veil is drawn before all these testimonies, because the people were not able to behold the glory which they cover with their curtain ...; for, therefore, God appears to us in a cloud, and his glories in a veil ... .[43]

Taylor saw a whole range of life 'in Christ and the Church' as 'sacramental in signification' in the Greek sense of *mysterion* or, to use Harry Porter's expression, 'a manifestation of the saving power of God in Christ'.[44] For Taylor, Christ 'perpetually offers and represents' His Sacrifice to His Heavenly Father within the Eucharist which of itself is a 'holy, venerable and unbloody sacrifice'. The holy table is 'a copy of the celestial altar' because salvation is a true part of eternity in which the Trinity share their life with redeemed creatures. The Beatitudes for Taylor are truly eucharistic. It is unlikely he knew of their place in the Orthodox Liturgy.[45]

This meant that for Taylor ministry had to be a sacrament and not merely an ordinance. Priests at the altar *diakonountes mesiteurein* – 'stand between God and the people, fulfilling a special and incomprehensible ministry, which "the angels themselves do look into" with admiration'.[46]

Archbishop McAdoo finds a persistent theme in all Taylor's

works of the heavenly altar with Christ representing the eucharistic sacrifice of His Church on earth, with the holy table corresponding below. He finds it not only in theological discourse but also in iconic illustration for books deriving their themes from Taylor, such as the frontispiece to C. Wheatley's *Rational Illustration of the Book of Common Prayer* (1714). McAdoo sees the origin of Taylor's image in his reading of St John Chrysostom's *De Dignitate Sacerdotali*, a work which he would have read in Latin and which he erroneously thought to be by St Ambrose.[47] If the worshipper partakes of the divine nature in the heavenly banquet, it followed that there must be a 'change of condition' and not merely a 'change of use' in the elements.[48] The elements must be 'holy in their change'.[49] The physical element is essential and cannot be extrinsic to Christ in His Presence: it must be 'presential', 'really exhibited' and then taken up by the Spirit into the eternal. All 'fantasms and ideas' which fell short of this gave no real understanding of the Eucharist.[50] Christ being 'really present' was the same as his being 'present in reality'. It had nothing to do with semantic or 'mathematical' arguments over identity with the body of 'Jesus born of Mary'.[51] Darwell Stone, too, found a strong Alexandrian influence in Taylor – the Eucharist as spiritually visible word, following on Clement's interpretation of John 6.[52] The Holy Spirit was the 'energiser' through the 'ministries of life'.[53] In his own personal liturgy of 1658, Taylor affirms the initiating role of the Spirit by inserting, as in the Eastern rites but not in the Roman, the affirmation 'Amen' after the Words of Institution – 'May this be so!'[54]

Taylor affirmed St John Chrysostom's idea of the 'life-bringing table'.[55] For him, arguments over what 'made' the Eucharist – words of institution or *epiclesis* – were beside the point. The words were essential to the 'completion' of the rite but only as part of 'a mystical prayer' which was in fact the true *epiclesis* – a Pauline groaning in the Spirit. The whole Eucharist was an office of intercession, passing from priest to God and from people to God. The Holy Spirit was not 'called down by the force of a certain number of syllables' but by the prayers of the whole Church presented at the altar by the priest, whose role, being sacramental rather than supernatural, possessed an essentially humble status – 'according to the energy of human advocation and intercession'. Priests were the 'collectors of the Church and instruments of adunation'.[56] Taylor thus bypassed altogether the Protestant-Catholic debate over whether the eucharistic sacrifice repeated that of Calvary or whether the priest exercised or shared in Christ's high-priestly ministry. Christ acted 'in a proper and glorious manner'; the priest acted 'properly' also, but on a different plane in parallel with Christ, his ministry 'wholly from God', a *mysterion* 'like to that of Jesus'. Hence, the importance of Taylor's use of the Liturgy of St James with its affirmation of the 'confidence' which God has given to His priests to 'present' themselves and 'represent' a holy and unbloody sacrifice for their sins and those of the people.[57]

Taylor bewailed how the Eucharist, the 'tree of life', had become an occasion for perpetual dissension. It was against his wish and disposition to add to that dissension, although at one point he was forced to by a local disputation in Wales involving a Roman priest. We know no more how Jesus Christ is truly present in the Eucharist, he said, than we know 'how a cherub sings or thinks'. The change which took place was change 'really enough' (*reipsa*) and that was sufficient to know.[58]

Like Forbes, he did not seek to heap odium on the Romanists for their scholastic notion of transubstantiation as such and he cautioned the household of faith against 'rhetorical words' which added to what offence already existed. His desire was ever to draw men away from the 'manner of the flesh' to the manner of spiritual grace and sacramental consequence in accordance with the Primitive Fathers. 'There our bodies are nourished with the signs and our souls with the mystery; our bodies receive into them the seal of an immortal nature and our souls are joined with Him who is the first fruits of the resurrection and can never die.'[59] Taylor was grateful to find in the Fathers a very wide range of expressions for the mode of the Presence – mutation, conversion, transition, migration, passage, transelementation, transfiguration, transformation. The *dynamic* was what mattered, not the *category*.[60]

It is therefore not surprising that Taylor enthusiastically advocated the eucharistic fast 'that we might express honour to the mystery'. He makes generous use of the *Trisagion* in his devotions.[61] In his form of Morning and Evening Prayer for use by faithful Anglicans under the ban of the Commonwealth he used the confession in the *Euchologion*, not that of the Book of Common Prayer, adding to it in the evening the prayer of St Ephrem, his object being to avoid the juridical implications of the Latin rite, reflected so clearly in the Prayer Book, and stress the element of prayer, since absolution was not an 'act of power' but an 'act of wisdom'.[62] He wished to hedge baptism by making it a function of the deacon and thereby reducing its forensic character, and he would have preferred confirmation and communion to follow on immediately from baptism. He wrote the first Anglican book on confirmation, ostensibly at the suggestion of his fellow Irish bishops after the Restoration but really out of a deep inner necessity.[63]

Given that most of his liturgical work was done in private under the Commonwealth, Taylor's liturgical style was cramped by the need to have short and inconspicuous services which would not attract the attention of the Puritan authorities. It was therefore Orthodoxy compressed.[64] Even after the Restoration, when he at last held episcopal rank, he was constrained by extraordinarily stringent circumstance. He could not, for instance, have introduced confirmation and communion immediately after baptism, surrounded as he was in Ulster by militant Scots Presbyterians who would have taken advantage of such a radical change to undermine his credit. For the same reason he held back on reintroducing unction, about which he had long felt strongly, because he knew there was no chance of persuading the Church of Ireland to adopt it corporately in face of a Roman majority. Like Thorndike, he contented himself with the thought that it was theoretically possible and meanwhile interiorized his understanding of unction in his personal prayers.[65]

Although Taylor wanted due acknowledgement in the Liturgy of the effect of God's 'Good ... Holy ... and Glorious Presence', the only significant liturgical advance that he could achieve during his brief time as Bishop of Down and Connor was a new form for consecrating churches, which was published in the year before his death. Many of the prayers in it were drawn from his Offices of 1658 and the whole has a distinctively 'Eastern' feel, minus the ritual, of course.

One may measure Taylor's frustration over what he was unable to do by his quite immediate idea of the Church's function, namely to bear witness to, and make 'more evident' the faith once delivered to the saints, under the guidance of the Holy Spirit who helped it to apply that unchanging faith to the conditions of any time. Any time but not *his* time! As the title of one of his tracts written during the Commonwealth – *The Liberty of Prophesying* – shows, he would not concede to the Puritans the monopoly of direct speech, nor was he afraid to call upon the Montanist Tertullian in his defence.[66]

Taylor's apparent public failure was symptomatic of the whole of Caroline Anglicanism after the Restoration. Aside from the Irish form for consecrating churches, the Carolines' insight into the Orthodox Liturgy gained no public embodiment. The royal warrant summoning the Savoy Conference in 1661, designed to reconcile the Episcopalians and Presbyterians, ordered a comparison of the Book of Common Prayer with 'the most ancient liturgies', but the plan was wrecked by the Presbyterians who wanted accommodation on less adventurous terms and said they could not find liturgies early enough for their liking. The research and thinking were there; so also, from the mid-60s onwards, was the opportunity of skilled practical observation in Greek lands; but the public encouragement was lacking and indeed the prevailing anti-popery of the 70s and 80s made it impossible to advocate in public what, to the untutored eye, smacked of rank popery. The routine teaching on worship in the Restoration Church tended therefore to be notional and prosaic. The secularity in English commercial society, which Cosin bewailed before the

Civil Wars, also blighted Restoration religion. It was as if, as Cosin put it, people's attitude was 'let the Church sink or swim, since they can live without it.'[67]

Despite this, let us not assume that there was no deep undercurrent. There was and it is best epitomized by Herbert Thorndike who, like many patristic scholars of his generation, patiently filtered his insights into the prosaic fabric of everyday Restoration church life. While Jeremy Taylor's Orthodoxy was unique, intuitive and emotive, Thorndike – in Bishop Stevenson's view the most comprehensive and balanced of the Caroline patristic scholars – was the least sentimentally attached to the Prayer Book although at cost to a total patristic witness. He was not susceptible to the Reformation taboos about such things as prayers for the dead and the invocation of saints, accepting patristically that remembering the dead was the corollary of the dead remembering the living. In this as in everything else he was cool and dispassionate. Although fully equipped to be a controversialist on eucharistic theologies in the grand mode (he had mastered the intricacies of the Claude/Arnauld controversy and seen to the bottom of Cardinal Guise's notorious questions), he doggedly refused to get bogged down in what he knew to involve a false antithesis between 'spirit' and 'substance', arguing that if the 'spiritualists' were taken literally there would be no need to attend the Eucharist at all. He accepted that liturgy was not a mental construct but a symbolic garment clothing men's minds in 'terms intelligible'. For him the real question was what was real, what was objective, what was *there*. The Eucharist was the objective promise of the Kingdom, just as the Law had been under the Old Covenant. He was satisfied that on this St Cyril of Jerusalem was precisely right. But the promise was for a people, the eucharistic community. That was the agent of consecration. Hence his unique suggestion, not realizable of course in the context of his times, that the 'Sanctus' should always be sung by the whole congregation.[68] The mental strength of men like Thorndike was the chief legacy which held Anglicanism together as a spiritual entity, rather than merely a legal and social establishment.

Bishop Stevenson in his recent study of the Caroline Anglican understanding of the Eucharist offers an explanation of why the Carolines always seemed to veer towards Orthodoxy and for the most part firmly (not to say aggressively) away from Rome. It is, he suggests, to be found in their refusal to see the work of the Incarnate Christ in primarily forensic terms (as both Rome and the Puritans tended to do in mirror-image) and their preference for a 'symbolic, pictorial and dramatic' model in terms of 'living sacrifice'.

This enabled Thorndike, Taylor, Cosin and even less overtly 'High Church' divines like Daniel Brevint (Dean of Lincoln, 1681–95) to accept a spiritual continuity between the early Christian vision of the Eucharist and the Israelite Sacrifice. Brevint had no doubt that the earliest Christian Church accepted this as axiomatic. Christ's sacrifice, said Brevint, was offered 'both in the fulness of time and in the midst of the habitable world, which properly is Christ's great temple spreading salvation', just as, in type, the burnt offering did in its smoke, the golden altar in its perfume and the candlestick in its light. Now all that was co-extended 'to all both times and places'. Stevenson notes that sacrifice was a major iconic feature of Restoration church art, evidenced in the pelican figures in such new altar pieces as those in St James's Piccadilly and All Hallows Lombard Street. One may find it also in many of the Restoration spiritual songs of Pelham Humfrey and Henry Purcell.[69]

That a gap remained between this Anglicanism and Orthodoxy is a consequence of the lack of an integral tradition of life and worship throughout the whole fabric of the Church of England. Intellectual, social and even economic reasons have been offered for it. Fundamentally, there was a lack of authority – an authority not of penalty but of life. There was of course still in seventeenth-century England a punitive authority which the Church could call upon with the aid of the State, to be enforced by the processes of Common Law; but increasingly this bore more upon Romanists and Protestant Dissenters than it did on the bulk of church members. The purely civil sanctions of excommunication, which had worked well under the Tudors but had provoked Puritan resistance under James I and Charles I, were transmuted into something else under the Puritan regime of the Commonwealth and could not be properly restored in their prescriptive Anglican form after 1660, for all the efforts of Archbishop Sheldon. The purely spiritual sanctions of the believing community, expressed in unvaried practice and buttressed by penance, had not really been there since the Reformation and now found voice only in the formal rhetoric of the Prayer Book exhortations and in episcopal visitations.[70]

The preface to the 1552 Prayer Book had spoken of the alteration and breaking 'these many years past' of the 'godly and decent order [of worship] of the ancient Fathers'. The fact was that the 'Justinian' concepts of Henry VIII had not been able to take the strain of popular Protestant conscience. For purposes of polemic against Rome it continued to have currency: John Jewel appealed to the Henrician idea of a sovereign empire in Church and State while appealing at the same time to the autonomy of the Eastern Patriarchates as a fact of life, albeit under Turkish yoke. The Carolines were quite prepared to locate ecclesiastical authority in the Canons of 1571 and 1604 as expressive of the *ecclesia katholike*, the 'Great Church'; as opposed to sectarian separation, which was capable of transforming the world, whose life was salvation, the divine life of the Trinity. As we shall see, only when the Nonjurors lost their hold on the Church-State nexus was any thought entertained of separating law from the soteriological function of the Church.

> If we be schismatics because we have left them [Rome], by what name shall they call themselves, which have forsaken the Greeks, from whom they first received their faith . . .? For though these Greeks, who at this day profess religion, and Christ's Name, have many things corrupted among them, yet hold they still a great number of those things which they received from the Apostles. They have neither private masses nor mangled sacraments, nor purgatories, nor pardons . . . Whole Greece and Asia complain how the

bishops of Rome, with the morts of their purgatories and pardons, have both tormented men's consciences and picked their purses.[71]

But this was rhetoric – equally empire and ancient patriarchy. The realities for the Church of England were increasingly elsewhere and greatly diffused.

Hooker built his whole edifice of 'ecclesiastical Polity' on the idea of 'Church-entitive' and 'organicall' and was hated for it by the Puritans. On paper his vision carries conviction and would find resonances in Orthodoxy.

It is not for a man which doth know or should know what order is, and what peaceable government requireth, to ask 'why we should hang our judgment upon the Church's sleeve' ... That which the Church by her ecclesiastical authority shall probably think and define to be true or good, must in congruity of reason overrule all other inferior judgments whatsoever.

Hooker actually quotes St Basil's Epistle 68 at this point for the 'bare consent of the whole Church' as always superior to that 'wrought by an agent singling itself from consorts'. He devoutly hoped that the Church of England was not 'so weak, nor so unstrengthed' that her law could not command obedience. But so it proved in the century following. Habitual consent for the soul's sake had been broken at a profound level and could not be put together again except in the minds of the deeply understanding. The Church of England could neither be 'inhuman and stern' nor apply the 'gentle yoke' of *oeconomia*.[72] It was a dilemma which haunted the Caroline divines. They might, like Crakenthorpe, invoke the sheer reality of the Eastern Patriarchs as an excuse for the Church of England's existence free from Rome, or like Laud argue the lack of logic in Rome's treatment of the Greeks as 'no Church'; seeing that they were 'so ample and large a Church'. But in practice they could not realize the Orthodoxy they admired from afar or identified with their reading of the

Fathers. All they could do was to meet Orthodoxy in principle on 'Exclusive Ground', i.e. the Councils which all accepted, and the Fathers.[73]

Anglican critical editions of the Fathers appeared regularly in the seventeenth century. In the first half they ranged from Henry Savile's edition of St John Chrysostom of 1613 to Ussher's Ignatian Epistles of 1644. Edmund Chishull, writing at the end of the century, saw the period of the Cappadocian Fathers as that of the Church's 'meridian light'.[74] Beveridge attempted an *eirenikon* on the *Filioque* from the Fathers.[75] He knew his Cappadocians well enough to be sure that they did not accept purgatory.[76] On the same ground Bramhall thought it could not be otherwise than that the Greek and English Churches should agree, seeing they had the same creed 'without addition or subtraction', the old liturgies 'with less variation than the Church of Rome' [presumably he means variation from the primitive norm] and the Fathers.[77]

However, the temper of Caroline reverence for the Fathers differed markedly from that of the Orthodox in the seventeenth century. They were the heirs of Hooker whose use of the Fathers, in Middleton's view, was 'an advance in historical understanding' and a reaction against the arid use of proof-texts in the Puritan controversy which relegated the Fathers to 'an appendage' rather than an integral part of the argument. By countering the Puritans not text by text but by attacking their assumption of a wholly fallen Church, Hooker was able to use the Fathers, 'not only where the consensus is grounded in Scripture, but also where it is not against Scripture in matters of doctrine and discipline' so as to find a legitimate place for reason in all ages of the Church. In so doing he tended to appropriate a 'patristic mind', incarnational and eucharistic and extending as far as *theosis* (or, as he and his successors would have preferred to say, 'participation'). The Carolines might still quote the Fathers occasionally by rote in anti-Roman polemics; they might also, like Cosin and Taylor, now study them according to historico-critical method. They were, after all, at liberty to do so because they were not enmeshed in an absolutely unbroken tradition of their use and reverence. They could stand back and look at them afresh.[78]

Taylor looked to the Church of the Fathers for a 'sensing' of Scripture, but he knew that they did not always agree. Furthermore, he knew from comparative textual study that Roman editors had corrupted some texts to their own apologetic advantage. The texts distributed in England by Constantine Palaeocappa in the early sixteenth century were suspect.[79] Taylor was aware of the danger of simply using the Fathers, as the texts had come down to him, as an ammunition dump to fuel controversy. He found them an 'excellent corroborative' in questions already determined by Scripture and therefore saw Tradition (the 'tradition of the Fathers') as 'morally and probably' confirming the sense of Scripture.[80] But he must ask himself of the Fathers, as he did everyone else, whether each individually were fit to be believed on this or that. There was nothing to be gained from quoting a Father out of context simply because it seemed to fit an argument, squeezing the poor man into a procrustean bed. God was not morally 'wanting to our industry' any more than he was to theirs. He blessed every age with understanding.

Beveridge agreed. A 'real truth', he said, must be tested, quoting St Basil in his support. Beveridge, whose ability to make critical analysis of patristic texts was enhanced by his prodigious knowledge of Syriac and Chaldean so that he could pursue common texts outside of the Greek world, realized clearly that in the study of both Scripture and the Fathers one needed to take account not only of individual passages *literatim* but also of what he called 'common notions' which 'from the beginning implanted in the minds of all Christians, not so much from any particular passage of holy Scripture as from all; from the general scope and tenor of the whole Gospel ... and ... from the constant tradition of the Apostles, so to speak ... For on any other supposition it would be incredible, or even impossible, that they should have been received with so unanimous a consent everywhere, always and by all.' By the same token this applied also to the reception of the Fathers where there was a common sense. This suggested that there was a 'patristic mind' which was more than the sum of its

parts and transcended particular errors.[81] In general the Carolines spoke of the Fathers much as individual Fathers spoke of
their own predecessors in the Faith. John Collinson notes in
his 1813 Bampton Lectures that the Fathers spoke of their
predecessors 'not indeed in terms of blind zeal and indiscrim-
inate attachment, but with respect and confidence.' John Colet
and Erasmus had sown such a humane way of looking at the
Fathers and it contrasts markedly with the sceptical approach
adopted in the 1630s by the French Reformed divine Jean
Daillé, the English translation of whose work as *Concerning
the Right Use of the Fathers in the Decision of the Controversies that are at this day in Religion* (1651) sparked off a
bitter print war in which the whole of Caroline erudition was
employed to defend the 'Anglican' position.[82]

In every age, said Taylor, the Holy Spirit was an 'eternal
band to keep our reason from returning to the darkness of the old
creation.' So reason and prayer must always go together in the
use of the Fathers. For this reason he was not afraid to quote
them, say, Hugh of St Victor, although Hugh came from an age
of papal corruption. In fact he made massive use of Thomas
Aquinas. Justifying himself, he quoted from Hugh's *Eruditiones
didascaliae* the need for judiciousness and discrimination. It
was all a question of balance. Like Hooker, he held that neither
Fathers nor Councils per se should restrain the Church, where
the need arose, from making a judicious reordering of worship.
Once again, Beveridge concurred. Taylor, like others in the
Caroline tradition, believed that the word of God must be
discerned from the 'pretences of men'. God, he said, was not
'wanting to our ministry' any more than to that of the Fathers;
He 'blessed every age with understanding of His truths' through
the Spirit, who was implicate both in prayer and right reason.
Taylor saw no impassable gulf between them. Mysteries were
'uncomprehended' rather than 'uncomprehensible'.[83]

Close as he was to the measured spirit of Orthodoxy,
Taylor was distrusted by the Anglican leadership as a 'wild
man', of 'dangerous temper' and 'apt to break out into extrav-
agances'. For that reason his old Oxford friend, Gilbert
Sheldon, banished him to an Irish see. This of course back-

handedly admits his potency. He was extravagant only in terms of the extreme intellectual timidity of High Churchmen at the time. Those trying to negotiate a compromise settlement with the Presbyterians feared that he might 'rock the boat' with his candour. Herbert Croft, Bishop of Hereford, was typical of the established thinking against which Taylor stood out. Croft thought the great authority of the Fathers in the early Church had not been normative for all time but simply a function of the superabundance of pernicious heresies in their own day. These heresies could only be quenched and people kept on the straight and narrow by massive and repeated quotation. But as for himself, he was quite prepared to ditch even the ante-Nicene Fathers as a bunch of chiliasts.[84]

The object of Andrewes and the Carolines had been, to use John Fell's description of Henry Hammond, to be 'perfect and ready in the sense of the fathers, councils, ecclesiastical historians and liturgies'. Thorndike, in his *Epilogue to the Tragedy of the Church of England*, held that the true English Reformation could only be secured on the basis of a further reform on the model of the primitive Catholic Church, which would 'distinguish that which is substantial from that which is not'; by (to use the title of another of his tracts) a process of 'Just Weights and Measures'.[85] But circumstances were against them. It might be, as the Tractarian Arthur Haddan opined in 1870, that the Carolines 'recalled and made sure' to Anglicans their place in Catholic Christendom, so that 'no single name, however influential, has ever succeeded in usurping the right of branding with its own designation the Church of this land' and so retained to them a 'title unbroken to be a branch of the Church Universal as it has existed from the beginning . . .' Certainly, he is right that they discouraged the 'crude speculations of a single generation' or a 'single crisis'.[86] But for all their profound patristic learning, they failed to make it possible for the Church of England to achieve a theological rapprochement with Orthodoxy, even in face of Rome. One should not therefore be surprised at how mistaken they could be when brought face to face with Orthodox on their own home territory.

Notes

1. See *The Glastonbury Bulletin*, VII, 88 (1994), 240–6, for the present writer's review of Litvack's *John Mason Neale and the Quest for Sobornost.*
2. *A History of the Holy Eastern Church: The Patriarchate of Antioch* (London, Oxford and Cambridge, 1873), pp. ix–x.
3. Ibid., p. lx; *A History of the Holy Eastern Church: A General Introduction* (London, 1850), para 42, p. xxvi.
4. Kathryn D. Hill, 'Robert Grosseteste and his work of Greek translation' in Derek Baker (ed.), *The Orthodox Churches and the West* (Studies in Church History, vol. 13) (Oxford, 1976), pp. 213–22. Cf. G. R. Stephens, *The Knowledge of Greek in England in the Middle Ages* (London, 1933) and Donald M. Nicol, *Studies in Late Byzantine History and Prosopography* (London, 1986), pp. 193–4. John of Basingstoke (d.1252) studied in Athens, allegedly with Constantina who may have been the daughter of Michael Choniates, Archbishop of Athens, although he denied the parentage. Whatever her lineage, by all accounts she was a brilliant teacher and polymath.
5. Joseph Gill, SJ, *The Council of Florence* (London, 1959), p. 296. See Deno J. Geanakoplos, *Byzantine East and Latin West. Two Worlds of Christendom in Middle Ages and Renaissance* (Oxford, 1966).
6. Steven Runciman, *The Great Church in Captivity: A Study of the Patriarchate of Constantinople from the Eve of the Turkish Conquest to the Greek War of Independence* (Cambridge, 1968), p. 289. Cf. W. Weiss, *Humanism in England during the Fifteenth Century* (Oxford, 1941), pp. 143–8.
7. P. S. Allen (ed.), *Opus Epistolarum Des. Erasmi Roterdami*, III (London, 1906), 947; E. F. Rogers (ed.), *The Correspondence of Sir Thomas More* (London, 1947), pp. 111–20; P. E. Hallett (ed.), *The Life and Illustrious Martyrdom of Sir Thomas More by Thomas Stapleton* (London, 1928), p. 41. See also E. E. Reynolds, *St Thomas More* (London, 1957), pp. 104–6. It is not clear why Arthur Middleton thinks there was a patristics revival at Oxford under the influence of John Colet. Cf. Middleton, *Fathers and Anglicans. The Limits of Orthodoxy* (Leominster, 2001), pp. 11–12. The revival does not seem to have occurred on any scale until the later years of the century and then largely at St John's College, where John Buckeridge taught St John Chrysostom, St Gregory Nazianzen and St Basil the Great, influencing the young William Laud in the direction of the Greek Fathers. In most of Oxford Calvinism was dominant and patristics at a discount.

8. Cf. E. E. Reynolds, *Saint John Fisher* (London, 1955), pp. 40, 47.
9. Runciman, op. cit., p. 290.
10. C. W. Dugmore, *The Mass and the English Reformers* (London, 1958), pp. 184ff. They agreed only that Christ was present as consecrator in every Eucharist.
11. Cf. K. J. Walsh, 'Cranmer and the Fathers, especially in the *Defence*' *Journal of Religious History*, 11 (1980), 234; Middleton, op. cit., pp. 21, 33; Dugmore, ibid., pp. 115, 184–5; Edward Burbidge (ed.), *The Remains of the Library of Thomas Cranmer* (London, 1892), p. 20; G. J. Cuming, 'Eastern Liturgies and the Anglican Divines 1510–1662' in Baker, op. cit., *The Orthodox Churches*, p. 231.
12. Cuming, ibid., p. 232; Cf. F. E. Brightman, *The English Rite*, I (London, 1915), I, lxvi, 178.
13. Cf. Dugmore, op. cit., p. 114.
14. Ibid., pp. 133–4; Cuming, op. cit., p. 232. Cranmer studiously ignored the more explicit Eastern material encapsulated in the Cologne Church Order. Cf. Cuming, p. 233.
15. Cuming, ibid., pp. 234–6; Middleton, op. cit., pp. 77–78.
16. A. M. Ramsey, 'The Ancient Fathers and Modern Anglican Theology', in *Sobornost*, Ser. 4, No. 6 (1962), 290.
17. Runciman, ibid.; *Christopher Angell, a Grecian who tasted many stripes and torments inflicted by the Turkes for the faith which he had in Christ Jesus* (Oxford, 1617), pp. [1], [7]. Cf. Sir Paul Rycaut, *The Present State of the Greek and Armenian Churches* (London, 1679), p. 132; Runciman, op. cit., p. 294; William H. McNeill, *Venice. The Hinge of Europe 1081–1797* (Chicago, 1974), pp. 162, 190–1, 209; cf. Colin Davey, *Pioneer for Unity: Metrophanes Kritopoulos (1589–1639) and Relations between the Orthodox Roman Catholic and Reformed Churches* (British Council of Churches, London, 1987). See also G. Hadjiantoniou, *Protestant Patriarch* (London, 1961).
18. Runciman, ibid., pp. 294–5.
19. Ibid., p. 296.
20. Ibid., p. 291. Mention should perhaps also be made of Sir John Finch, who was Professor of Medicine at Pisa before going to Constantinople as ambassador. Cf. Edward Carpenter, *The Protestant Bishop. Being the Life of Henry Compton, 1632–1713, Bishop of London* (London, 1956), p. 361. Archbishop Laud was kept thoroughly informed by Pocock and others (presumably Roe and Wych) of the events leading up to and following Cyril Lucaris' murder. Cf. Laud to Pocock, 8 April 1640, regarding Cyril's successor, Cyril Contari. 'I hear no good yet; what it will please God to work by him I know not.

It may be he hath shown the Turk a way, in the death of Cyril, how to deal with himself [i.e. by his conspiracy against Lucaris with Turkish connivance] ... I heard before your letters came to me that the Patriarch who succeeded Cyril was like to suffer. And certainly he deserved it, and that in a severer manner than is fallen upon him. Yet I cannot but say there is charity, and perhaps wisdom, in preventing the execution that might otherwise have fallen upon him.' *The Works of the Most Reverend Father in God William Laud DD* (Library of Anglo-Catholic Theology, VI, pt. 2, Oxford, 1857), 580.

21. Runciman, ibid., p. 290.
22. Cf. Everyman edition of Burton (1896), I, 70 and the Sherwood Sugden version of Browne, edited by W. A. Greenhill (Peru, Illinois, 1881), pp. 8–12.
23. William Forbes, *Considerationes Modestae et Pacificae Controversiarum*, II (posthumously published in 1658), (Library of Anglo-Catholic Theology, Oxford, 1856), 208–9. For a modern edition of the Joachim-Lutheran exchange, see George Mastrantonis (ed.), *Augsburg and Constantinople: The Correspondence between the Tubingen Theologians and Patriarch Jeremiah II of Constantinople on the Augsburg Confession* (Brookline, Mass., 1982).
24. Cf. Bramhall, *Works* (1672), p. 636 and *Works*, (Library of Anglo-Catholic Theology, I, Oxford, 1842), 279. See the article on Pearson and F. Sanders in the *Dictionary of National Biography*.
25. Cf. Günter Thomann, *Studies in English Church History* (2nd ed., Stoke-on-Trent, 1993), pp. 59, 62.
26. Laud read Elias Metropolitan of Crete on Gregory Nazianzen's *Orations* in a Latin translation published by Billius at Paris in 1630. He also read something on the Council of Florence which persuaded him that Bellarmine was wrong in claiming that the Easterns believed in purgatory. *Works*, op. cit., I (Oxford, 1847), 133; II (Oxford, 1849), 384–5. Cf. T[homas] B[arlow] (Bishop of Lincoln), *Popery; or, The Principles and Positions Approved by the Church of Rome* (London, 1679), pp. 15–18, 27. See McNeill, op. cit., pp. 208–9. See George A. Maloney, SJ, *A History of Orthodox Theology since 1453* (Belmont, Mass., 1976), esp. p. 156.
27. Cf. Richard Crakenthorpe, *Defensio Ecclesiae Anglicanae*, edited and published posthumously by John Barkham, 1625, reprinted in the Library of Anglo-Catholic Theology, Oxford, 1847.
28. They were printed together as *Leitourgeia ton Hagion Pateron*.
29. Cf. Cuming, op. cit., p. 235. See the distinguished Orthodox

study by Nicolas Lossky, *Lancelot Andrewes the Preacher (1555–1626). Origins of the Mystical Theology of the Church of England* (Oxford, 1991).

30. Laud to Ussher, ? April 1638, in *Works*, op. cit., VI, Pt. 2, 521.

31. Thorndike knew Scialach and also the Latin translations of the Ethiopian Liturgy (Rome, 1549) and the Malabar-Malankara Liturgy (Coimbra, 1606). This, together with his encyclopedic knowledge of the Greek liturgies, gave him an overview of liturgical structures. The numerous variants he found implied for him 'continuous alteration' and not the permanency which Byzantines and others claimed. 'For as the Latin and Greek prelates added or changed, upon occasion, divers things afterward, in the liturgies which they received from the Apostles, so it is meet to think was done, according to the occasion of times, by those of Alexandria and Egypt.' (Presumably by 'Alexandria' he meant the Greek Patriarchate and by 'Egypt' the Coptic.) See his *The Religious Assemblies and the Public Service of God* (1642) in *The Theological Works of Herbert Thorndike*, I (Library of Anglo-Catholic Theology, II, Oxford, 1844), 264–5. He knew Masius's work on the Liturgies of St James and St Basil as translated from the Syriac versions into Greek. Cf. ibid., pp. 340, 353, 362. He appears to have made a comparative study of Eastern *anaphoras* and was aware that the only accessible version of the Ethiopian Liturgy lacked a *sursum corda*. Ibid., pp. 341, 351–14. Nicholson's *Plain and Full Exposition of the Catechism of the Church of England* (1655), which was very widely used in the Restoration period, shows a wide range of such liturgical reading, though it comes out only cryptically. Cf. Henry McAdoo, *The Eucharistic Theology of Jeremy Taylor Today* (Norwich, 1988), pp. 149–50, 154.

32. *The Works of the Right Reverend Father in God John Cosin, Lord Bishop of Durham* (Library of Anglo-Catholic Theology, I, Oxford, 1843), pp. 87–105, 130, 311; II (Oxford, 1843), xvii; IV (Oxford, 1851), 7, 28, 55, 75, 152, 160, 181–94, 228, 246, 260ff, 272, 462, 466ff; V (Oxford, 1855), 193–4, 355, 408; VI (Oxford, 1857), Pt. 1, 109ff, 120, 221–2; Pt. 2, 670; Affidavit copied by Thomas Baker, Smith MS 47, f.21, Bodleian MSS 15654. See also Kenneth Stevenson, *Covenant of Grace Renewed: A Vision of the Eucharist in the Seventeenth Century* (London, 1994), p. 97; W. J. Sparrow Simpson, *The Prayer of Consecration* (London and Milwaukee, 1917), pp. 149–51.

As will become apparent in later chapters, the Arnauld/Claude controversy was provoked by Antoine Arnauld who brought together a portfolio of 'testimonies' allegedly signed by Greek patriarchs, bishops and abbots to the effect that they believed as a doctrine of faith the teaching of the Council of Trent on transubstantiation. Ironically, although this served the strategy of the Jesuits and Franciscans in the eastern Mediterranean, Arnauld was a known leader of the 'Jansenists' who were the object of Jesuit attack in France. The French ambassador in Constantinople, the Marquis de Nointel, through whom the testimonials were collected and transmitted to Arnauld, was also a Jansenist. There may have been a private agenda here on the part of the Jansenists to deflect Jesuit attentions from their alleged heresies. Arnauld's publication provoked a counterblast from the Protestant minister of Charenton who questioned the methodology involved in the collection of the testimonials and argued that what they appeared to say was *prima facie* unlikely. For further details on the background see the forthcoming paper by Archimandrite Efrem Lash as mentioned in the Preface.

33. John Smith of Durham to Thomas Smith, 29 February 1703, Smith MS, ff.209–10, Bodleian Library; Middleton, op. cit., p. 182.
34. Harry Boone Porter, *Jeremy Taylor, Liturgist* (Alcuin Club, London, 1979), pp. 16–18, 72–74, 78.
35. Thomann, op. cit., p. 51.
36. Ibid., p. 45.
37. Dugmore, *Mass*, op. cit., pp. 95–96.
38. Hooker, *Laws of Ecclesiastical Polity*, IV, 9.1; V, 55.14, 55.9; 56.1; 56.7; 67.3; 67.4; 67.5; 67.7; 67.11; 67.12; 67.32–34; 78.2. See also Stevenson, op. cit., pp. 26, 28–30, 33–34; J. E. Booty, *The Divine Drama in History and Liturgy* (Allison Park, Pa, 1984), p. 144; Darwell Stone, *History of the Doctrine of the Holy Eucharist*, (London, 1909), II, 246ff.

For Andrewes' sense of 'living the Mystery', see the excellent summary by Middleton, op. cit., pp. 128–36, which relies heavily on Nicolas Lossky's *Lancelot Andrewes, the Preacher*, op. cit. Lossky identifies Andrewes' sense of tradition as 'a way of living in time in the light of eternity which recapitulates past, present and future. Everything is lived in contemporaneity with the reality of the Gospel'. (p. 340). Middleton infers from this that in his controversy with Cardinal Bellarmine, Andrewes had to place his emphasis on moral authority rather than on coercive jurisdiction (op. cit., p. 119). For Andrewes' instinctive recapitulation of the Fathers, see Middleton's judicious comments, ibid., pp. 124–6. A. M. Allchin had noted in advance of Lossky the 'patristic quality' of Andrewes' preaching. See his *Participation in God* (London, 1988), p. 15.

39. Richard Field, *The Church* (1606), cited by C. W. Dugmore, *Eucharistic Doctrine in England from Hooker to Waterland* (London, 1942), pp. 55, 57. Dugmore, ibid., p. 40. Forbes was perhaps the most outspoken of all the Carolines in affirming unequivocally the eucharistic sacrifice as a patristic teaching which could not be evaded by anyone who professed reverence for the Fathers. As far as he was concerned, there was a total patristic consensus. See a sensitive analysis of his view in Stevenson, op. cit., pp. 82–83, citing his *Considerationes*.
40. McAdoo, *Eucharistic Theology*, op. cit., p. 48. Ibid., p. 50.
41. Ibid., pp. 97–100. Forbes was confident that the concessions made by the Greek delegates at Florence on the question of purgatory were immediately repudiated by the Greek Church at large, citing as his authority Mark of Ephesus (*Considerationes*, pp. 115–7). He assumed therefore that the modern Greek Church was faithful to the Fathers whose minds were 'quite alien' to the idea of purgatory, notwithstanding occasional verbal infelicities. Purgatory and prayers for the dead were not in his view logically linked. In this he agreed with Thorndike and Cosin (pp. 74, 88).
42. See Carroll's introduction to Jeremy Taylor, *Selected Works* (New York, 1990), p. 55.
43. See Taylor's *The Great Exemplar (1649)* in *The Works of Jeremy Taylor*, XIX, edited by Heber and Eden (1852), 9, cited by Stevenson, op. cit., pp. 201–2.
44. Porter, op. cit., pp. 87–88.
45. Stevenson, op. cit., pp. 116–18, 121–2, 124–5.
46. Taylor, *Clerus Domini* (1651), cited by McAdoo, *Eucharistic Theology*, op. cit., p. 95.
47. Taylor, *Holy Living* (1650), cited by Porter, op. cit., p. 62; McAdoo, ibid., pp. 71–3, 82ff, 99, 154, 176.
48. McAdoo, ibid., p. 154.
49. Ibid., p. 86.
50. Ibid., pp. 190–1, citing *The Worthy Communicant* (1660).
51. See Chapters VI and VII of McAdoo, passim.
52. Darwell Stone, op. cit., II, 33.
53. McAdoo, op. cit., p. 202.
54. Porter, op. cit., p. 133.
55. McAdoo, op. cit., p. 46.
56. Taylor, *Clerus Domini*, cited by McAdoo, ibid., pp. 97–99, 102.
57. McAdoo, ibid., pp. 99–100, 105–6.
58. Ibid., pp. 109–11, citing *The Real Presence Spiritual in the Blessed Sacrament* (1654).
59. McAdoo, ibid., p. 133, citing *A Disuasive from Popery* (1664);

McAdoo, ibid., pp. 132, 162, citing *The Real Presence; The Rule and Exercise of Holy Living* (privately printed 1650 or 1651), p. 2.
60. McAdoo, ibid., p. 64, citing *The Great Exemplar* (1649), *Discourse XIII.*
61. Porter, op. cit., pp. 46–48.
62. Ibid., pp. 96, 99, 103.
63. Ibid., pp. 30, 34, 37–8, 131.
64. The *proskomide* was drastically shortened for this reason. Cf. ibid., pp. 72–74, 78.
65. Ibid., pp. 114–6.
66. Ibid., pp. 114–5. Taylor, *Disuasive*, cited by W. J. Sparrow Simpson, op. cit., p. 70. Also of God's acknowledgement and acceptance of the prayer of the Church as he accepted the gifts of Abel, the Sacrifice of Noah, the service of Moses and Aaron, the peace-offering of Samuel, the repentance of David and the incense of Zachariah.
67. Cuming, op. cit., pp. 236–7. See Beveridge's *Ecclesia Anglicana Ecclesia Catholica; or, The Doctrine of the Church of England consonant to Scripture, Reason and the Fathers* [a commentary on the Thirty-Nine Articles] in *The Theological Works of William Beveridge DD* (Library of Anglo-Catholic Theology, VII, Oxford, 1845), p. 478. Some Restoration divines, like Simon Patrick, George Bull, Isaac Barrow and William Stillingfleet, who were influential preachers, never fully escaped their Presbyterian background in the Commonwealth. Anthony Horneck, a vastly influential preacher at the Savoy, brought to his ministry a German Protestant mind-set though he formally converted to the High Church. Cf. Dugmore, *Eucharistic Doctrine*, op. cit., pp. 111–16, 120ff.
68. Thorndike, *Of the Laws of the Church* in *Works*, op. cit., IV, Pt. 1 (Oxford, 1852), pp. 26ff, 82; 'The Reformation of the Church of England better than that of the Council of Trent', *Works*, V (Oxford, 1854), 544, 546. Thorndike was aware in detail of the Venetian Greeks' answer to the Twelve Questions of Cardinal Guise. He understood them to intend 'transelementation' throughout the whole eucharistic action rather than localized transubstantiation. Ibid., IV, Pt. 2. See Stevenson, op. cit., pp. 140, 142, 147–8.
69. Cf. Stevenson, ibid., pp. 102–3, citing Brevint's *Christian Sacrament and Sacrifice* (1673); see also pp. 175–7; Sparrow Simpson, op. cit., pp. 45–47. See also James Dymocke, *The Great Sacrifice of the New Testament* (London, 1686).
70. Middleton, op. cit., p. 54.
71. Cf. W. M. Southgate, *John Jewel and the Problem of Doctrinal*

Authority (Cambridge, Mass., 1962), p. 194; John Jewel, *An Apologie or Answere in Defence of the Church of England*, tr. Anne Cook (Lady Bacon), (London, 1564), Jelf edition (London, 1848), p. 194. Cf. Samuel Hudson, *A Vindication of the Essence and Unity of the Church-Catholick visible*, reprinted by Edmund Calamy (London, 1658); Hooker, *Ecclesiastical Polity*, V, 7.2–4; 8.4.

72. Significantly, Nathaniel Marshall, who knew a great deal about the 'declension' of penitential discipline in the West, showed little knowledge of the corresponding discipline in the East. See his *The Penitential Discipline of the Primitive Church* (1714) (Library of Anglo-Catholic Theology, Oxford, 1844). This imbalance was fairly general, but one may cite as exceptions not only Cosin but also Thorndike and Peter Gunning. Thorndike learned of Orthodox penitential discipline from Morinus' *De Poenitententia*, whose sources were as up-to-date as Patriarch Jeremias II (i.e. 1580s). Peter Gunning, Bishop of Chichester, collated patristic evidence on the Lenten fast into a system which he assumed had continued validity. It is worth nothing that Thorndike was also familiar with some aspects of Greek matrimonial practice, which he held in low regard, seeing it as having 'imbased and corrupted' the Church's life. He derived his information possibly from Matthew the Monk or Arcudius. See his 'Laws of the Church' in *The Works*, op. cit., IV, Pt. 1 (Oxford, 1852), pp. 297–8, 330–1, 353–4. Gunning's work, which grew out of a sermon which he delivered before Charles II, was reprinted in the Library of Anglo-Catholic Theology in 1845.

73. Crakenthorpe, *Defensio*, op. cit., pp. 86–87. Cf. pp. 134–5, 138–9; Laud, 'True Relations of sundry Conferences had between certaine Protestant Doctours and the Jessuite called M. Fisher' (1626) in *Works*, op. cit., II (Oxford, 1849), p. 29. See also [M. D.], *A Seasonable Advice to all True Protestants in England* (London, 1679), p. 21. Laud certainly believed the Greek Church had erred (though, like Bramhall, he inclined to think the issue was, as Bramhall put it, a 'mere logomachy' or 'manner of speech'. However, not every public error denied 'Christ the Foundation'. The whole Greek Church had not lost the Holy Spirit and so remained a true Church 'in the main substance'. Laud thought it cruel of Fisher to dismiss a Church 'whose Cross is heavy already'. Ibid., pp. 25–27, 30. See Bramhall's 'A Replication to the Bishop of Chalcedon' [a Roman bishop *in partibus infidelium*], in *The Works of the Most Reverend Father in God John Bramhall DD*, II (Oxford, 1842), pp. 260, 597, 629. Thorndike likewise was convinced that both

the Roman and Greek Churches rained 'salvation . . . upon both sides'. While both, he believed, carried an element of fault for schism, probably neither was guilty of idolatry. Faith had been sufficiently guarded by the first six Councils. See his 'Reformation of the Church of England', op. cit., in *Works*, V, p. 498; also Chapters XII, XIII and XIX passim.

74. Edmund Chishull, *A Charge of Heresy* (London, 1706).
75. Beveridge, *Ecclesia Anglicana*, op. cit., pp. 173ff.
76. Ibid., pp. 473, 486.
77. Bramhall, *Replication*, op. cit.; *Works*, II, pp. 85–86. Middleton, op. cit., p. 96, citing John Luoma, 'The Historical Perspective of Richard Hooker: A Renaissance Paradox', in *The Journal of Medieval and Renaissance Studies*, viii (1977), p. 45 and 'Who Owns the Fathers? Hooker and Cartwright on the Authority of the Primitive Church' in *The Sixteenth Century Journal*, viii (1977), p. 45; Middleton, pp. 99–100.
78. Cuming, op. cit., pp. 231–2.
79. McAdoo, op. cit., p. 157.
80. Ibid., pp. 24–25, 31.
81. Beveridge, op. cit., pp. 365, 385. Thomann, op. cit., p. 64. On reason, Taylor cited with approval Aquinas, *Summa Theologica*, 2-2, q. 180, 3 and 4c, and Hugh of St Victor, *Eruditiones*, *Patrologia Latina*, CLXXVI, pp. 741–836, stressing especially p. 772. Cf. Beveridge's Preface to Vincentius, *Against Heresy* (reprinted, Oxford, 1851), p. vi and his *The Importance and the use of the Oriental Languages (1658)*.
82. John Collinson, *A Key to the Writings of the Principal Fathers of the Christian Church who flourished during the first Three Centuries* (Oxford, 1813), p. 13; Middleton, op. cit., p. 209.
83. McAdoo, op. cit., pp. 24–25, 31, 45.
84. McAdoo, op. cit., p. 204. *The Legacy of the Right Reverend Father in God, Herbert, Lord Bishop of Hereford . . .; Or, a Short Determination of all Controversies we have had with the Papists by Gods Holy Word* (London, 1679), pp. 43–45, 56, 64–66. Croft had been a Roman convert in his youth and had studied at both St Omer and the English College in Rome. Drawn back to Anglicanism by Bishop Morton of Durham and patronized by Laud, he nevertheless ended up under the Restoration boxing the compass theologically. He fiercely combatted Popery in his diocese and advocated pan-Protestant union. See the article on him in the *Dictionary of National Biography*.
85. Cf. Fell's 'The Life of Dr H. Hammond' appended to Hammond's *A Practical Catechism* in his *Works* (Library of Anglo-Catholic Theology, Oxford, 1847), p. cxxx; Thorndike, *Works*, II, I, pp. 120–4.

86. Haddan in Archibald Weir & W. D. MacLagan (eds), *The Church and the Age: Essays on the Principles and Present Position of the Anglican Church* (London, 1870), pp. 231–3.

CHAPTER TWO

ACCIDENTS OF LOCATION: THE ARCHDEACON AND THE CONSUL

In the first of a series of picture postcards from the Orient which began to open up the world of Orthodoxy to the Anglican cognoscenti, we shall consider (not too perversely) a Frenchman, though a devout Anglican, forced into a distant exile by the English Civil Wars, and a diplomat with an un-English name who did an honest job in a dishonest profession and along the way made some fair if unflattering comments on the Greek religious character.

Isaac Basire

Isaac Basire de Preaumont was born in Rouen in 1607. His father was a Huguenot of the lowest order of the French noblesse. He studied at the Universities of Rotterdam and Leyden, where he conceived an intense and unusual interest in the hypostatic union, purgatory and indulgences.

How and why he moved to England is not clear. All that is known is that having done so and conformed to the Church of England, he was ordained to the diaconate in 1629 by Bishop Morton of Coventry and Lichfield. There can be no doubt after reading his letters and diaries that he adopted both England and its Church with sincerity and zeal. Very soon he was Morton's chaplain and followed him on his translation to Durham in 1632. His fixation with establishment and his attachment to monarchy probably dates from Charles I's visit to Durham in 1633. He soon became chaplain-in-ordinary to the King and was made Archdeacon of Northumberland by Morton in August 1644. He was not left in peace for very long to exercise that office because of the Civil War, but his conscious exercise of visitorial duties when he was restored to it at the Restoration was beyond compare.[1]

Basire moved straight from being a Huguenot to being an Anglican High Churchman. Puritanism was not for him. By 1634 he was confessing to Gerard Vossius at Leyden that he regarded the Greek Fathers as only inferior in authority to the Holy Scriptures. He wrote in terms of 'sacred antiquity'.[2]

In 1651, because of the Puritan supremacy and his ejection from the archdeaconry, he began an extended tour of the Near and Middle East 'to note the progress of Christianity from the earliest ages'. He had taken advantage of not only the spate of English editions of the Fathers as background but of all that was available on the Fathers in continental centres like Leyden. Presumably he had also read Sir Thomas Roe's *Relation* of 1627. Roe (or Rowe) was English ambassador to Constantinople and gave many Greek and Arabic manuscripts to the Bodleian Library at Oxford, including a Greek Bible of fabulous origin (attributed in legend to Thecla). He had sought to protect the Greek Church against Ottoman oppression.

Basire reported that while on Zante he spread among the Greeks 'the Catholick Doctrine of our Church, the sum whereof I imparted to sundry of them in a vulgar Greek translation of our Greek Catechism ...' According to his account this drew down on him both envy and persecution, not from the Greeks but from the Latins who had a large presence on Zante through the Venetian and Genoese influence. In Morea, he said, the Metropolitan of Achaia asked him to preach twice in Greek at a meeting of bishops and clergy. The sermons were 'well taken'. He left behind him there also his Greek Church of England Catechism. At Aleppo, where he stayed some months, he had frequent conversations with the Patriarch of Antioch to whom, yet again, he gave the Catechism, though this time in Arabic. At Jerusalem he was received with much honour not only by the Greeks (which is hardly surprising as he must by then have accumulated many letters of introduction from Greek bishops) but also by the Romans. Perhaps they had got wind of his activities and decided it was better to humour than to seek openly to discredit.

The Patriarch of Jerusalem expressed to Basire his desire for communion with the English Church. After some 'velitations' about the validity of Anglican orders, the visitor was let into the church of the Holy Sepulchre at half-price – i.e. at the priests' rate. He then ventured into 'Mesopotamia' and met some Armenian bishops (he was not quite sure who they were but said 'Armenians most of them'). He arrived at Constantinople in 1653 shortly after the Turks had intruded a patriarch, as was their wont, and thereupon betook himself to the 'true patriarch', talking with him about intercommunion 'salve conscientia et honore'. At the same time he did not neglect to nudge his Beatitude about the need for a 'Canonical Reformation of some grosser Errours'. He was very conscious of acting for the exiled Charles II as his chaplain-in-ordinary and lived in daily hope of receiving royal instructions. It is ironic that Basire should have been talking to a deposed and humiliated patriarch at a time when the 'true Church of England' was itself degraded and dispossessed.

Basire planned a visit to Egypt to 'take a survey of the Churches of the Cophties' and to 'conferre with the [presumably Greek] Patriarch of Alexandria', to complement the other three, 'partly to acquire the knowledge of those Churches and partly to publish ours . . .' He never got to Egypt because he was sidetracked to Transylvania. During his travels Basire collected several confessions of faith – Greek, Armenian, Jacobite and Maronite. These he presumably kept with him during his time in Transylvania as advisor to the Prince. They would not therefore have been known to others until after his return to England at the Restoration.[3]

Basire was aware that not all the Greek clergy were ignorant or looked down upon. The protopresbyters in Zante and also some of the clergy he met in Lebanon and Syria were held in high regard and even had precedence over nobles.[4] He gave credit where credit was due. In this he proved more generous than some.

Archbishop Juxon and Bishop Brian Walton of Chester urged Basire to publish the confessions he had collected, but clearly he did not do so immediately upon his return from exile.[5]

What use Basire himself made of his first-hand experiences was affected by his a-priori assumptions about church history and in particular the church history of England. He was influenced by Simon Birkbeck's work on Protestantism which sought to show that for fifteen hundred years after Christ 'divers guides of God's Church have in sundry points of religion taught as the Church of England now doth'. Friendship with Nathaniel Ward, a fierce anti-papist, encouraged him to think much of 'our holy land' and to resent the papist intruders. In his will of September 1676 he affirmed that 'having taken a serious survey of most Christian Churches, both Easterne and Westerne' he had 'not found a paralell of the Church of England, both for soundnes of Apostolicall Doctrine and Catholicque Desiplin'.[6]

But above all other assumptions which influenced him and 'straightened' his estimate of the Orthodox Churches was his vehement propagation of the dignity and autonomy of the imperial British Church.

> Gildas the Wise writeth, That Britain almost from the age of the Apostles, had Bishops, who communicated with the rest of the world in Pacifique and formed letters, even from the beginning of the Gospel. Tertullian in his Book against the Jews, Num. 43 of Pamelius's Edition, after hee [sic] hath reckoned up all the Catholick Churches throughout the world, adds, And the Britains holds, inaccessible to the Romans, are subdued to the yoak of Christ. And Pamelius upon the said place, out of Bede, and Polydore Virgil, confesseth, That Britain had publickly received the whole Evangile, not onely in the time of Marcus Antoninus Verus, under King Lucius, but asserts also out of Gildas, from the beginning of the Gospel ... With Gildas not onely Tertul-

lian giveth suffrage but also Origen; yea and St Athanasius glorieth, That Bishops passed out of Britain to the Council of Sardis, wherein Athanasius' absolution was obtained ... The same thing teacheth Chrystome; And that the Catholick Bishops came from Britain to the Council of Ariminum is manifest out of Severus Sulpicius, Theodoret, Hierome, Ruffinus, Socrates, Zozomen, cited by Harpsfield. That the Britannick Church kept this Communion and Unity of Rule with the Gallicane, to the coming of St Augustin into England; ... and it appears out of the first book of the History of the English Nation, Harpsfield and other English Writers, That the Gallick Church sent into Britain St German and Lupus, before the coming of Augustin into England, to succour the Britannick Church. And Bede relates, That Aegilbert a Gallick Bishop resided no small time in Ireland, being imployed in reading upon the Scripture; Moreover it appears out of Bede, Harpsfield, Surius and others, That Hilda the Nunne of Calice was sent into England by St Aidan, and had communicated with the Britannick Church. But on the other side presently, when as she lived in the Monastery at Calice, that St Malo, Bredon, Samson, Polensis, about the year 550, communicated with the Gallick and Aremorick Churches ... Now it appears out of Bede that neither Britains, nor Scots, would communicate with the English, and their Bishop Augustin, more than with Pagans, as Huntingdon speaks; and the reason was, because Augustin seemed to deal with them uncanonically, by constraining them to receive him for their Arch-Bishop, and to submit themselves to the mandates of Foreigners, when as the ancient manners of their Church required, that they should act all things Synodically among themselves ...[7]

These words by an English Benedictine monk and 'moderate Romanist' in ill-favour with the pope, from a tract passed from hand to hand among Anglican exiles in Paris in the last years of the Commonwealth, were commended by Basire on his return to England and fairly represent his viewpoint. He always began by giving priority to canonical legitimacy: that which was canonically legitimate had a pre-emptive right to be considered orthodox also. His knowledge of canon law and how it related to civil law was considerable and he thought he could use it to refute Roman claims over the English Church without resorting to classical Protestant polemic. He easily manipulated the 5th Canon of Nicaea and the Cyprianic privilege to show that Augustine 'invaded' the 'Britannick Church' and so made the Reformation legal settlement appear to be a simple matter of restoring common dignity and decorum by overthrowing lawlessness, albeit lawlessness covered by centuries of use. The Church of England could then be contradistinguished from 'Cabals and Conventicles' of all sorts 'now adayes', which he regarded as a cancer on its 'sacred body'.[8] For Basire the external polity of the Church anywhere depended on the Prince, although of right it devolved upon the clergy. The power to call synods, order fasts and festivals, distinguish parishes, dioceses and provinces were at one and the same time rightly royal and episcopal powers, while the power to fix the hierarchical degrees of bishops 'so that this man is a Bishop, that a Primate, the third Metropolitane . . .' was a strictly princely power. He applauded the Henrician Parliament's description of Henry VIII as 'the Emperour of Britain'.[9] In this Basire was an immaculate Byzantine, but the very completeness of his Byzantinism paradoxically protected him from any modesty or deference toward the Greek Church or any possibility of conceiving that that the Greeks might be doctrinally sounder than the Church of England.

Although Basire did not publish in detail on the usages of the Greek Church as some of his successors did, his influence was pervasive and immense and the mere knowledge that such a colossus of Patristic and Canonical learning had moved among Greek bishops and preached to them prepared his readers and associates to attend to more detailed reports.

Sir Paul Rycaut

Sir Paul Rycaut was Secretary to the English Embassy in Constantinople between 1661 and 1668 and then went on to become English consul at Smyrna. He was a man of some learning, knowing Greek, Arabic and a smattering of Armenian – all languages necessary to trade in the Middle East. He was a Fellow of the Royal Society. He was not a profound theologian, but he could assess and arrange to orderly practical fashion areas of theological importance. His main published works were his *The Present State of the Greek and Armenian Churches* (1679) and *The History of the Present State of the Ottoman Empire* (1686).[10] His method was very concise and economical compared with his clerical contemporaries but none the worse for that since for all their scholarly apparatus they proved no more accurate as observers than he was. His aim was to be purely factual, not polemical. In his address to the King he confessed that he was squeamish about 'Disputations' and 'Wranglings' and all too conscious of his scholarly limitations. He inclined to reconcile and cover over blemishes in the Body of Christ when they were not 'plain Heresie'. Syllogisms, he was convinced, never convicted anyone.[11]

Paul Rycaut was a marvellous travel writer. He describes how he found altars all over Asia Minor concealed in 'secret and dark places ... rather like Vaults or Sepulchres than Churches, having their Roofs almost levelled with the Superficies of the Earth, lest the most ordinary exsurgency of structure should be accused for triumph of Religion and to stand in competition with the lofty Spires of the Mahometan Moschs'. Rycaut took this architectural feature of the landscape for a parable of Christ suffering in His Mystical Body. He honoured the humility and patience of that Body under peevish persecution, especially when, with Turks and Greeks mingling to the extent that they did, speaking the same language, allowing their children to play together, it was difficult to have a classic spirit of martyrdom. He noted too how by a subtle manipulation of privilege, even at the level of the children, the overlords constantly tempted Christians to apostasize.[12]

Yet, like other literary tourists, Rycaut was not averse to touristic vandalism. Visiting the site of Philadelphia he was shown 'a wall of Mens bones . . . which is so well cemented, and the bones so entire, that I brought a piece thereof with me thence'.[13]

For Rycaut, as for Basire, the weakness of religious systems other than their own was to be found first in morality and only derivatively in dogma.[14] He had little doubt that the Byzantines brought nemesis on themselves by their 'delight in ease', luxurious security, avarice and faction, pontificating that Providence did not ordinarily dispose things 'without rational Causes and Previous Disposition . . .'[15] The frequent depositions of patriarchs he saw as due entirely to clergy coveting their seats; this opened up constant possibilities of bribery and inducements, of which the Turks simply took advantage, even if it meant sometimes hanging or garroting the incumbent patriarch to make way for another as expeditiously as possible. Patriarch Methodios avoided that fate in 1670 only by being able to quickly take refuge in the house of the English ambassador. Because of this incessant competition, the Church was perpetually in corporate debt – in 1672, according to the then Bishop of Smyrna, to the tune of £350,000. The Turkish Treasury rigorously called in its debts or else imposed enormous interest charges. This strange economy produced a situation in the 1670s of veritable musical chairs at the Phanar in Constantinople and the price of the patriarchate shot up from £10,000 to £25,000. So reduced were the patriarchate's finances that patriarchs could no longer be installed with the ancient ceremonials; they literally crept into office. Sophistically, this was excused on the ground that without such a rapid changeover and the accompanying exchange of cash, many metropolitans would literally starve.[16]

Although Rycaut saw part of the explanation in the 'light and vain humour' of the Greeks as a people, he also took the point of poverty. The reason, as he saw it, why the clergy

asked fees for everything and even bought their own ordination was that society was poor and the Greek people in any
case ungenerous.[17] Rycaut noted that among the Armenians,
benefices had just as much monetary value as among the
Greeks and for the same basic reason. In the Armenian
Church the rites of passage had their price. To some degree
he was prepared to be more indulgent towards the Armenians
than he was towards the Greeks, because the Armenians had
endured a long period of subjection to the Persians before they
fell under the Turks. He noted that they genuinely believed
themselves exonerated from the charge of simony on this
count alone.[18]

Rycaut's feelings about Orthodox penitential discipline
were ambivalent, partly because of his low estimate of the
Greek character and partly because he had accepted with
reluctance the need for his own Church to hold its penitential
discipline in abeyance because of the chaos created by the
Puritan revolution, but he hoped to see it restored 'in more
seasonable times'. He wanted to believe, because he was
proud of his Church, that this had been a wise judgement in
the Spirit of God.[19] It is obvious that he felt very vulnerable
in this, – admitting, as he did quite openly at the outset of his
book that the 'Easterns' looked at the Reformed Churches of
the West and saw only that they neither kept the Fasts, nor
made private confession, nor used the sign of the cross (except
in baptism). It was as if he heaved a great sigh of relief in
saying that at least the Church of England had retained an
ordered liturgy, the calendar of feasts and the baptismal use
of the cross. It is also clear that like Jeremy Taylor he valued
the Orthodox understanding of confession as the 'oyl of
prayer'.[20] That said, he had no illusions about the way
penance actually operated in the Greek Church. He was well
aware that as far as the laity were concerned, less penance was
required or expected of the 'labouring and common people'
(for whom confession once a year was thought sufficient) and
those with 'leisure and convenience of living' (who were
expected to confess four times in the year). He was also aware
that in the Armenian Church, and probably also the Greek, a

monetary 'peace' offering was expected of the penitent by the priest, not merely as an 'atonement for sin' but also as an appeasement or satisfaction of 'the indignation of the Priest himself'.[21] He was keenly aware of the very high and easy use of excommunication among both the Greeks and the Armenians and suspected that this was due to a desire on the part of the desperately poor priests to mulct the people for the privilege of having it lifted. In this regard, he described with some evident distaste the caste distinction made between equally poor clergy and laity when it came to their treatment at death, with both the bishops and priests anointed with consecrated oil while the laity were 'only washed after the manner of the Turks, and fashion of the Eastern parts of the World.'[22]

Rycaut reported that the Greeks were 'ill instructed, or rather not taught at all' in the truths of their faith. Sermons and catechizings were alike rare, even in the context of the Liturgy, which tended to be performed perfunctorily. Not surprisingly, he thought, the common people contented themselves with an *Opus Operatum* kind of religion and so manifested in their lives very little of the power of godliness unless one excepted penitential exercises which were often the only 'Axel' of community solidarity in a state controlled by infidel aliens. Rycaut indignantly exhorted his readers to value the light of the Gospel which shone 'in our Islands', the daily lectures heard in Anglican pulpits, the knowledge of the Scriptures which Anglicans had in the vulgar tongue, and the commentaries on the Divine Mysteries which were readily to hand. Mechanicks, he assured them, were 'more learned and knowing than the Doctors and Clergy of Greece', even though Englishmen, he had to confess, feared too little the discipline of the Bishop and had scant regard for penance and fasting.[23] He held an even lower opinion, if that were possible, of divine learning among the Armenians, who did not seem to possess many books of divinity in their monasteries. Armenian monks, he said, spent most of their time conning only one book the *Lives of the Saints* by Gregory of Stat.[24] Otherwise they knew little of their religion except the details of the lenten disciplines and the calendar.[25] He was not surprised, therefore, to find little that could be called technical sacramental language among them, not even a term equivalent to 'sacrament', so that it was impossible for them or anyone else to say with certainty whether they believed in two sacraments or seven. Needless to say, given this degree of ignorance, he did not see how they could very well be held to be either Eutychians or Monophysites![26] At a much earlier date, he was sure, the domination of the Turk had been due to an enfeeblement among the Greeks and Armenians, induced not only by levity and a weak moral sense but also by 'Ancient doctrinal janglings' spiced with malice. But Tradition, based on once sophisticated reasoning, albeit now ossified, had enabled the modern Greek at least to adhere to the 'proper Basis and Pillar of their Faith in face of gross humiliations.' If God had removed their bright candlestick they certainly delighted still to dwell in 'the twilight of Batts', preserved from the western entanglements of such recondite matters as justification by faith by their naive trust in an 'active and prolifick Grace'.[27]

Rycaut seemed grateful that their priesthood was their 'Regimen' and protection, and rejoiced that, loyal to the admonitions of St Paul, they took their worldly disputes to the bishop rather than go through the Turkish courts. They were thus bound insensibly in their lives to the canons, the calendar and the Liturgy, entrusted doctrine to the 'Safe Pilotage' of their leaders. He suspected that this was the reason for the Muslims' good opinion of the sanctity and efficacy of the Christian religion.[28] The only misgivings he had on this score was that their very constancy to Tradition bound them to some fantastic notions, such as (in the celebration of the Dormition) that all the rivers of the world flowed into the Nile in homage to the Holy Family's refuge from Herod in Egypt. This 'oriental proclivity' he found even more pronounced among the Armenians, whose fascination with 'Spirits' made him feel queasy.[29]

As to Eastern Liturgy itself, he frankly found it 'tedious and indiscreet', even *St James* which he claimed he had witnessed going on for five hours.[30] One can understand this if one remembers that one thing that Basire valued in the Anglican system was its brevity, even in the Catechism.[31] High Church Anglicans must have returned to the *status quo ante bellum* with great relief after the prolixity of the Puritans. Then was not the time for prodigal imagery.

Rycaut closely observed, with almost prurient interest, the communion practices of those among whom he moved. The Armenians, he tells us, administered the Holy Eucharist to small children at their baptism by rubbing their lips with it; young acolytes licked the priest's fingers after he had dipped them into the wine as a kind of pledge or foretaste of full communion; adults received in both kinds but mixed together, Armenian priests put no water into the wine and the eucharistic bread was unleavened, &c &c. All this observation became too much for him and he blurted out his dismay at how far the practices he had observed fell short of the simplicity of the Last Supper narrative which he evidently thought had been preserved in the Reformation traditions by the Church of England, albeit other reformed Churches had been tainted with sectarianism.[32] Like nineteenth-century Tractarians observing Catholic Apostolic worship at Gordon Square, Rycaut confessed to a sneaking reverence for the way the Armenian Church celebrated its Liturgy before dawn so that the common people could attend before going to work.[33] He noticed also, with at least complacency, that among the Greeks the observation of lesser feasts was 'retrenched for the sake of the poor who had to live by their daily labour' and enjoined in their entirety only on monastics and secular clergy who had 'nothing else to do'. This aspect of *oeconomia* evidently pleased him. He was even more impressed by what he understood to be the practice (although he does not claim to have observed) of the prospective communicant asking pardon of those in the church and being prepared to retire uncommunicated if anyone challenged.[34]

There were aspects of Orthodox eucharistic practice of which he was unsure; for instance whether Orthodox understood the adding of water to the wine to be of dominical institution or simply 'of long antiquity'. He inclined to the view of Vossius that it grew from a concern in the early church that the close proximity of Eucharist and agape should not give rise to the suspicion of intemperance. Like many other observers, he was confused by the reverence given to the elements at the Great Entrance before they were 'consecrated' and the Spirit invoked. It was as if the worshippers expected some 'miraculous benefit' by the 'beams and influx' of the sacrament even before it *was* the sacrament. He had questioned Orthodox clergy about this, but all he could derive was the suggestion that the 'unconsecrated' elements had the 'immediate capacity and disposition' to be a sacrament and were therefore treated reverently. This puzzlement was part of a wider one about the implications of Orthodox behaviour in the Eucharist for what they really believed about the Presence. He was aware that despite reverencing at the Great Entrance, they did not prostrate themselves before the consecrated species nor expose them for public adoration as the Romans did. Did this mean that their belief in the Real Presence was really quite 'moderate' and that Cyril Lucaris's presentation was actually fully consonant with the Eastern Tradition, Roman expressions in the Confessions of Moghila and Dositheus notwithstanding? He was persuaded by some fellow westerners, probably including John Covel, that terms like *metousiosis* and *metamorphosis* were themselves 'lately formed' to accommodate the Greek language to transubstantiation and he wondered if the effort of trying to adjust the languages had thrown them completely off balance. What they really needed to be saying, Rycaut thought, in order to be loyal to the spirit of their Tradition, was that the Body and Blood were given 'under the Covering of [the elementary species] of bread and wine' and nothing more. Uncertain as he was of the wider context, he could not adjust to the widespread attitude of worshippers to the *Antidoron*. If they saw the blessed bread as a 'representation or shadow' of the Holy Eucharist, why did they so often seem to value it *more* than an infrequent communion, even to the extent of receiving it fasting and abstaining from sexual intercourse beforehand? However, he could see that in the circumstance of the ordinary faithful scarcely ever communicating in the proper sense, this exaggerated devotion to the shadow at least fended off a 'coldness of spirit'.[35]

One aspect of Orthodox public worship which deeply moved him was the way in which the 'minor orders' and humblest functions, even down to trimming the candles, were seen as a call of the Holy Spirit.[36]

Rycaut had less respect for the administration of the other ordinances or sacraments. He noted that the marriage canons were observed more in the breach than the practice. He attributed this to the profound poverty of the clergy which tempted them to wink at infringements in return for a 'consideration'. Patriarchs could vary their judgement in one case several times, each time in return for money, 'leaving the ignorant soul as well confused in his love as in his Conscience'.[37] He sympathized with resentful young clerical widows at the ban on second marriages, not only because they feared that they might not be able to maintain a continent life but also because they feared that the claim to 'innocence' implied by the 'Dove' medalion on their hats could be belied by the state of their hearts or their loss of self control. He could not take seriously the idea of 'sacred consanguinity' used to ban the marriage of godparents and godchildren.[38] The incidental ceremonies associated with Orthodox matrimony, such as 'sugared Confections' eaten with a spoon, struck him as frivolous 'Toys' which were 'too mean and low' for the exalted state of marriage.[39]

On the doctrines of the Descent into Hell and the state of the departed, Rycaut was confused. He gravely misunderstood the Descent into Hell though he appreciated well enough the difference between Roman Purgatory and both the Greek and Armenian ideas about the 'Middle state'.[40] The 'barbarous lamentations' of the women at funerals and anniversaries struck him as not only 'extravagant' but 'undecent' inasmuch as it infringed St Paul's strictures against 'mourning like those without hope' (1 Thess. 4:13). The fact that they could turn it off like a tap and go sit 'under the shadow of some Tree' and guzzle wine made their offence the worse.[41]

Not surprisingly, he could see no great difference between

Greek and Latin prayers to saints and angels save that in the Greek Church it was less overwhelmingly enjoined at every turn. He saw ikons as a mere concession to 'Gentilism' whereby objects like fountains were once thought to have miraculous powers. He described the ikon as 'an ill-favoured sort of flat painting'. It was danger to the ignorant Christian, scandal to the devout Muslim; and it prevented conversions from Islam. Since it was not an essential part of worship, the ikon should be 'wholly taken away'.[42] The publication of Rycaut's book in 1679 with these sentiments in it, at the height of the Popish Plot scare, can only have made more certain the ruin of the scheme for a Greek church in London, as we shall see in the next chapter.

Although Rycaut firmly believed in a life of order and discipline, Orthodox asceticism left him bemused. He records without undue comment what he believed to be the fasting and abstinence rules for monks in general and strict ascetics in particular, but he jibbed at the idea that if a man was 'sick to death' and could theoretically be revived by prescribed food, it was better that he die than sin by consuming.[43] His mind boggled at what he understood Armenian fasting to be. A lenten table in the west, he declared, would serve as an Easter dinner in Armenia! Since they were only allowed the use of the dregs of olive oil during fasts, he was not surprised that everyone kept off sexual contact during Lent, because they must have smelt rank.[44] He tried to formulate a rational theory for explanation of such idiocy, and the only one he could come up with, was that since nations like the Armenians had always been more abstemious and less addicted to excess than the northern and western nations, they could progressively and imperceptibly reduce their diet until they virtually faded away: in other words, fasting was 'natural' to them, not a supernatural grace.[45]

Given these misgivings, it was inevitable that Rycaut should have difficulties with Mount Athos. He found the physical aspect of it 'as horrid as Caucasus'.[46] And yet, although he found somewhat comic how the monks competed for who could surpass in 'a holy and seraphic way', he was, against all his prejudices, impressed by the unusual erudition of the Athonite monks (mostly, he thought, on the Cappadocian Fathers) and their 'lively sense of God and of his service'. They seemed to him not merely 'real and moral good men' but men 'something touched with the Spirit of God'.[47] His problem with their learning was that it was so constricted. It seemed to him that they despised both Latin and Hebrew and also philosophy and mathematics as 'unnecessary for men who lead a mortified and spiritual life'. He also baulked at their self-censorship which caused them to keep nothing at variance with the Seventh Ecumenical Council, or books by 'those whom they call Hereticks'. The slovenliness with which they kept their libraries with 'books piled high one on the other, without order and method, covered with dust, and exposed to the Worm' offended his sense of humaneness.[48]

Rycaut was impressed by how the grandeur of the Athos Liturgies induced 'the Vulgar' to leave behind gifts out of sheer reverence and devotion, even in spite of their normal Greek 'narrow-hearted'-ness; but at bottom he could not reconcile their professions of poverty with the amount of treasures they had amassed. Could monks really be wealthy misers, 'starving amidst the heaps of gold'?[49]

Rycaut was in Greek lands at a time of more than usual pressure from the Latins to induce Orthodox to conform to Rome. As a practical man of the world with a keen sense of the proprieties, he tried to see this issue straight and not to exaggerate or misinterpret. He was anxious to disabuse his readers of the oft repeated inanity that the Greeks repaid Rome's excommunication with their own each year, like Punch and Judy knocking each other over the head. They could not do such a thing in the last analysis because in Orthodox ecclesiology one Church could not make a blanket excommunication of another, having no jurisdiction to do so. Only Rome thought that it could do that.[50] On the other hand, after visiting Athos, he understood perfectly the intensity of Orthodox feeling against Romish intrusion ever since the shotgun marriage at the Council of Florence.[51]

He questioned Orthodox carefully everywhere he went on

how the Latin intrusion had come about. Not least intriguing is his analysis of how it happened in the Armenian Church. There he believed the rot set in with one man in the early thirteenth century, Ovan de Kurnah (Rycaut's transliteration), who had 'a wandering head, and a genius towards Learning, somewhat more curious than the generality . . .' This man, he believed, visited France and Italy via Poland and on his return disseminated western ideas among his co-religionists, 'which seemed unto them [even the "wisest"] to be all new matters, and high notions' which won their 'admiration and applause'. He thus implied that many small Latin ideas were thus absorbed into the fabric of church life, although when Ovan went on to preach Papal primacy his influence was 'leavened' and he was frozen out by patriarchal disapprobation.

As a result there was a schism, with one branch adhering to the pope with a church in Rome. Rycaut knew the text and sources of the Armenian rite and witnessed the liturgical worship of both communities finding the Uniate form 'much differing' from the original and 'squared acording to that of the Latines'.

While he was in Italy for several months in 1678, rumours abounded that the Armenian Patriarch and thirty-six of his bishops were about to submit to Rome; but nothing happened and Rycaut did not show any surprise. Not only was he virtually certain that nothing on that scale *could* happen but he was sure that if a new survey was done among the Armenian clergy it would produce views much closer to those of the Church of England than to Rome, especially on the Eucharist.[52]

Rycaut was under the impression that the Latins over a long period of time had encouraged the Turks to lean heavily on their Christian subjects in the hope that it might induce them to turn to Rome for succour. This could be the only reason why there were so many Romish priests in the Greek islands. They certainly did not yet have a constituency there, but they assiduously published books in vulgar Greek. One of their most effective books, by the Jesuit Francois Richard, was banned and burned by the Patriarch of Constantinople around 1661. The Patriarch threatened to excommunicate those who read it. The Latins had the advantage of unlimited cash and thereby maintained well-stocked schools, while the Greek schools, such as they were, were, said Rycaut, fit habitation only for owls. Hence the number of aspiring Greek scholars drawn away to Italy and there subverted because of their incapacity to question Roman ideas in terms of their own tradition. The situation was at its worst in the Aegean and Ionian Islands. But Rycaut was assured from his observation that although the Latins drew Greeks there to their 'better ordered services', they did not often win their allegiance. Nevertheless, the situation had been dire until Metropolitan Ignatius Neochari of Scio persuaded the Turks to expel all Roman Catholics for better security against Venice. He asked that all those who might remain should be required to be subject to his jurisdiction. The Latins refused this indignity and decamped to Adrianople, protesting to the Porte because they left many fine churches behind. Somehow, through French influence, they bribed the Porte so far as to get the restoration of some of their churches and therefore a presence once again in the islands.[53]

Rycaut knew this was connected with the efforts of the French Ambassador to the Porte, the Marquis de Nointel, to subvert the Greek Church in Jerusalem and its control of the Church of the Holy Sepulchre by stirring up riots. In that case the Vizier Ahmed Pasha was not to be bought or intimidated and the Greeks retained their position in the Holy Places. Rycaut thought that possibly the English Ambassador had had something to do with outcome.[54] He knew precisely the strength of the French diplomatic system with the Turks, the title of Padeshah which the Porte had accorded to the French King, the value of their cash; but he also knew – from the inside – that the Turks' current esteem of the French was not as great as the French would have the world think. 'I have heard the wife of the Lord Chancellor Samosade say, that the French gained that title of Podeshaw to their King by craft and subtlety, and was never fully examined or considered ... It is true, that there was a time when the French Ambassador was called to secret Councils, and admitted within the wall of the

Seraglio to private meetings and debates of the Turk; but it was when the French plotted and openly assisted in transportation of the Turks, for the Invasion of Italy; but since that time, and especially in the year 1664, through the force given the Emperour, and the Bravado upon Barvary, the French hath always (and that not without some reason) gone declining in the good opinion and esteem in the Ottoman Court'.[55]

Rycaut doubted the practicality of Nointel's strategy of factitiously documenting the Greeks' 'acceptance of transubstantiation' as a means of tying them to Rome and to the French cause against the Habsburg Emperor. He doubted it even more in regard to the Armenians, even if some of the clergy might think signing a statement could tend to their 'Honour and Profite'. Though it was at a meeting between Nointel and the Armenian Patriarch that the wider plot was first conceived, when he moved among the Armenians Rycaut detected a strong undertow of resistance to what was afoot. Clergy freely told him that the endorsement of transubstantiation was only to be found in one document, an *Epitome of Doctrine* which had been signed 'by only a minority of the bishops'.[56] Even if a few Orthodox, including bishops, were won over to Rome, he doubted if it would have any ecclesial significance, given the way the Eastern Church was structured. Even the habitual bribery could go only so far.[57]

Rycaut had sanguine hopes that with a little encouragement through English diplomatic channels the Church of England could secure the Greek Church against Roman subversion. Like other seventeenth-century High Churchmen he had in his armoury of apologetics the writings of Archbishop Marc-Antonio De Dominis in his 'Anglican' phase. De Dominis' model of the *via media* had been shown to have substance in the light of the murder of Cyril Lucaris with the connivance of the French and the Latin Church.[58] Greeks had had prophecies indicating the Tsar as their deliverer. With the strength of its commercial arm in the eastern Mediterranean, England could secure for its own Church this honourable role.[59] He urged upon his readers that some of the negative images the Greeks had in their minds of Reformed Churches in the West were deliberately sown by the Romanists in their efforts to induce submission. This is how the Jesuits had been able to discredit the Confession of Cyril Lucaris. For his own part, he was sure that Cyril's mature views were based on his observation of Anglicanism under the Royal Martyr, with its churches 'trim'd and adorned in a modest Medium between the wanton and superstitious dress of Rome, and the slovenly and insipid Government of Geneva'. The realistic Anglican estimate of the 'state of Souls after separation' and 'reverent Opinion of the Holy Sacrament of the Eucharist' must have made its mark.[60] Here then was the *kairos*. But he warned against anyone thinking that 'prepossessions to a Party or Tenent [sic]' could win the day. That is where the Papists and the French had come unstuck. Unity must be the goal but unity based on something more stable than clever formulas.

Notes

1. W. N. Darnell (ed.), *The Correspondence of Isaac Basire, D.D.* (London, 1931), pp. 1–4, 43–44, 207.
2. Ibid., p. 12.
3. *A Letter Written by the Reverend Dr Basier [sic] to the Honourable Richard Brown ... Relating His Travels, and Endeavours to propagate the Knowledge of the Doctrine and Discipline established in the Britannick Church among the Greeks, Arabians, &c* (London, 1661), unpaginated.
4. Basire to ? 22 April 1665 in Darnell, op. cit., pp. 234–5.
5. Basire to Edmund Castell (Professor of Arabic at Cambridge), 20 September 1670, ibid., p. 291.
6. Ibid., pp. 6, 29, 312.
7. F. Barnes of the Order of St Benedict, *Select Discourses concerning Councils, the Pope, Schism, The Priviledges of the Isle of Great Britain, &c.* (London, 1661), pp. 24–29.
8. Darnell, op. cit., pp. 15–16, 18, 32, 36, 41, 113. Sir Richard Brown called this work an 'excellent Diatribe'. (Preface). See also Darnell, op. cit., pp. 115–20.
9. Basire, *The Ancient Liberty of the Britannick Church and the Legitimate Exemption thereof from the Roman Patriarchate* (London, 1661), pp. 9, 15, 23–25, 11.
10. Runciman, *The Great Church in Captivity*, op. cit., p. 308.
11. Rycaut, *The Present State of the Greek and Armenian Churches, Anno Christi 1678* (London, 1679), pp. [7]ff.

12. Ibid., pp. 12–15.
13. Ibid., p. 75.
14. Ibid., Preface, p. [11].
15. Ibid., pp. 4ff.
16. Ibid., pp. 97–98, 102–2, 107–8. He thought the other three patriarchates were relatively less venal than Constantinople because they were a long way from the seat of Turkish power (pp. 112–3).
17. Ibid., pp. 114, 136, 252.
18. Ibid., p. 439.
19. Ibid., Preface. He insisted that the principle had been preserved in the Exhortation and in the Caroline sermons and writings.
20. Ibid., pp. 263–4, 266.
21. Ibid., p. 438. One should perhaps not understand the word 'indignation' in quite the petty sense it has now.
22. Ibid., pp. 438–9, 444.
23. Ibid., Preface.
24. Ibid., pp. 430–1.
25. Ibid., pp. 419, 422.
26. Ibid., pp. 431–2, 409–11.
27. Ibid., Preface; pp. 372–3.
28. Ibid., pp. 17–18, 19–21, 126. Rycaut has a curious disquisition about the attitude of the Church of Georgia to the age of baptism which reflects on his idea of the force of prescriptive tradition. He understood that originally the Georgians did not baptize until the age of fourteen, but 'Preachers' were constantly sent among them by the Patriarch of Antioch who pressed them 'to conform to the practice of the Ancient Church'. Being a people 'very tenacious of the Doctrines they once received', they eventually compromised at eight years in order not to completely lose face. Ibid., p. 170. He also saw the horror with which the Greeks viewed excommunication as a function of the force of common tradition. They could not face the thought of being shut out from the sacraments even though in point of fact they rarely received. Hence the popular Greek myth that the bodies of those dying excommunicate lay preserved by demons from the natural corruption of all flesh. For this reason their loved-ones bought post-mortem release from the Patriarch so that they instantly dissolved 'into the first Principles of Earth'. Ibid., pp. 273–83, 290.
29. Ibid., pp. 374ff., 396–407.
30. Ibid., pp. 317, 320.
31. Basire to Antoine Leger (Reformed minister at Geneva), n.d. [probably 1653] in Darnell, op. cit., p. 123.
32. *The Present State*, op. cit., pp. 433, 435.

33. Ibid., p. 408.
34. Ibid., pp. 157–8, 200. He understood that the Armenian laity were not expected to observe more than ten feasts in the year (p. 422).
35. Ibid., pp. 178–80, 182–14, 189, 197.
36. Ibid., pp. 202–3.
37. Ibid., pp. 308–9.
38. Ibid., pp. 169, 201–4. He was aware of a recent stop put by the Patriarch and the Mufti to casual marriages between Christian women and Muslim men in Romania. That way round the Turks would not have cared so much had not the Patriarch reminded them of the heinousness of Turks uniting themselves to the bodies of women nourished on swine's flesh and wine (pp. 314–7).
39. Ibid., p. 310.
40. Ibid., pp. 298–304, 410, 422–4. He understood the Armenian belief to be that the dead were 'intercepted in the way' to heaven or hell and 'lodged together in the same place, which they called Gayank, which is the Eighth Heaven where the Stars are, and have there no joy or grief but what proceeds from a good or bad Conscience'. Those with only venial sins were relieved by the alms and good works of the Faithful. The righteous dead did not then see the face of God but were 'filled and replenished with certain beams of his glory and Divine Illumination'. Further, he understood that the Mother of God and possibly Elijah were in a different category.
41. Ibid., pp. 295–8, 445.
42. Ibid., pp. 334–6, 329–30. Rycaut had some justification for his negativity inasmuch as often in his travels he encountered the attribution of crude physical powers to ikons as if they were talismans independent of moral worth (cf. pp. 148–50).
43. Ibid., pp. 187–8, 205, 208. However, he realized that some spiritual directors advised such people to eat and then make their confession.
44. Ibid., pp. 415–6.
45. Ibid., p. 425.
46. Ibid., p. 217.
47. Ibid., pp. 244, 262.
48. Ibid., pp. 259–61. For comparison, see the reaction of the modern phil-Orthodox Anglican scholar, A. M. Allchin in his *The Dynamic of Tradition* (London, 1981), p. 28.
49. *The Present State*, op. cit., pp. 224, 248.
50. Ibid., pp. 291–2.
51. Ibid., p. 228.
52. Ibid., pp. 427–30, 452. Rycaut noted the existence of an

Armenian monastic order named after 'Surp Dominicos', but he
could find nothing distinctively Roman about it (p. 424).

53. Ibid., pp. 27–30.
54. Ibid., pp. 349–55.
55. Rycaut, *The History and Present State of the Ottoman Empire*
(London, 1686), p. 174.
56. Rycaut believed that this was the document discussed at
Nointel's meeting with the patriarch in 1674. He had seen a
copy of it in Armenian and had had help from a bishop in
construing it. It seemed to him, even in translation, more like
the 'contrivance of some Fryer of the Romish Church' than an
authentic Armenian expression of belief. Both the style and the
thought forms were wrong. It spoke in Latin terms of the saints
in heaven when the Armenians did not believe the saints were
presently in heaven. Cf. *The Present State of the Greek and
Armenian Churches*, op. cit., pp. 172, 176.
57. Ibid., pp. 450–1.
58. Ibid., Preface.
59. *The History and Present State of the Ottoman Empire*, op. cit.,
pp. 172, 176.
60. *The Present State of the Greek and Armenian Churches*, op. cit.,
Preface.

CHAPTER THREE

'RABBI' SMITH AND THE GRAND DESIGN

Thomas Smith (1638–1710) studied at The Queen's College, Oxford, taking his MA in 1663. He was made Master of Magdalen College School, Probationer Fellow of Magdalen College in 1666, full Fellow the following year, Dean in 1674, Vice-President in 1682. His time as chaplain in Constantinople fell between becoming Fellow of Magdalen and Dean.[1]

He brought back from Constantinople several Greek manuscripts for the Bodleian Library and gained the nickname of 'Rabbi Smith' because of his oriental enthusiasms. Under James II he wanted to become (indeed expected to become) President of his college, but he bowed to the King's wishes to have a Roman Catholic, Anthony Farmer, in that post. Though he lost his fellowship in the subsequent shake-up and left Oxford, he remained loyal to the King and refused to take the oaths to William and Mary at the Revolution, becoming one of the first of the Nonjurors. For a time he was custodian of the Cottonian Manuscripts. He continued to correspond with Greece. As many as 138 volumes of his papers are lodged in the Bodleian.[2]

Smith was a polymath and widely recognized as such. He possessed a large library from which Sir Paul Rycaut borrowed in the preparation of his own book. In 1664 John Pearson, Master of Trinity College, Cambridge and, as we saw in Chapter 1, a precocious Patristics scholar while still a boy at Eton, sent a student to Smith who was planning to edit

Aristinus, Balsamon and Zonaros on the Greek Canons, confident that he would be able to help him. Smith himself later projected an English critical edition of the Liturgies of St Basil and St John Chrysostom because he had no confidence in the Venetian edition. He was interested in astronomy and mathematics and was fluent in Italian. He became a fund of knowledge on the state of the western continental Church in the eighth and ninth centuries and on the Anglo-Saxon charters.[3]

After Smith had been forced by his conscience into Non-Jury, Samuel Pepys praised him for his 'Abundant Humanity' and William Trumbull told him that he admired his 'unwearied Piety and Labours in Promoting Goodnesse and contributing so much to the Interest of the Established Church of England, in this degenerate and Apostasting (sic) Age.' In 1706 he himself modestly told Bishop Thomas Ken, the deprived Bishop of Bath and Wells, that he had always tried 'to do right to the Church of England.' He did, however, develop a hearty loathing for English domestic politics and its factions during the Popish Plot crisis, congratulating his friend Sir Philip Warwick for choosing the better part by retiring from the 'éclat' of such things to spend his life in meditation (in which he would do more good, said Smith, than if he was advanced to the 'highest dignity in the State'). In another letter to Warwick he speaks metaphorically of the 'discontented Passengers, who ready to be caste away by the unskillfulness of the Pilots, grow more desperated and enraged, and please themselves with the poor satisfaction of throwing them overboard first before they themselves are swallowed up by the quicksands'.[4]

Whatever he was before his chaplaincy at Constantinople, he was never thereafter a narrowly bookish man. He took a very close interest in international politics, declaring in 1678 that France was becoming more of a danger to Europe than the Turk, being consumed by 'ambition and thirst for fame' to the detriment of 'business', and that Louis XIV had now become 'the Dread of Christendome'.[5]

Some time after Smith went out to Constantinople, Sir Daniel Harvey was appointed as Ambassador to the Porte.

Pearson assured Smith that he would be happy under Harvey's roof because Harvey had always had 'an exemplary kindnesse for a Scholar'. Not surprisingly, therefore, Smith decided that Harvey needed a briefing on how the Greeks functioned in Constantinople. Simultaneously, George Etheridge, Harvey's secretary, was attempting to brief the Ambassador on Turkish ways. The Greeks, said Smith in his memorandum, had maintained 'the face of a Church, in despite of all opposition'. Had it not been for their Liturgy and the maintenance of their feasts, strict fasts and festivals, Christianity would long since have been destroyed in 'the East'. The Turks, he said, preyed upon them continually. He provided Harvey with a list of the living patriarchs (i.e. those ruling and those involuntarily redundant). He gave it as his opinion that the present Patriarch Methodios seemed trustworthy, but he warned Sir Daniel that several of the bishops were 'not satisfied in his Government' and, to his present knowledge, had 'Purses enough' to 'unpatriarch' him by bribing the Vizir if they had a mind to it. He urged the Ambassador to distinguish between the monastic and the secular clergy, implying that the latter tended to be less reliable. Smith was to have given Harvey a further briefing on the differences between the Greeks and Rome, but ill-health intervened and Smith returned prematurely to England.[6] Harvey evidently adopted Smith's advice. He took in the deposed Patriarch Parthenios as his house guest at Pera. Beza Sargeant reported to Smith, by then back in England, that Parthenios thought he was not without hope of being restored and indeed Sargeant later reported that Parthenios had indeed 'got back' – for the fourth time – 'by money and friends', the 'friends' presumably including Harvey.[7] Smith's role at Constantinople may have made him enemies. This might explain that later he was receiving letters from a Greek woman called Theodosia who said that she had to be very discreet in writing to him.[8]

Smith was a staunch High Churchman of the Caroline School. According to his biographer in the *Dictionary of National Biography*, Thomas Seecombe (an ardent admirer of Orthodoxy in the Victorian period who devised his own

Orthodox lifestyle), he shared with Sir Paul Rycaut a strong desire for rapprochement with the Greek Church. He accepted the chaplaincy at Constantinople out of an 'inbred curiosity' about it, but his great desire for rapprochement appears to be the fruit of his time there. He seems to have made a promise while he was still in Constantinople to publish his findings in due course. Hence his *Account of the Greek Church*. This work, typical of his scholarship and standing at Oxford, was published first in Latin in 1676 with a dedication to Bishop John Fell of Oxford, warmly applauding the Bishop for his promotion of scholarship, and later in English.[9]

In his preface 'To the Reader' Smith notes with a sense of frustration that the major authoritative works by modern Greek scholars were never brought out in new editions and so remained rare in the West, 'scarce to be met with'. His book was designed to make good that deficiency. He determined to avoid relying too heavily on popular piety and to concentrate on the offices, confessions and catechisms of the Greek Church. He was aware, and did not disguise from the reader right at the outset, that many aspects of popular piety scandalized the puritanical Moslems and had disquieted devout Protestant observers.

One remarkable feature of his approach was a deliberate avoidance of quoting the Fathers. He wanted his account to be an existential picture of the modern Greek Church, unclouded with ideal images of what that Church might or should be according to its 'title deeds'. He did, of course, revere the Fathers, like all the Carolines. His decision was therefore purely methodological.

Smith was well informed about Cyril Lucaris' time as Patriarch of Constantinople, having not only read his *Confession* but also compared various accounts of his kidnapping and death by those who were in Constantinople at the time and could be directly questioned. It is worth nothing that, for Smith, Charles I was a 'Martyr, of Blessed and Glorious Memory' and he seems to have placed Lucaris on the same level.[10] Some aspects of the Greek Church immediately appealed to him as a member of a recently persecuted and degraded Church, especially its maintenance of a 'due Subordination ... among the Ministers of holy things'; even in the midst of their desolation. Without this he was sure 'Confusion' would have overwhelmed them, as it very nearly overwhelmed the Church of England. He reported that all Greek Christians attributed any happiness and quietness they enjoyed to their patriarch and noted the extraordinary respect given to him by the other patriarchs even though they did not owe their own positions to him.[11] He admired and wondered at the way 'the poor Greeks', under such 'sad pressures from the stupid and blasphemous Turks' maintained 'with all imaginable constancy' the 'entire profession of the Mysteries of Faith, as they were believed and acknowledged in the first Ages.'[12]

Smith's book was part of a dialogue involving Henry Compton, the Bishop of London, designed to obtain some provision for Greek Christians in England. He indicated in his dedication to Compton that he had discussed this plan in Constantinople. We shall return to it later. Sir Steven Runciman describes the book as 'well informed, frank, but fairly sympathetic'.[13]

As may already be guessed, Smith saw the modern Greeks as stupified and deprived of all material honour by the Turks, so that they no longer had any hope of change. Unlike Rycaut, he does not feel moved to give space to prophecies of delivery from subjugation by Russian might. The birthrate among the Turks was notoriously low, so their subjugation was, in his view, in a sense illusory, resting for its force on renegade Christians prepared to sell their faith for office.[14] Nevertheless, the Greeks at present lacked the courage to overthrow it. Like Rycaut, he well appreciated the disruptive effect of greed for 'Dignities' on the body ecclesiastical. It resulted, he said, in a restless passion which marred the peace and interest of the whole. The quick succession of patriarchs in his own time was due, he thought, at least as much to 'horrid Quarrels' among the Greeks themselves as to the rapacity of the Turks. It led to shameless bribery of Turkish officials by the competing parties and accumulating debt to the Church. He was not surprised that the Turks exploited it for all it was worth. He told readers that even in his own short time in Constantinople there were four patriarchs and ex-patriarchs milling around looking for support from the foreign ambassadors. He had the lowest opinion of Parthenios who, he said, was widely hated for his 'imperious carriage and cruel exactions', for which he was banished to Cyprus.[15]

In Smith's view, the Greek bishops as a whole badly needed 'sober and peaceable counsels', otherwise their disputes and conspiracies would 'fatally' enclose them in an inextricable knot.[16] They hardly had an enviable task, because since the fall of Constantinople several metropolitans had lost their suffragans and some bishoprics had become purely titular because the sees had been depopulated of Christians. Chalcedon, for instance, was now but a poor Muslim village.[17]

Yet all was not lost. Smith admired the lower clergy for their spirit in face of acute adversity. At a time when, in the West, menial duties to King or noble house were no longer performed by the well-born, he was impressed by the way the most menial duties were performed for the patriarch by their deacons.[18]

The widespread ignorance and lack of training among the clergy disturbed him. He knew from the fate of Metaxas's printing press in 1627[19] how impossible it had been for the Greeks to print their own texts under the jealous eye of the Turks. Only the good offices of Sir Thomas Roe had managed to get the Metaxas Press set up in the first place. On it Cyril Lucaris had printed his *Confession*, whose dedication to Charles I had of course ensured Roman and French opposition through the Porte to any further printing.[20] Smith noted, however, one additional and unnecessary obstacle to popular instruction, the fact that many clergy preached to the ignorant *hoi polloi* in unintelligible scholarly Greek.[21]

Given all these disadvantages, Smith was convinced that Orthodoxy had survived among the Greeks since the Turkish conquest because of their devoted observance of feasts and fasts. This he saw as a providence of God. Even children and those of a lower capacity understood their importance and flocked together in great numbers for the festivals of the

Saviour's birth, death, resurrection and ascension. The commemoration of the Apostles and Great Martyrs gave believers courage in their distress.[22] He admired the monks on Mount Athos for the special way they had aimed to keep up 'the credit of their first Institution'. They were self-sufficient, frugal and industrious, albeit 'painfull and severe', and this had preserved them from corruption.[23]

Before he went to Constantinople, Smith had long discussions on the fasts and calendars with the priest Jeremias Germanos when the latter visited Oxford. This exchange continued in Constantinople and must have provided Smith with a unique way into understanding the Liturgy.[24] He was, however, sceptical (and thought the Greek scholars were also), about the New Testament ascription of Liturgies to St Peter, St Mark, St Matthew and St James, although he gave more credit to the St James than the other three, even if it was not 'received' but simply 'noted' in Canon 32 of the Council in Trullo, and was only used in the Church of Jerusalem (and then only once a year), as an act of piety on the feast of St James. He was even more scathing about claims for the Liturgies of St John Chrysostom and St Basil deriving in anything like their present state from those authors. Such ascription could not even be excused on the ground of 'ancient Piety'. Textual criticism, he was sure, would refute it.[25] Indeed, this was but part of a broader scepticism about blanket claims made by the Greeks that the present praxis was wholly in line with the Fathers *literatim*.[26]

Before arriving in Asia Minor, Smith knew from Rycaut that he could not expect much stately 'glory and splendour' in most Greek churches since they had been 'overwhelmed' by the Turks. In the event he did indeed find them 'narrow and mean'. No doubt they had been deliberately kept so in order that they should be less of a temptation to the infidel to despoil. In the event of natural disasters such as earthquakes or fires wrecking a church, the Turks forbade rebuilding without complex permits and bribes. Some churches in Constantinople had been burned down in a 'dismal' fire around 1660. Only a few of the wrecks had so far been restored.[27]

Like so many Englishmen after him, he found Greek chant difficult to take. It was, he said, 'very mean and pitiful ... without figure and the relishes of art'. The lack of organs and bells he attributed to fear of the Turks, other explanations notwithstanding. When one considers that he published in English in the year when Henry Purcell was coming to his maturity as a composer of church music, and older contemporaries like William Blow and William Child were at the height of their powers, Smith's dismay is understandable. Child's pupil, Benjamin Rogers, was organist of Smith's own college at Oxford from 1664 until 1685 and the standard of singing in chapel must have been very high. The issue at stake here was not compositional brilliance (Rogers' harmonies are described as dull) but seemliness, decorum and articulation. This to Smith's mind seemed notably lacking among the Greeks.[28]

In spite of the music and the tawdriness of the 'décor', Smith was deeply moved by the Liturgy. Alone among our main writers he actually gives a testimony to the spiritual impact which it made on him. He could not believe that any Christian who attended would not be moved to tears and sighing. For his part, he experienced 'great strugglings and yearning in his bowels.'[29] He was attuned to the simplicity of the offices, describing them with respect and affection.[30] The attentiveness of the people to the *Synaxarion* of the saints and martyrs caused him to marvel, as did the way in which quite humble people brought their offerings of bread, wine, oil, candles and incense. He knew this was the 'Primitive' custom. He knew also that the patriarch reciprocated by providing letters of introduction to the very poor commending their need to the better off. The Turks had tried to abuse this practice by sending their well-provided Christian slaves to the patriarch, but the ruse had not worked. Altogether, Smith had a more generous estimate of the ordinary Greek than Rycaut, noting how even the poorest 'scraped some money together' for poor relief or to give to the Church as a thank offering.[31] Neither was he so supercilious as some at the way in which the faithful could swing from being 'grave and serious' to being positively 'dramatic', as in the footwashing on Holy and Great

Thursday.[32] The eucharistic fast won his respect even when, on Holy and Great Saturday, it led to some fainting in Church. However, he did know that people exercised their own *oeconomia* in cases of 'human infirmity' and took with them to church bread, dates and figs to consume on the side.[33] Like Rycaut, he was struck by the practice of asking mutual forgiveness before approaching communion, and also, like Rycaut, he applauded the latitude practised over confession in the case of poor working people, finding it in accord with the High Church interpretation of the Prayer Book rubrics and the exhortation not to burden people with 'unjust scruples'. Like others, he merely regretted that the clergy felt the need to commute penance for cash, which could be as grievous to poor people as a heavy fast and looked to the outsider like 'avarice and juggling'.[34]

For a man so genuinely 'moved' to describe the Liturgy as 'tedious' and 'pompous' cautions us not to read too much pejorative meaning into the seventeenth-century use of such words. That he realized time was not necessarily oppressive to those used to it is clear in his comment about the clergy taking turns to relieve each other 'when tyred' during the very long vigils. The longest service he appears to have attended was seven hours.[35]

While the fundamental character of Greek worship was congenial to Smith, some specific aspects repelled him. He disliked 'extravagant' or 'fulsome' language in worship and therefore could not take the Theotokos hymns (presumably, in particular, the *Akathistos*). The word 'protection' in those hymns offended him. He did not understand incense, seeing it simply as 'perfuming the church'. He was 'perplext' by the 'multitudinous vestments'. He had qualms about the placing of the small particles beside The Lamb on the paten with prayers for pardon, lest this bring purgatory in by the back door when it had been expelled from the front.[36] He was disgusted at the way worshippers drank 'greedily' of holy water and rubbed their eyes with it, and he found offensive the way in which the clergy defended their use of leavened bread against the Latins or 'Azimites', regarding their language as unreasonable and intemperate (even though their usage corresponded to his own), and seeing their attitude as leading to the ridiculous superstition about a portion of the Saviour's own leavened bread at the Last Supper being in the Emperor's chapel when it was sacked by the Latins in 1204. While accepting the genuine and devout need for reserved sacrament in times of persecution and dispersed congregations in the early Church, he could not see any justification for the Orthodox's modest and inconspicuous mode of reservation in modern times, when there were plenty of churches and little direct persecution.[37]

Smith's greatest misgiving – it cannot be regarded as more than that because, confessedly, he was unsure what was at stake – was over the great reverence shown by worshippers to the elements at the Great Entrance, with some bowing, others prostrating and a few kissing the priest's stole. This engendered in him confused emotions. Why was it happening? What did it imply? He was not impressed by the explanations to be found in Symeon of Thessalonica and Gabriel Severus. He would not have been so upset if there had been corresponding devotion later in the Eucharist, but there noticeably was not. So, like Rycaut, he was bemused and not a little offended.[38]

Smith was so entangled in the theological arguments over *latria* and *dulia* as attitudes of worship that he entirely missed the main point about ikons, which he dismissively labelled as 'painted figures'. Because he had not even begun to understand the theology of ikons (clearly his patristic studies had stopped short of John Damascene) his mind revolved incessantly round 'extravagant respect', excessive prostrations and crossings.[39]

Some Orthodox attitudes he found harsh and contradictory. He thought it 'hard and cruel' to doubt the salvation of infants who died unbaptized (this was a theological preoccupation of other contemporary High Churchmen too, including Jeremy Taylor, while on the other hand Henry Dodwell in his controversy with Edmund Chishull a few years later appeared to some to be even more rigorist than the Greeks; so it was hardly something on which High Churchmen had a common mind).[40] In contrast, Smith found the ease with which divorces were obtained 'upon several light and frivolous accounts', giving the husband virtually *carte blanche* to get rid of his wife when he tired of her, contrary to the Greeks' own theological professions, both a scandal and a practical evil which seemed 'past all remedy; there being no other way left at present to satisfy a people who are so prone to revenge where they have conceived a grudge, or to make new love after a dislike of the match' but by 'this most unjust and horribly abused indulgence.'[41]

Behind the seeming contradictions, Smith detected a legalism which tainted Orthodox ideas of sanctity in the special realm of ritual and sacrament. He noted the taboos (always of a sexual nature) restricting who could be communicated. Wives of married priests and old women who had taken a religious vow were regarded as 'clean', some others not. There seemed to be gradations of holiness just as legalist as under the Old Law. This is interesting because on the whole Smith does not make as much fuss as some others about legalism within the Orthodox system. As already stated, the Greeks' attitude to fasting, which others condemned as legalism, he thought 'oftentimes to be admired', and on the whole he praised their exercise of excommunication as 'a preservative of true religion'. So where he condemns he is perhaps deserving of some respect.[42] What he clearly found offensive was anything smacking of taboo such as cultic attitudes to purity. Scruple regarding even casual contact with proscribed substances during fasts turned his stomach.[43] Perhaps for very much the same reason, he was uneasy at the timidity of Greeks at the thought of 'unshriven ghosts' knocking importunately at the doors of the living in hours of darkness, a timidity so extreme that some would not answer a call at the door during the night, even if they thought they recognized the voice, lest it be a deceiver masquerading as the known person. In the same way, like Rycaut, he was dismayed at the myths about the bodies of the excommunicated lying bloated and 'undissolved' in the grave. He suspected that priests used such superstition to hold the people to the canons.[44] In addition, one may note his horror at the sheer venom with which the

Greeks hated the Armenians.[45] What he seemed to be suggesting was that there was a profound moral flaw in the Greeks which cut across whole segments of their life while leaving the central eucharistic core of their faith untouched.

Like Rycaut, Smith devoted some space in his book to the attempts by the Latins to subvert the Greek Church and the use they made of eucharistic doctrine to do so. He swept to one side the specious argument used by the Latins to discredit the Greek stance on the *Filioque*, involving the suggestion that there was something significant in the way the fall of Constantinople fell on Pentecost Tuesday. One might as well argue, Smith said, that the Kings of Jerusalem were guilty of some Christological heresy because they lost Rhodes to the Turks on Christmas Day![46] He understood the real issue of the *Filioque* and the Orthodox position on it very well, deploying his terms with some subtlety.[47] He had made a detailed study of Patriarch Jeremias's letter of 1576 to the Wittenberg divines, Peter Moghila's Confession, and the decree of the Synod of Bethlehem-Jerusalem of 1671. On the basis of a systematic comparison between these he was sure that he knew precisely how the Latin influence had foisted on the Greeks a false appearance of Roman eucharistic doctrine between Lucaris and his own time in Constantinople. Jeremias had been modest in tone and assertion; the Latin spokesmen had been rash. There was clearly a hidden agenda.[48] On the Synod of 1671 he found the Constantinople Patriarchate strangely slippery when asked innocent questions. The reason was not hard to find: it was the deft deployment of cash among the Orthodox leadership by the agents of the Latin West. The Roman emissaries had blatantly taken advantage of the Greeks' poverty and distress by their offers of assistance. For Smith, as for so many other observers in this period, the proof of Roman depravity was to be found in the way they had engineered Cyril Lucaris's deposition and murder, simply because he stood in their way and in the way of French diplomatic ambitions. From his study of Lucaris's life and from his interviews with some of those around at the time, he believed he knew exactly how many Greeks had studied within the Venetian sphere of influence, at

Venice and Padua, and had been suborned in the Jesuit and the French influence. Lucaris's fate had been outstanding because of his mental acuity and the danger he presented to the Franco-Jesuit strategy; but many others, Smith believed, had been intimidated and had had their lives ruined by this financial juggernaut.[49]

The ramifications of the Franco-Jesuit plot were beyond Smith's ability to ascertain; this left him with grey areas in the back of his mind about which he was quite honest. For instance, was the Formula of the Seven Sacraments adopted by the 1671 Synod actually part of the plot?[50] John Covel was to be later convinced that the Synod was a fiction, with no real assembly or deliberation, a put-up job to ratify a private agreement already reached between Parthenios, some other bishops and the Latins. Smith was honestly not so sure.

Smith was familiar with the Arnauld/Claude controversy over the Orthodox and Transubstantiation. Indeed he saw himself as a friend of the Huguenot Claude and knew his book *La défense de la Réformation*, published in 1673.[51] Whatever the politics of the plot to get the Greek bishops to endorse Roman eucharistic doctrine, Smith was convinced that the eucharistic language of both Patriarch Jeremias and Patriarch Cyril Lucaris precluded an identity of Greek understanding with Latin transubstantiation as formulated by the Council of Trent. The Greek terms did not determine the 'manner': that was not their purpose. Smith saw the Greek understanding of change in both Baptism and the Eucharist as implying contextual not 'natural' change. Even such a word as *metamorphosis* was not found in earlier Greek writers but first appeared in a treatise of Gabriel of Philadelphia in the sixteenth century. Gabriel was not uninfluenced by his residence at Venice. Smith thought Gabriel's exact contemporary, Patriarch Jeremias, more authentic. He located the major shift in language as taking place between 1643 and 1662 and finally gaining the tacit approval of Patriarch Parthenios, who had studied under the Jesuits at Galata and was 'wholly governed by them'. The 1671 Synod was simply a means by which the Latinizing bishops, in defiance of historical fact and the 'Faith of their Ancestours', could give an appearance of satisfying their paymasters when there was 'no hope or likelihood' of securing a real consensus in that direction. He accorded to the conspirators 'great eloquence and wit', as well as keen political sense in realizing that what was important was to convince their Roman paymasters that something significant was happening even when very little had in fact changed.

In the light of his analysis, Smith was frankly dismal about immediate prospects. If the Roman Church triumphed in its designs upon the 'present Greeks', he said, 'we need not envy them a victory, which they have gained by such base and treacherous Arts, not to say Bribery'. In his own experience, whenever the implications of transubstantiation had been put to the Greek clergy they had invariably 'stood amazed'. But they seemed so overawed by events that all they could do was mutter about 'a great Mystery'. Such was the nemesis of years of dissimulation. Once they sold the pass on eucharistic doctrine, he had little hope that the bishops would stand firm on the *Filioque*. However, he still nurtured the hope, based on his observation, that even if the bishops caved in, the people, the *laos*, would stand firm in their Tradition.[52]

In this, as we shall see in the next chapter, he had a sounder Orthodox sense than his successor John Covel for whom the only role of the laity was 'follow my leader'.

However, his interpretation of Greek eucharistic teaching and the authority of Cyril Lucaris did not go unchallenged among his fellow High Churchmen. One of his most frequent correspondents was Henry Dodwell, a fellow of Trinity College, Dublin. Dodwell was anxious to learn of Smith's experiences even before Smith had returned to England. In a six-page closely written quarto letter to an unnamed correspondent which was subsequently passed on to Smith, he betrays his itchy curiosity but also rehearses at somewhat tedious length and with great erudition conclusions to which he had already come in his reading. Smith does not seem to have been in a hurry to satisfy him. In a letter of April 1673, which betrays some past tension between the two men, Dodwell declared:

My present earnest desire is to be aquainted with the present state of the Greek Church, how they are affected to the Protestants, and particularly how the actions of their late Patriarch Cyrill are resented, whether his party be at present considerable, together with the learning they are most addicted to, and what kinds of MSS are preserved and valued in their Libraries. If your other studies would permit, I think your labours in this kind would not only be a favour to me but a gratification to the publick and very seasonable at this juncture wherein men are somewhat more than usually intent on the Popish controversyes; besides that this argument will be more acceptable for being new and more intirely your own, without the assistance of other Authors.

Dodwell urged Smith specifically to write an account in Latin.[53]

Dodwell was a persistent man. He followed this up just under three months later with a plea to be told what the Greek Church thought specifically of 'our communion' and 'our opinions', 'whether they lay such stress on those points, wherein they agree with the Papists and differ from us, concerning the adoration of Images and Saints and the B Sacrament &c.', and which of these was in his opinion 'the most prejudicial to Communion', to the extent that 'they would reject us from their Communion' and 'refuse to communicate with us'. Patriarch Jeremias II ('Jeremy') eventually grew 'very high' with the Lutherans in the previous century and he feared 'the like Temper in the moderns'. He seemed to imagine that there might be some Anglican tenets which the Greeks thought 'erroneous' and 'yet tolerable', i.e. not so entirely 'pernicious' that they were obliged to separate. How really desirous were they of the peace of Christendom and how willing 'to receive a better information'. Whatever became of Metrophanes Kritopoulos who spent so long at Oxford 'to be educated'? Could he have been active in propagating Lucaris's opinions? Dodwell at the time of writing this clearly had no idea that Metrophanes had himself attained a patriarchate, although amusingly he quotes the Patriarch of Alexandria not realizing who he was and only later realized his faux pas.[54]

Dodwell also wanted more precise information on what techniques the Jesuits were using to reduce the Greeks to the Church of Rome and how far these techniques had succeeded. Then came a characteristic laconic statement: 'They are so considerable a part of the Catholick Church, that I should highly value them if they were a little more cultivated than I doubt they are ...'[55] He went on pestering Smith to publish his findings, fearful that he might abandon the project, then rejoiced that Dr Cave had persuaded him to 'resume'.[56] Meanwhile he insisted on clearing up certain things. Did the Greeks now communicate only in wine? This was such an important issue with the Romans that he relied on Smith's 'candour and experience' to put him right. For the sake of the 'Catholick peace of Christendome', which he knew Smith valued in his 'Zeal for Truth', he must speak out. 'That you may therefore see that I am not destitute of Testimonies even of the modern Greeks the words of Jeremias are very express as to the Communion in both kinds, that they do approve of ours and disapprove of the Roman practice in this particular ...' And what of the communication of infants? Jeremias seems to make it 'very plain'. Dodwell spends a page and a half in his minute handwriting worrying around his latter question, resorting to a Latin authority on Coptic practice and determining to check further with 'Persons' and 'modern books' as to whether infants received the Body by way of the smallest particles of the margarita in the chalice, fearing that the modern Greeks had somehow modified the practice since the days of Jeremias. He seemed obsessed with the mechanics of it. What if an infant could only 'suck'? Did the Greeks perhaps think that by dipping the spoon into the chalice at least the 'virtue' of the margarita was imparted to the infant? Or perhaps they consciously communicated only in wine 'on account of the Doctrine of Concomitancy, that is on account of the natural inseparability of the natural Blood of Christ from his natural Body'; or yet again perhaps it was simply

because of the 'natural incapacity of the children to receive
more' and that, on the principle of spiritual communion the
children were thought to receive the benefit when unable to
receive the substance. He is not satisfied with relying on the
testimony of mere 'Itinerants' who are 'apt to speak according to their interests'. What was needed were testimonies from
some of the Greeks' 'leading men, either their Patriarch or
some Metropolites, or at least some Bishops'. He advised
Smith in his book to distinguish carefully between his authorities and what he himself witnessed, so that the reader might
know if he spoke 'on the Credit of Books' or on his 'own
particular knowledge.'[57]

Dodwell's neurosis about accuracy and authority stemmed
from the battle he was then waging in defence of the Creed
against the Socinians. Similarly, his obsession with the
communion of infants had to do with his current preoccupation with the 'Pelagian Controversyes' concerning what was
necessary for salvation. He told Smith that he abhorred all
'dissimulation', always called a spade a spade and, though he
had 'very great value for Catholicke Peace', he would never
pursue it at the cost of fudging an issue. This, he believed,
was a 'suitable season' in 'Divine Providence' for the good
blessings promised to peacemakers, but those blessings must
be sought in strict fidelity to truth and fact.[58]

After he had read Smith's book in Latin, Dodwell said he
wished it had been even more detailed on the Greeks' unwrit-
ten traditions, especially those which might be 'of use in our
occidental Controversyes', and he wished for more on the
disputes surrounding Lucaris and what the present Greeks
thought of him. Smith saw Lucaris as the victim both of 'ignorant and mercenary Greeks' and of unscrupulous Latins 'who
out of great zeal to the Roman See, very disingenuously'
treated the Patriarch 'not only as a Dishonest man who gained
the Patriarchates, first of Alexandria and then of Constantinople, by money and 'by evil arts' but also as one who dissem-
bled his views and told the English and Dutch Ambassadors
what they wanted to hear.[59] Dodwell, for his part, could not
believe there was no smoke without fire. He saw Cyril as

plainly teaching a virtualist understanding of the eucharistic presence in Chapter 17 of his *Confession*. 'The words are as plain ... as our fathers could desire them ...' Cyril had claimed this not only in the name of his 'primitive forefathers' as delivered to them by Christ (on which Dodwell could agree, being a virtualist himself) but also in the unanimous name of his 'immediate ancestors', and the problem for Dodwell was that he did not know 'with what probability' this 'could have been pretended', not only because several of Cyril's near contemporaries (including Jeremias II) denied it but also because Hugo Grotius, who knew him personally, was 'dissatisfyed in the integrity of his acting in the name of the Greek Church'. Therefore, unless Thomas Smith had found otherwise during his sojourn in Constantinople, he thought there were 'very great and probable presumptions of his singularity', especially in the light of the relatively recent teaching of Gabriel of Philadelphia, 'a great stickler for the Greek Church' and no 'Latinizer'. Cyril, as far as Dodwell could see, had not consulted 'the sense of the generality in any fair and equal way', nor with the 'privity or approbation of any considerable persons'. Even Claude in his controversy with Arnauld could only claim that Lucaris was endeavouring to return to 'ancient doctrine', not that he represented 'the present sense of the Greeks'.[60]

Having read the correspondence between Jeremias II and the Lutheran divines,[61] Dodwell had come to the conclusion that Jeremias evidently supposed Transubstantiation. He was struck by the 'pertinency of the sense and the emphaticallness of the words' in the Patriarch's reply, likening them to those of Mark of Ephesus and Nicolas Cabasilas, albeit both those earlier theologians were excoriated by the Latins. Cabasilas at Chapter 27 of his exposition of the Liturgy 'playnly denyd' the 'figurative sense' in favour of the 'naturall'. 'To the same intent also he conceives the presence of Christ in the sacrament to be such as that he is seen and felt (expressly denyd by Cyril in his condemnation of our Adversaryes doctrine) by which you may perceive how little presumably he spoke to the language of his predecessors.' Dodwell found a consistency in

Greek statements as far back as the ecumenical Council of Lyons (1274) 'when there were less false Latinizers among the Greeks' than later at Florence. At the time of Lyons, Euthemius appealed back to Gregory of Nyssa and John of Damascus – 'non dixit autem, Haec sunt *signa* corporis et sanguinis meus, sed, Haec sunt corpus et sanguis meus'. 'So also', he adds, 'those curious disputes, which for a while troubled the Greek Church in the Empire of Alexius Comnenus whether the body of our Lord in the Eucharist were corruptible or incorruptible must needs have supposed its presence in the naturall sense . . .' He found the testimony of Simonas of Gaza particularly telling because of his defence of a 'natured change' in the elements occurred in the context of a general defence of the Christian faith against the Muslims. (All his distinctions were predicated on a strict realism, e.g. how the unity of Christ's Body can be reconciled with the division of the bread.)

Dodwell was unconvinced by the argument of Peter Martyr Vermigli and Martin Chemnitz that the Greeks at Florence dissented from Transubstantiation. The most one could say was that the Greeks were leaving the Council just as the Armenian delegation of whom the doctrine was required were arriving and so had no opportunity to say anything one way or the other. Dodwell reluctantly concluded that Greek eucharistic understanding was a by-product of the Iconoclast controversy, in which Christ was understood by the defenders of ikons to have made the Eucharist an ikon of his Humanity and so left no room for lesser 'resemblances' or 'natural similitudes' since the elements, once consecrated, were very 'truth and reality'. The denial of attributes after consecration was thus a consequential 'innovation from the generall doctrine of their ancestors'. Those who were against images were thus against transubstantiation for very logical reasons while those who were *for* images 'were the most jealous abetters of Transubstantiation'. A study of the iconoclast Council of Frankfurt and the writings of John Scotus Erigena would bear this out. He was sure that upon inspection it would be found that the iconoclastic position lasted only just so long as the doctrine of

Transubstantiation was not yet universally received. This, thought Dodwell, would explain the otherwise strange silence of the Patriarchs of Constantinople and Jerusalem at the Lateran Council (1215) 'wherein at length the word of Transubstantiation was first broached'. Therefore the Greeks at Florence kept quiet either out of prudence for the sake of their own reputations or because, by then, 'the contrary could not easily be proved'.

Dodwell is a useful foil to our main witnesses. In spite of his pedantry, he had a sharp mind for deception. He constantly harped on the need for 'pertinency' in the use of authorities rather than accumulating citations of little context and variable value. In his long letter of 2 June 1670 he wrote: 'a man has need to be cautious what authors he trusts' and how he uses them, 'considering that the doctrine of transubstantiation is not so much the denyall of an old article of faith' as the introduction of a gloss which might be 'false' while not utterly contradicting the old. There was, he said, 'nothing more prejudiciall to the Common wealth of learning than the tenaciousness whereby some otherwise excellent Persons maintain their private opinions', for this deterred 'ingenious persons' from attempting improvements against 'prevayling prejudice'. He urged that in the eucharistic controversy they 'deal like indifferent and impartiall enquirers of Truth' and not 'like factious abetters of partys' (a practice 'too frequent even among our modern as well as ancient controversialists'). If the true eucharistic doctrine really had been replaced by an innovation among the Greeks, it seemed 'most difficult' to him to discern it before the controversy was explicitly raised and the Church had had a chance to declare her sense of it, by which time the waters had already been muddied.

Dodwell knew that getting the 'sense' of the Greek Church rather than relatively private views within it, was not easy. One of the difficulties, he foresaw, would be that under the Turks the Greeks had not been much used to Synodal procedures. Where they *had* declared themselves for some pressing reason, they had sometimes 'extremely altered' the tradition in particulars according to 'occasions and places', mixing up the 'ancient' with the fortuitous. In such a situation the only fixed measure regarding their eucharistic belief might be how in practice they adored the 'Exterior Elements' during their Liturgies. The difficulty there was that Rome tended to claim all such usages automatically for their own case. How, then, was one to evaluate the equal 'honour' given to the elements between the blessing of the Prothesis and the Great Entrance on the one hand and the Words of Institution and *epiclesis* on the other? He was aware that 'Sacramentall change' was associated by the Greeks with the *epiclesis* and the infusion of warm water. It was clear to him as an armchair critic who had never been present at an Eastern Liturgy but on the basis of pure logic that the acts of liturgical 'adoration' could not of themselves 'conclude' anything in respect of theories of presence and therefore of transubstantiation. All this meant that it was especially important to decide what 'presumptions' were necessary for distinguishing when modern Greek writers were speaking in the sense of their Church and when they were speaking their own. One had to adopt a methodology for dealing with the more general use of the Fathers in their handling of Scripture in this matter – where they agreed with the papists, where they agree with 'us'. The crucial break-off point was, in his view, the ninth century when the eucharistic controversy began to separate out in recognizably modern form.

From a distance it was clear to Dodwell that the Greeks of the islands and the mainland littoral were now 'more or less Latinized' either as a result of the Council of Florence or through the influence of the sophisticated Venetians owing to the 'natural servility and flattery and barbarousness of the [Greek] nation'. He hoped that Smith had not been reading too much 'barbarious modern Greek' which reflected this modern modification. He was also well aware of the tendency for Greeks long resident in Italy for studies to say things by way of compliance, even if they had read the earliest Fathers and had some idea of the 'sense of the Apostles'.[62] He was cautious about giving weight to contemporary English scholars who had converted to Rome because converts' 'excessive bitterness' laid them open to the suspicion of partiality. A cradle Latin was always more reliable.[63] He urged upon Smith the compilation of a comprehensive catalogue of all texts which were 'doubtful or counterfeit' yet 'certainly ancient and therefore useful for the history of church tradition.'[64]

Dodwell was undoubtedly a great scholar. The breadth of his reading was staggering, embracing the writings of St Efrem the Syrian and modern writings about the Copts which led him to suspect that the controversy over Dioscuros and Eutyches was abating.[65] His weakness was not a scholarly but a spiritual one. Although unquestionably a High Churchman, he seems to have had little access to the mystical theology which linked Andrewes, Cosin, Laud, Taylor and Thorndike and which gave access to a deeper, kingdom-centred understanding of the sacraments and the Church. He had a rather mechanistic idea of grace and of divine action in the Eucharist, seeing Transubstantiation as simply a 'change' which required 'the omnipotence of God to affect it', something which enabled 'materiall elements' to be 'operative on an immaterial soul'. Since in his perspective this was required of both the 'realist' and the 'virtualist' view, the former, the Roman, view was superfluous by the principle of Ockham's Razor. Divine action by types and antitypes 'and memorialls of the passion of our Lord was as effectual a presence as any change in the species'. The Roman view was in any case abhorrent because it 'corrupted' the elements.[66] Smith seems to have sensed a serious limitation in Dodwell's mind. When Dodwell announced his commentary on St Barnabas with copious notes on the 'mystical interpretation of Scripture', his colleague somewhat blanched at it and hoped his friend Dr Hudson would look over it very carefully 'that no prejudice may accrue to our holy religion by any Singular opinions he may possibly advance it'.[67] Quite possibly he felt that Dodwell was the very last person to write a commentary on anything 'mystical'!

Smith's book, it will be remembered, appeared in Latin in 1676 just as the national hysteria over a popish plot at home was beginning to build up over the conversion of the heir to the throne James, Duke of York, to Rome. The hysteria reached its peak between 1679 and 1680, the year of the publication of an English version. All that Smith wrote concerning the French and Jesuit plots in the Eastern Mediterranean was tailor-made to the plot mania, not least among High Churchmen who already nurtured feelings of vulnerability from the Commonwealth period and feared any further encroachment on what Jeremy Taylor had described, typically, as 'my dear mother, which is the best church on the world'.[68] Thomas Ken, a mild-mannered man and a very High Churchman, declared after a visit to Rome in 1675 during the Year of Jubilee that if 'not actually "Satan's seat", Rome was at least the presence-chamber of Mammon.'[69] The plethora of anti-popery tracts in these years stressed the necessity to maintain the 'Established Religion'. Although one tract used the autonomy of the Eastern Patriarchates as a stick with which to beat Rome, another characterized the 'Grecians' as well as the Romans as 'adorers of a consecrated wafer as their God'.[70]

We know from Smith himself that the publication of his book was part of a scheme already floated by Henry Compton, the Bishop of London, at his urging, to succour 'the poor distressed Bishops and Priests' of the Greek Church. In his dedication Smith says that the Bishop has 'merited of the Greek Church' for giving its persecuted members somewhere to 'fly unto'. There is a suggestion in this dedication, however, that Smith does not altogether think Compton's scheme is workable. This was to prove prescient – so prescient indeed that it is surprising that others did not pick up the warnings before embarking on ill-judged and exceedingly ill-timed projects for Greek education in England.

By raising this issue as the ground of his publication and at the same time disclosing what appeared to be devastating evidence of popish plotting elsewhere in the world, Smith was, to say the least, getting into deep waters. He obviously tried to mitigate any undesired inferences by likening Bishop Compton to the moderate Romanists Carlo Borromeo and Francis de Sales. In fact the book's publication, as a way of promoting the grand design to help the Orthodox, was an unmitigated disaster whose failure was built into it not only because of the hysterical atmosphere of the time but chiefly because of the contradictions built into Smith's own scenario for an Anglican-assisted Greek community in London.

There had been a small Greek commercial colony in London since the beginning of the century, hence, the interest in publishing Christophoros Angelos' account of the Church's persecution which was discussed in Chapter 1. The printer Nicodemos Metaxas settled in London. By the 1670s there was a resident priest, Daniel Vulgaris. Vulgaris took the initiative in 1674 in asking the Privy Council for a church they could use. He suggested as a quid pro quo that all the Greeks in London would become English subjects: he himself became one in 1675. Nothing, however, had happened when Joseph Georgirenes, the 'retired' Metropolitan of Samos, arrived in England in 1676 with the objective of getting Greek service books printed.[71] Vulgaris took advantage of the Bishop's presence, knowing it could not fail to impact on Bishop Compton. A subscription list was opened. Interestingly, the Duke of York gave generously (presumably he had not read the anti-Roman passages in the Latin version of Smith's *Account*) and accepted the dedication of a book to be published by Georgirenes on the Island of Samos (presumably he had not read that either). As we saw in Chapter 1, James had some direct experience of Orthodox at worship in Paris during the Interregnum.[72] A site was chosen in Crown Street, Soho, and the building, St Mary's, was completed in 1677. Then came the backlash.

Anti-Popery sentiments were directed against Metropolitan Joseph by a dishonest servant, Dominico Cratiana, who had absconded with funds to Bristol and covered himself by laying charges against the Bishop of being a 'secret Papist' before the Bristol magistrates. It was easy enough to make the charges in the heightened atmosphere of the time, especially in the wake of the dedication of Georgirenes' book to the Duke of York. In the process, the Metropolitan was ingeniously entangled in the murder of Sir Edmund Berry Godfrey, simply because the disreputable witnesses testified that Sir Edmund's body had been put on a horse behind the Greek church. The driving force behind this charge was the Vicar of St Martin-in-the-Fields, who had resented the building of the Greek church on his patch. Bishop Compton, who sat on the sub-committee of the House of Lords 'Plot' Committee to investigate the murder had an open ear to the vicar. It would be interesting to analyse the Bishop's line of questioning in the enquiry to see if there was any evidence of 'leading' the witnesses. The Metropolitan was hampered at the same time by the scandalous behaviour of a priest called Ciciliano who had attached himself. All this did not augur well for the future of the Greek church. Cratiana had turned up in Bristol and, according to Gilbert Burnet, one Bedloe, an associate of Titus Oates and Isaac Tonge, the authors of the Popish Plot, and 'a man of very vicious life' who had defrauded many people, made allegations about Godfrey's murder before the Bristol magistrates. So there may have been collusion between Cratiana and Bedloe to smear the Greeks.[73]

Smith made it clear in his Dedication, in terms which Compton and the general reading public could understand, that his objective was not simply charitable relief. Those Greeks who came to England either out of curiosity or love of learning could be 'reduced' from 'those errours and corruptions which have of late crept in among them, by bringing them into a nearer and more familiar acquaintance with the Doctrin and rites of Worship establisht in the Church of England.' Knowing Smith's pre-occupation with the Latin infiltration of the Greek Church since the early part of the century, in particular the efforts made to tie the Greeks to an affirmation of transubstantiation, it is tempting to understand the term 'of late' literally and see his whole objective as one of de-Latinization. But in fact Smith gave more hostages to fortune. There are in his Dedication hints of restricting the Greeks in their use of the church building in Crown Street in other more fundamental ways. He writes of allowing them to use such worship as was 'decent and inoffensive' and 'essential to their Religion'. This implies a value judgement on his part which might conflict head-on with Orthodox feeling. Clearly, in the existing social and legal context, they would not be allowed to go in procession in the streets with ikons and relics. But what of their behaviour inside the church? There could well have been public concern even about this, because members of the public would be free to walk in.

In the event, the restrictions imposed by Bishop Compton were draconian and showed immense insensitivity. There were to be no ikons in the church, nor any prayers to the saints. Any priest officiating there would have to sign a repudiation of transubstantiation and of the Synod of Bethlehem-Jerusalem.[74]

News of this got to the Patriarch and Synod in Contantinople and they were understandably offended. Sir John Finch, the English ambassador to the Porte, was summoned to give an explanation. Finch was subjected to very close interrogation. Intellectual though he was, he was at a great disadvantage in not being fluent in Greek and having to reply in Italian which was then translated into Greek by a priest who had been briefly in London in 1677 and knew a little of the background. The ambassador came away from the ordeal convinced that the Greek bishops had stridently affirmed their agreement with Rome on transubstantiation, although in reality all they appeared to have said (and said with vehemence, it is true) was that the Body of Christ Crucified was present in the Liturgy. There was also a failure of communication over the importance accorded in England to the 1671 Synod. Apparently it did not seem to them to be all that significant for their faith. If what Covel reported about it to England was true, viz. that it was no real deliberative synod but simply a collecting of signatures by Latinized bishops who were *parti pris*, it is hardly surprising that the Patriarch and his synod were not forthcoming on it or that Compton and his advisers should have wished to make it a test case.[75]

It appears that Finch, under pressure, had admitted that Greeks in London would not be allowed to repudiate the *Filioque* in their worship and would not be permitted to acknowledge the authority of the Patriarch, as they came within the jurisdiction of the Bishop of London and the Royal

Supremacy. On hearing all this, the Patriarch refused to bless the scheme.[76]

The former Metropolitan of Samos, who had been sidelined in these negotiations, was unable to cope with the crisis and the Anglican hidden agenda, for want of sufficient English. In this weak situation, he put to Archbishop Sancroft a proposal for training Greek students in England 'in the true Doctrine of the Church of England'. Somehow he thought this would edify people back home in the Greek lands. It was this proposal which Benjamin Woodroffe of Christ Church, Oxford, took up ten years later, albeit after Sancroft himself had become a Nonjuror and lost his primacy.[77] The original idea was for twenty to thirty Greek students to settle at Gloucester Hall in Oxford (now Worcester College). The idea was that of Thomas Smith, who in 1677 lobbied Compton and gained his support. There was a simultaneous project to get students from the Unitas Fratrum or Bohemian/Moravian Brethren to Oxford or Cambridge and seems to reflect a desire in the Restoration Church to break out of ecumenical isolation. The Moravian project fell through. Metropolitan Joseph took up the idea while still in England in 1682, but by then it had been whittled down to 'about 12 Scholars out of Greece'. Sancroft was, to say the least, slack in his response, despite reminders from Compton. Compton's motive was evidently to use the scheme as a means of proselytizing or at least combating the Latins in Greece. Sancroft probably had no such idea. Compton designated Woodroffe as 'President' of the students but nothing started until 1698 and then the students who came were so badly treated that they left, some of them ironically tempted by the Romanists to move to Paris, which was precisely what Compton did not want. Patriarch Gabriel III banned all further Greek students at Oxford.[78] Meanwhile, the church in Soho was rendered virtually useless to the Greeks by the intolerable restrictions placed upon it. The Greek community tried to sell it but found their title technically unsound. Possibly the Anglican authorities contrived things hoping that the building would fall to them. It did so when the Vicar of St Martin-in-the-Fields turned the Greeks out in 1682.[79] There was no further attempt to establish a Greek church in London until 1721. Thomas Smith's irenic hopes had seemingly collapsed in ignominy. He had, however, managed to leave an impression of the Greeks and their Church in the mind of his associates in England which looked fairly hopeless. John Wallis, the Laudian Professor of Arabic at Oxford from 1674 to 1738, wrote to him in 1698 that whatever their sad condition might be now under the Turks, if they exchanged 'the Turkish slavery for that of Rome, I don't doubt they would change for the worse'. Wallis cited the case of the Hungarian Protestants who passed from Turkish control to that of the Habsburg Emperor and suffered for it. Wherever the Jesuits functioned, he said, it was always the same. In another letter Wallis referred to Rome's 'new and negative Religion'.[80] Long after Smith's return to England, he appears to have been involved in sending copies of Pococke's modern Greek translation of the Church Catechism and parts of the Prayer Book Liturgy to Greece to encourage his Greek friends, possibly having found a way around the efficient Jesuit methods of intercepting such materials.[81]

After the Revolution Smith became a Nonjuror. He did not live long enough to be involved in the Nonjurors' negotiations with the Patriarchs between 1716 and 1722, but it has to be assumed that he influenced them in their thinking. Alone of all the Nonjurors, he had experience of living among the Orthodox. But it would seem that the one thing he could not convey to the future negotiators was that sense of spiritual immediacy in the midst of the Orthodox Liturgy which above all had so much impressed him.

Notes

1. He was chaplain from 1668 to 1670 and immediately preceded John Covel.
2. See the entry on Smith in the *Dictionary of National Biography*.
3. Rycaut to Smith, 17 May 1669, 20 May 1673 and 28 July 1681, Smith MS 53, ff.153, 157 and 159, Bodleian Library; Pearson to Smith, 7 October 1664, Smith MS 53, f.25; Sir Paul Rycaut to Smith, 5 April 1682, Smith MS 55, f.161; Smith MS 45,

passim; Smith to Sir Philip Warwick, 24 July 1678, Smith MS 66, f.81; Humfrey Wanley to Smith, 30 May and 25 July 1697, Smith MS 54, ff.79–80, 89–90; Smith to George Hickes, 13 May 1699, Smith MS 63, f.15; Wanley to Smith, 20 June 1697, Smith MS 54, ff.83–85; Hickes to Smith, 10 December 1697 and 22 May 1702, Smith MS 50, ff.101, 123; Smith to Wanley, 8 June 1697, Smith MS 66, ff.67–70.

4. Pepys to Smith, 18 May 1695, Smith MS 53, f.31; Trumbull to Smith, 26 May 1709, Smith MS 54, f.9; Smith to Ken, 19 December 1706, Smith MS 64, f.33; Smith to Warwick, n.d. 1678, Smith MS 66, f.90.

5. Smith to 'Mr Younger', 8 June 1678, Smith MS 63, f.4; Smith to Sir Philip Warwick, 14 July 1678, Smith MS 66, f.82.

6. Pearson to Smith, 26 July 1668, Smith MS 53, f.27. A suggestion as to how much Smith was in Harvey's confidence is to be found in Rycaut's letter to Smith of 17 May 1669, Smith MS 55, f.153. For Smith's memorandum to Harvey, see quotations from it in Etheridge's letter to Joseph Williamson, assistant Secretary of State, 3 May 1670, State Papers 97/19, f.150–v and Harvey to Williamson, ? November 1670, ibid., f.158, Public Record Office.

7. Sargeant to Smith, ? January 1671, Smith MS 53, ff.169.

8. Cf. Theodosia to Smith, 18 June no year, Smith MS 53, ff.177–8.

9. *An Account of the Greek Church, as to its Doctrine and Rites To which is added An Account of the State of the Greek Church, under Cyrillus Lucaris Patriarch of Constantinople, with a Relation of his Sufferings and Death* (London, 1680), 'To the Reader'.

10. Ibid., pp. 225–6.

11. Ibid., pp. 71–72.

12. Ibid., pp. 195–6.

13. Steven Runciman, *The Great Church in Captivity*, op. cit., p. 293.

14. *An Account*, op. cit., pp. 15–17.

15. This reference to Cyprus is perhaps more pertinent than he knew. Franz Georg Maier has found the tendency for Greek bishops under the Turks to become exploiters of their own people to be especially marked in seventeenth-century Cyprus. He cited evidence from C. D. Cobham, *Excerpta Cypria* (Cambridge, 1908) that many Greek Cypriots blamed their bishops for their 'misfortunes', especially their debts. The Archbishop of Cyprus speculated in corn in collusion with the Turkish Governor, frequently seizing the whole annual produce for export at an arbitrary valuation. As late as the second decade

of the nineteenth century the same charge was being made by British travellers. The theory was advanced that such rapacity was worse in Cyprus than elsewhere because of the special status of the Archbishop as Ethnarch. Cf. F. G. Maier, *Cyprus from earliest time to the present day* (London, 1968), pp. 114, 121, citing J. M. Kinneir and W. Turner.

16. *An Account*, op. cit., pp. 80–83.
17. Ibid., pp. 84ff.
18. Ibid., p. 79.
19. The then English Ambassador, Sir Thomas Roe, had made this printing press possible. But the Jesuits soon persuaded the Ottoman authorities to impound the press, and Nikodemos Metaxas took refuge at Roe's house. Roe managed to have his revenge on the Jesuits by securing their banishment from the city for so long as he was in post, but when he returned to England the following year the Jesuits surreptitiously returned, so nothing whatever had been gained. Cf. V. J. Parry, *A History of the Ottoman Empire to 1730* (Cambridge, 1976), p. 151.
20. *An Account*, op. cit., pp. 263ff.
21. Ibid., p. 17.
22. Ibid., pp. 18–19. Cf. George Etheridge to Joseph Williamson, 3 May 1670, PRO, SP97/19, f.150–v. Daniel seemed unaware of the religious differences which had caused the Cossacks to revolt against the Poles, so it is a pity that Smith's advisory role was cut short. Cf. Harvey to Williamson, ? November 1670, SP97/19, f.158.
23. Ibid., pp. 99–100.
24. Ibid., p. 46.
25. Ibid., pp. 121–4.
26. Ibid., 'To the Reader'.
27. Ibid., pp. 51–55.
28. Cf. Kenneth R. Long, *The Music of the English Church* (London, 1972), p. 245; Edmund Fellowes, *English Cathedral Music* (5th ed., Rev. J. A. Westrup, London, 1969), pp. 116, 124–5. See also Nicholas Temperley, *The Music of the English Parish Church* (London, 1979).
29. *An Account*, op. cit., p. 30.
30. Ibid., pp. 221–30.
31. Ibid., pp. 28–29, 78–79.
32. Ibid., p. 41.
33. Ibid.
34. Ibid., pp. 143, 160–1, 180.
35. Ibid., pp. 27–28; cf. p. 133.
36. Ibid., pp. 205–11, 231, 232–4, 237. He mitigated this by opting

for Cyril Lucaris's explanation over that of Gabriel of Philadelphia.
37. Ibid., pp. 153–5; 171, 216.
38. Ibid., pp. 133–5. It may be noted that James Dymock detected the same defect in Anglican worship in a small devotional manual of 1686, *The Great Sacrifice of the New Law*. See Part V.
39. *An Account*, op. cit., pp. 211–14, 230–1.
40. Ibid., p. 109.
41. Ibid., pp. 190–3.
42. Ibid., pp. 155, 158, 183.
43. He singled out those 'strangely devout, or rather superstitious' who showed such attitudes in throwing away perfectly good vegan food during a fast which had been accidentally 'contaminated' by a drop of oil or wine. Ibid., p. 36.
44. Ibid., pp. 183–6.
45. Ibid., p. 48.
46. Ibid., p. 202.
47. Ibid., pp. 198–9. The case made by Parthenios against Cyril Lucaris was, in his view, synthetic. He cites Lucaris's letter to Wytenbogaert to prove it.
48. Ibid., 'To the Reader'.
49. Ibid., p. 240. His clinching argument was that in the eyes of the Jesuits Lucaris had to go, once he openly denounced the Union of Brest–Litovsk incorporating the Ukrainian Orthodox into the Roman obedience. The Jesuits had engineered this. For some time Cyril had to endure in effect a Jesuit Anti-Patriarch, Cyril Contari, Metropolitan of Beroea, on his doorstep, waiting to walk into his shoes. Cyril of Beroea had in tow the Metropolitans of Adrianople, Larissa, Chalcedon, Cizicum and Naupactus, all of whom lived in or near Constantinople and were in French pay, as were the Metropolitans of Sophia and Acrida whom Cyril Lucaris had deposed. Smith's sources for these allegations were Nathanael Conopius, Protosynkellos to the Patriarch, and Edward Pocock of Christ Church, Oxford, who as English Chaplain at Aleppo was in Constantinople when Cyril was murdered and who, as mentioned earlier, made a detailed report to Archbishop Laud. That written report was lost during the Civil Wars, but Pocock gave Smith the substance of it in conversation. Cf. pp. 253–4, and *DNB* 'Smith', 'Pocock'.
50. Ibid., p. 107.
51. Smith to Hickes, 21 June 1704, Smith MS 63; Bodleian MS 15669. See also Lord Winchelsea to Smith, 31 May 1676, Smith MS 47, f.58, Bodleian MS 15654.
52. Ibid., pp. 144–53, 197.

53. Dodwell to Smith, 23 April 1673, Smith MS 49, f.49.
54. Dodwell to Smith, 1 August and 26 September 1676, Smith MS 49.
55. Dodwell to Smith, 12 July 1673, Smith MS 54, f.111.
56. Dodwell to Smith, 12 July 1673 and 17 April 1675, Smith MS 64, ff.111, 115.
57. Dodwell to Smith, 25 September 1676, Smith MS 49.
58. Dodwell to Smith, 3 July 1675 and 21 April 1676, Smith MS 49, ff.121, 126.
59. Smith to Dean Lloyd of Bangor, 30 June 1678, Smith MS 64, f.145.
60. Dodwell's comments here and in the succeeding paragraph come from a very long letter to an unknown correspondent dated 2 June 1670 which was passed to Smith and is contained in his papers, Smith MS 45.
61. For a modern text of the exchange in English with scholarly commentary, see George Mastrantonis, op. cit.
62. Dodwell to Smith, 2 June 1670, Smith MS 45, f.1.
63. Dodwell to Smith, 26 September 1676, Smith MS 49, f.131.
64. Dodwell to Smith, 19 June 1671, Smith MS 45, f.9.
65. Dodwell to Smith, 23 May 1667 and 1 August 1676, Smith MS 49, ff.45, 127.
66. Dodwell's letter to an unknown recipient, 2 June 1670, Smith MS 45.
67. Smith to Hudson, 12 July 1707, Smith MS 63, f.49, Bodleian MS 15667.
68. Jeremy Taylor, *Deus Justificatus*, cited by H. R. McAdoo, *The Eucharistic Theology of Jeremy Taylor Today* (Norwich, 1988), p. 35.
69. Cf. F. A. Taylor, *Thomas Ken* (London, 1896), pp. 24–25.
70. [M.D.] *A Seasonable Advice to all True Protestants in England in This Present Posture of Affairs. Discovering the Present Designs of the Papists* (London, 1679), p. 21; *A Rational Discourse Concerning Transubstantiation, in a Letter to a Person of Honor, from a Master of Arts of the University of Cambridge* (London, 1676), p. 41. This last pamphlet could well have been by John Covel who, as Chaplain at Constantinople, was obsessed with the issue of transubstantiation. Typical of the tracts in this period are *The Pope Outlaw'd, or the Catholick Looking-glass* (1674); *The Proselyte of Rome call'd back to the Communion of the Church of England* (1679); [Anthony Egan], *The Papist Design Detected and the Jesuits Subtill Practises to Ruine and Subvert the Nation, discovered and laid open* (1678); [L. Williams], *Christianity Abused by the Church of Rome* (1679); James Salgado [ex-O.P.], *The Romish Priest Turn's Protestant* (1679); *Dr Martin Luther's*

Prophecies of the Destruction of Rome and the Downfall of the Romish Religion (1679); *A Relation ...* (1680); *The Pope's Cabinet Unlocked* (1680). These are just a few of the published tracts collected in a bound volume by a concerned member of Sion College at the time and show how easy it was to stir up hostility against the Greeks in London and against the Metropolitan of Samos in particular. There are similar collections in St John's College, Cambridge, and the Founder's Library at the University of Wales at Lampeter.

71. Cf. Runciman, op. cit., pp. 294, 296–9.
72. According to Sir John Finch in his evidence to the Patriarch of Constantinople in 1679, Charles II also donated generously. Presumably the royal brothers conferred together on what was the most prudent thing to do in the circumstances. Runciman, ibid.
73. Ibid., p. 298. Cf. Stephen Knight, *The Killing of Justice Godfrey* (London, 1984), p. 298. 'A coroner's jury', says J. P. Kenyon, 'brought in a verdict of wilful murder by some person or persons unknown, but for this formula the popular mind substituted two words, "The Papists". While Godfrey's corpse was brought back for an elaborate lying-in-state which lasted ten days, London was gripped by the kind of panic not seen since 1666'. Chains were placed across city streets, Jesuits were arrested, the City Chamberlain, Sir Thomas Player, uttered in his panic the classic words, 'He did not know but the next morning they might all rise with their throats cut'. By February 1679 alleged murderers had been tried and executed. The three men who found Godfrey's body dumped on Primrose Hill were all from St Giles Fields, which was very close to the Greek church. J. P. Kenyon, *The Popish Plot* (London, 1972), pp. 89, 92, 302, 306. Kenyon's opinion was that Godfrey's murder was most likely to have been ordered by members of the London underworld because of grudges held against him as Justice of the Peace. He had always been aware of this animosity and had walked the streets with a bodyguard. For Bedloe, see Burnet's *History of His Own Time*, abridged by Thomas Stackhouse, 1724, Everyman edition (London, 1906), p. 155.
74. Edward Carpenter, *The Protestant Bishop. Being the Life of Henry Compton, 1632–1713, Bishop of London* (London, 1956), p. 360.
75. Historical Manuscripts Commission Report on the *Finch MSS*, pp. i, 148, cited by Carpenter, ibid.
76. Ibid., p. 362. Carpenter's comments on the breakdown are theologically naive.
77. For an introduction to the Woodroffe plan, see Runciman, op. cit., pp. 300–4.

78. Rawlinson MSS, 985c, f.5 and Tanner MSS 36, f.187, both in the Bodleian. Carpenter, op. cit., pp. 362–3. Under Woodroffe the students were required to study the Greek classics and the biblical commentaries of the Fathers (not, by implication, other works of the Fathers). Woodroffe tried to flatter Patriarch Callinicus with an elegant letter in his best Greek, lauding the Church of England's indebtedness to the Fathers, and he partly succeeded in his aim. But the scheme ended miserably for all that, labelled by people in Oxford as 'Woodroffe's Folly'. Edward Stephens, a phil-Orthodox who will appear again in this discussion, tried to revive the idea a few years later, with a view to a Greek house of studies in London; but although subscriptions were solicited, there was not sufficient interest to set it going. Cf. Runciman, op. cit., pp. 301–4.
79. Ibid., pp. 298–9.
80. John Wallis to Smith, 21 December 1691 and n.d. Smith MS 54, ff.55, 60.
81. Cf. James Smith to Thomas Smith, 10 April 1701 1703, Smith MS 53, f.206.

CHAPTER FOUR

'AN INGENIOUS PERSON'

John Covel and the 'Poor Silly Greeks'

Sir Paul Rycaut told Thomas Smith that he was confident John
Covel would continue his good work in Constantinople. But in
our account of early Anglican attitudes to Orthodoxy, John
Covel is an irritant and a maverick. He succeeded Thomas
Smith as chaplain to the English ambassador at Constantinople and accumulated far more material than Smith. More accu-
rately one should say more than Smith published: Smith's
papers in the Bodleian are on a scale which suggests that there
may be more than appeared in the book. Yet Smith published
within a decade of his chaplaincy and exercised influence on
Anglican opinion, while Covel sat on his material throughout
the rest of his life, claiming that duties at Cambridge left him
no time to organize and publish. Covel's dilatoriness is all the
more extraordinary when one considers that William Sancroft
as Dean of St Paul's, Peter Gunning the then Bishop of Chichester (described by Sir Robert Southwell as a 'Seraphic Man'
and a mystic) and the great patristics scholar John Pearson
then Master of Trinity College Cambridge all suggested to
Covel in advance a study of the Greek Church as part of his
tour of duty, with a view to publication. It is known that he
made early attempts to write *something*. It is unlikely that he
altered significantly such early drafts as he may have made
when he returned to the task in the last years of his life, over
forty years later.

His background may throw some light on the anomaly
without entirely explaining it. A grammar school boy from

Bury St Edmunds, he studied at Cambridge during the Commonwealth. It is possible that he studied medicine; he certainly studied botany and became something of an expert on exotic plants. It is thought that one reason why he accepted the chaplaincy so readily after a successful career at Cambridge was that he thought it would enable him to pursue his botanical interest and bring back specimens for his University's botanic garden. William Hunt in his article on Covel in the *Dictionary of National Biography* suggests that he had more of a natural bent to the physical sciences than to theology. That could explain why when he resigned his chaplaincy in 1676 he did not immediately return to his fellowship at Christ's College but indulged his botanical interests in Anatolia. His researches brought him immediate fame and helped to win him, in a manner characteristic of that pre-specialist age, the post of Lady Margaret Preacher as well as several sinecures including the post of Chancellor of York Minster when he finally came to rest in Cambridge.[1]

The timing of Covel's return to the early drafts on the Greek Church in 1722 on the verge of his death could be politically significant. It coincides with the closing phase of the Nonjurors' ill-fated negotiation with the Greek patriarchs which we shall examine in the next chapter. This raises the suspicion, in view of his marked lack of motive over forty years, that he may have been put up to it by senior figures, perhaps even by Archbishop Wake, as part of an effort to discredit the negotiation and thereby also the Nonjurors by offering to the reading public a highly critical account of the state of the Greek Church. Of course, if such a motive had existed, it would never have been admitted, since Wake was himself in flattering correspondence with the Greek patriarchs in an effort to warn them off the Nonjurors.

Covel's record in itself is hardly one of conciliation. While at the Hague as chaplain to Princess Mary, the eldest daughter of James Duke of York, he affronted Mary's husband, William Prince of Orange, by writing in private correspondence (it was alleged) that the Prince mistreated the Princess. William had him dismissed. Covel, a man with an eye for the main chance, wrote to Prince William in October 1685, following the crushing of the Monmouth rebellion against James II. Implacably opposed to James's popery, he was probably one of those who from an early stage in the reign saw William as the only possible agent of pressure on the King through his daughter. He probably also wished to hedge his bets as a senior Cambridge man in the event of Princess Mary succeeding to the throne in the absence of a male heir. In his somewhat egregious letter, he referred to himself as 'the most unfortunate Covel' of 'unlucky Name' and tried embarrassingly to exculpate himself from the consequences of his loose pen. As in due course Master of Christ's College, his controversial 'beautification' of the College chapel, which involved destruction of older fabric, earned him some distrust among the fellows, who noticeably failed to pay for the work out of their own pockets. Although Valentine Ritz's late portrait shows him as a 'jolly well-looking man of an open countenance', this public image may have been misleading. It is true that Covel procured many books for his college library, but apart from a 'Greek' *Euchologion* in Arabic, his criteria of choice appear to have been wholly literary and antiquarian, rather than reflecting in any obvious way a theological interest.[2]

According to Sir Steven Runciman, Covel amassed a large fortune in the silk trade while chaplain at Constantinople. This was made possible by the funding of the chaplaincy not by the state but by the Levant Company.[3] Before his death he dedicated his magnum opus to James Harvey, Duke of Chandos, partly because of the previous Duke's connections with Turkey, partly because James was Governor of the Levant Company and Covel knew him and his wife through often being their house-guest at Sudeley Castle. During his time at Constantinople, Covel's conversational Greek became fluent and this later made him a useful guide to Greeks visiting England. It also enabled him to converse with Greek clergy without the need for an interpreter, both in Constantinople and in his travels in Anatolia.[4] On his return to England he flattered himself on being an expert on the Greek Church and made it known that he wanted to be consulted about it on all occasions. He claimed acquaintance with patriarchs as well as ex-patriarchs (which is hardly surprising since, as we have already seen, ex-patriarchs were two-a-penny, thanks to Turkish policy). He wrote of Metropolitan Methodios being 'at our house'. He claimed acquaintance with many abbots and several senior monks on Mount Athos and that he had actually introduced Sir Paul Rycaut to the Holy Mountain.[5]

Covel was clearly an intellectual magpie and could manipulate language, albeit in a style which was already old-fashioned in 1722 when his book finally appeared. He was not as well grounded in theology as Thomas Smith and frequently fell back on philology as a substitute for exegesis.[6] His mind easily ran off from scholarly citation to animadversions on being bled or on being snubbed by the French ambassador! To be fair, this trait could have become worse between his chaplaincy and his final draft written in advanced old age.[7] There is already a hint in a letter he wrote to James Crauford dated 2 March 1675 that he was always somewhat indolent when it came to detailed transactions.[8]

Influences at Christ's College when Covel was an undergraduate may have a relevance for his later conduct. One of his tutors was another Thomas Smith who in 1651 published a translation of the Huguenot Jean Daillé's fiercely destructive 1631 treatise on the Fathers which portrayed them as 'vague, uncertain and obscure'.[9]

Both the format and a good deal of the detailed argument of his book suggests that Covel's chief conscious intention while at Constantinople was not so much to succour the Greeks as to 'do down' the Latins. The more exotic information that he offered on Greek ecclesiastical customs reads like just that – mere icing on a cake which was an extensive diatribe against the Roman doctrine of transubstantiation. Indeed, if Covel had published immediately on his return to England it would have greatly contributed to the anti-popery hysteria which was then seizing large parts of the country. As already suggested, there is some reason to suspect that one item in the pamphlet war of the late 1670s – *A Rational*

Discourse Concerning Transubstantiation – may have been anomyously his. Certainly when he came to write the final version of his book, using notes made in the 1670s, his attitude towards the Orthodox seems to depend on whether he wishes to present them semi-benignly to set off the Papists or whether to consider them as an object of anthropological curiosity, in which case he could be quite savage about Orthodox attitudes and practices.[10]

In his enormously long and rambling preface, Covel talks of the 'Many learned men all over Europe' who, during the sixteenth and seventeenth centuries, had been 'very inquisitive' about the ecclesiastical constitution and doctrines of the Greeks.[11] He is forward in admitting that before his own excursion to the east he was plied with questions by Sancroft, Gunning and Pearson, who wanted to know more than their reading told them. It would have been enlightening to know what these questions were. If Southwell's description of Gunning is anything like correct, then his questions, and possibly also Sancroft's, may have been more profound than Covel could handle or even comprehend. At the height of the Popish Plot Gunning demonstrated both his spiritual discernment and his brave immunity to mass hysteria by standing in the House of Lords and opposing a proposed oath against popery on the ground that the Church of Rome was not idolatrous as alleged. According to Darwell Stone's estimate of him, Pearson's questions, although erudite, are likely to have been less profound and therefore more to Covel's liking. His magisterial *Vindiciae Epostolarum S. Ignatii* of 1672 placed Pearson on a collision course with the radical critics of the Fathers, but only on text-critical grounds.[12]

In retrospect, Covel wishes the reader to understand what was not strictly true at the time, namely that he accepted the chaplaincy in order to study Greek theology, particularly the theology of the Eucharist, of which, he said, 'we had but slight account at home'.[13] He had, he claimed, been given 'a particular charge' in this regard and he had prepared himself for it while on board ship by discussing the issues which needed examining with the consular chaplains to Aleppo and Smyrna.[14]

The reason why the Greek experience was relevant at all to combating popish Transubstantiation had to do with a public controversy, already touched upon, between two continental scholars – Antoine Arnauld of the Sorbonne, the Papist (always referred to in English sources as 'Arnold'), and Jean Claude, the Huguenot minister of Charenton. Arnauld had used a large team of researchers among the Latin missionaries in the eastern Mediterranean to produce 'Testimonies' to show that the Greeks believed in Transubstantiation. Claude espoused an opposite view.[15] Of course both men, Catholic and Protestant, were *parti pris* and therefore scarcely objective. They had interests to serve in relation to which the Orthodox were simply pawns. Arnauld produced a large quarto volume of testimonials; Claude proceeded to shoot them down as either misunderstanding what had been asked to just downright fiction. Covel said that he had learned of the Arnauld/Claude controversy shortly after arriving in Constantinople and promised the Revd James Crauford to 'double' his 'diligence' and 'quicken' his research into the matter. He asked Crauford to send him a copy of the quarto volume in which Arnauld had published what he claimed to be Greek testimonials in favour of Transubstantiation. Crauford, who appears to have been in correspondence with Claude, promised to do this and lend him any other help he could. He also assured Claude that Covel would help him, but there is no indication that he did this with Covel's approval. Crauford, for his part, was convinced in his convenient isolation that Claude's 'proofs' were 'a most authentick' rebuttal of Arnauld's testimonials. Actually Claude had a letter from a Frenchman living at Colchis to the effect that some of the testimonies were 'meere fictions and others quite otherwise than they were told'. Crauford thought there was a reasonable question that the whole quarto volume as published might prove the same if 'diligently Enquired into'. He warned Covel that 'a great deal of prudence and discretion' was required in distinguishing between documents of this kind because the Roman emissaries were more subtle than the Greeks. He feared that getting at the truth might be a labour too great for one man. It is worth noting a separate subtle twist. Arnauld was a leading Jansenist. When his scholarship was accidentally dragged into the Popish Plot debate, those English Romanists who were falsely accused of treason tried to use him as a counterweight to the Jesuits, who for most of the English population were synonymous with popery.

The difficulty which both Claude and the Anglicans had in trying to spike Roman geopolitical strategy was how to distinguish between those Greeks who had 'anywise drunk in the Roman principles' at source by studying in Italy or indirectly by reading uncritically the semi-Roman Confession of Peter Moghila, Metropolitan of Kiev, and those who had simply inherited, albeit in more or less unscholarly form in many cases, the Orthodox tradition of earlier centuries. Clearly, what was needed was testimonials from Greeks who had not in any way been contaminated by Roman contact. Had the Latins been more subtle and less arrogant they would have realized that this was important for them too. But to make any such distinctions was next to impossible without more detailed knowledge of Greek society than any of the western controversialists possessed. Some senior Greeks had plainly received pensions from Rome while others willingly anathematized the Pope and all his works simply to gain favour with those Greek clergy (especially on Mount Athos) who were inveterately opposed to Rome as the inspiration of the 1204 sacking of Constantinople, no matter the doctrine.[16]

James Crauford assumed that most of Arnauld's testimonials were 'Impostures' and expected Covel's researches on the ground to confirm this to be so. But the exercise was tainted from the outset. Sir Daniel Harvey, Covel's patron and the first ambassador whom he served, had already promised Arnauld to testify that the Greeks did indeed believe in transubstantiation. He later withdrew this offer, probably on Covel's advice, pleading that it might make him appear a Papist in England. The French ambassador apparently charged Covel with preventing Harvey from testifying as he first promised. Covel countered by claiming that it had never been his ambassador's intention to so testify in the first place. In reality, he and Harvey were aware of some 500 testimonials which the Ambassador Nointel wished to use on behalf of the Jesuits but thought might not stand up to judicial examination. Conveniently for his reputation, Covel was not around at the crisis point between the two ambassadors, as he was in bed with a fever – or so he said! There was some sniggering in certain quarters about this.[17]

Such muddying of the waters was unfortunate for Covel's polemical enterprise because it was of vital importance to the Protestant camp to prove Arnauld's evidence to be an imposture pure and simple. This would discredit Rome and boost 'the whole Reformed Churches'. Covel had other reasons also for wanting to be seen in this matter as a reliable observer. Immediately on his arrival in Constantinople he hastened to ingratiate himself with Henry Bennett, now Earl of Arlington, the Secretary of State, and with his second-in-command, Joseph Williamson. He suggested to them that he could be an extra pair of ears in addition to those of the ambassador. Indeed, he did report a good deal of commercial information to Williamson. Sir Daniel Harvey, the ambassador, came to value Covel's general services, so much so indeed that on his unexpected deathbed in Belgrade he confided to his chaplain the arrangements he wanted to be followed in the interval before the arrival of a new ambassador. Covel appears to have been very fluent in Italian and therefore was the better able to assess the intentions of the Venetians and Pope Clement IX's involvement with the French government. Since the two main functions of an English ambassador to the Porte were, as the Earl of Winchelsea put it, to report on Turkish military dispositions and to protect the commercial interests of English merchants, Covel was a useful spy. Successive ambassadors saw their task at Constantinople as irksome. Winchelsea in the 1660s found his efforts to 'penetrate into the intentions of the Turkes to maintaine, or breake the peace' difficult enough, given the 'violent heat of the Country', the 'unwholesome-nesse of the Ayre' and the awkward tendency of Turkish officials to take advantage of any gentlemanly accommodation on 'small matters' by flying higher and becoming ever more 'insolent'. Furthermore, he was aware of the tendency of the Turks to play western diplomats off against each other by means of flattery. In a coded message to Henry Bennett he said, in effect, that if plenteous reserves of cash were not made available to him, he could not get very far with 'the Porte'. Winchelsea discovered that the Imperial and Venetian residents took every opportunity to set the English 'by the Ears with the Turke ...' He held the Venetian Grillo mostly responsible for this, and it is interesting that Covel spent some time with Grillo, presumably on behalf of his master. Covel found out why 'Bailo' Grillo would not assist Nointel in collecting signatures for his Transubstantiation testimonials. This was of political as well as theological interest to an English ambassador. Thomas Smith had got on well with Winchelsea because the Earl was interested in theology and detested the Jesuits, so much so that when he received intelligence that the shock troops of the Papacy, who had so often 'set the World together by the Ears' (note his fascination with listening!), were suffering a dispute in their headquarters in Rome, the ambassador was well pleased. While Smith had been helpful to the incoming Sir Daniel Harvey in briefing him on what he knew best, the state of the Greek Church, its corporate strength in its Liturgy and Feasts, as well as its weaknesses, the more worldly Covel was able to serve a political function as well.[18]

It is worth asking how much help the ambassadors were to their serviceable chaplain in combating the theological subversion of the Marquis de Nointel and thereby upholding the autonomy of the Greek Church. Winchelsea had been his own man in ecclesiastical matters and did not always take the Greek side. On one occasion he had intervened in a dispute (previously mentioned) between the Latin and Greek bishops on the formerly Venetian island of Scio where he thought that the Greek bishop had behaved very badly by trying to take possession of a Latin church building, refusing rites of passage to Latins and requiring Latins about to be priested to seek his licence first. (He had even demanded that his Latin counterpart leave the island altogether on the grounds that he

had tried to make a profit out of his services.) Both bishops
with their entourages made for Adrianople where the Grand
Vizir had his summer residence. They shouted it out. The
Greek bishop intimated to the Vizir that it would not be in
Ottoman interests to have a bishop in their territories communicating with Rome and Western Christian Princes. Perhaps
he also offered money. At any rate, the Vizir put the Latin
bishop and his whole party into gaol for fifteen days. Meanwhile, Winchelsea worked behind the scenes, persuading the
patriarch that his metropolitan was a 'proud and turbulent
spirit' who should be disciplined. This having been done, the
Vizir released the Latin party in return for a 'consideration'
of 15,000 dollars. Winchelsea told Secretary Bennett in
London that the patriarch stood in his debt in the matter. He
knew that the French put a good deal of pressure on Greek
merchants and was on his guard against any French duplicity
in that quarter. After Covel came on the scene 'the Intriguing
Embassador Monr Nantelle' (sic) and his instrumentality in
the 'Glorious Work' of collecting testimonials was a matter of
some ribaldry in the English Embassy, thanks to Covel's
counter-intelligence.[19]

Winchelsea had not been particularly worried by French
bluster, even when they stationed a warship in the Bosphorus.
Sir Daniel Harvey suspected that Nointel was under great
pressure from Versailles to get more concessions from the
Turks and was not succeeding. When their ambassador was
recalled, the weakness of the whole French position, including its ecclesiastical department, became apparent. Harvey
warned, however, that the English must be always vigilant,
and his successor, Sir John Finch, took a similarly cautious
view. Covel could therefore rely on his warnings about
Nointel being heeded and, as we shall see, if French intrigue
with the Porte caused a patriarch or a senior bishop to be
'displaced' – perhaps for refusing to sign one of Nointel's
ready-made testimonials – such an ecclesiastic, should he
survive at all, had welcome refuge in the ambassadorial residence. Therefore, although Finch was for a long time in ill-
health and indolent about making detailed reports to London,

Covel ensured that a minimally anti-French and pro-Greek ecclesiastical policy was maintained at the embassy and there were supplies enough of bibles and prayer books through the diplomatic bag to enable 'dialogue' to take place with the Greeks as occasion demanded. At the end of the day (depending on how the 'Turkish War' was going), there was always the Russian interest in the Holy Places to provide a counterweight to the French. In 1679 this proved potent and the 'Gran Tsar' became the 'Greek Protector'.[20]

So much for the context of Covel's account. Now for the mentality behind the 'evidence' he presents on the Greek Church.

To have been among the Greeks at all must have been a great pain to him. Unlike Basire, Rycaut and Smith, he had a gut distaste for modern Greeks. To him they were always 'the poor silly Greeks, quite overspread with Aegyptian Darkness'.[21] He was told to expect to find them more or less perfidious and he was not disappointed. A slightly later English ambassador, Sir William Turnbull, described one Alexander Mauro Cordato as an 'odious' and 'covetous wretch'. When Covel met this same man he did not describe him so colourfully, yet his invariable reaction to and expectation of the ordinary Greek came little short of it. 'The Greeks are the Greeks still', he wrote in his diary: '. . . For falseness and treachery they still deserve Iphigeneia's character of them in Euripides. Trust them and hang them'.[22] They had, it was true, some natural wit, but even so they always came off the worse with the Latins because they lacked the Latins' sheer stamina.[23] They had no real aristocracy (a black mark in Covel's book for he was a social snob) and their feelings (here we have a social revelation equal to many learned dissertations) were uniformly those of 'our Mob, or the Vulgar, in England'.[24] 'The common People in the East, Priests or Laymen, are wonderfully ignorant and illiterate; and you will find among the very Metropolites and Bishops themselves very few who will pretend to any deep or speculative Notions in Divinity'.[25] This, of course, was due to their lack of 'Academies or Schools for instructing students' under Turkish rule.[26] But for Covel mere lack of formal education was made worse by a congenital lightheadedness which in a perverse way he found reflected even in the proportion of wine to bread which they consumed in communion: 'a merry Treat', he said insensitively, 'something to drink but nothing to eat'. The Christian Greeks had less craft or artistic skills than their ancient forebears, so much so that Covel was absolutely confident that he could always tell the difference between a modern and an ancient Greek building. He wrote in his journal of the Patriarchal Chapel at the Phanar that it was 'a miserable poor, despicable thing'. Of its possible former magnificence 'not one fair footstep is now to be found.' All the ikons were poor and the pillars 'crude and slovenly'.[27]

It has to be said that Covel did not reserve his scorn only for the Greeks. As may have been anticipated from his use of the epithet 'Aegyptian Darkness', he was at least as scornful of the Copts ('those miserable Wretches, sufficiently noted by all for their horrid Confusion and Ignorance') and the Armenians, who cared nothing for each other, so riven were they with feuds. In fact he found the whole Christian Middle East a hotbed of murderous hatred, and in this he included the Jews for good measure. All the factions under the domination of the Turk each used whatever few advantages they had to do down the others with the Ottoman authorities, who in their turn 'ate money out of them right or wrong'. In his view the problem the Greeks had was not that they were being extremely persecuted by the Turks, which patently they were not for the most part, but that their venality made them pliable to the Turks. For this reason, the bishops of either party – Latinizing or traditional – could never rely on firm support from anyone.[28] The only time the Church had positively gained at the expense of the Latins was at Jerusalem under Patriarch Sophronicos when a massive use of gold and silver by the Greeks had overwhelmed the Franciscan hold on the Turkish vizir and temporarily regained for the Church the control of the Holy Sepulchre. This had been as long ago as 1590 and Covel could see only a progressive declension of Greek integrity since that time. In his experience few Greeks had the heart for martyrdom, or even a spirit of great endeavour. Accommodation and follow-my-leader, not *koinonia*, was the norm.[29]

On account of this weakness, the Greek Church had enjoyed real security under Turkish rule only during the time of the first two post-conquest Patriarchs of Alexandria. (He meant here the Greek, not the Coptic Patriarchs.) Thereafter, Greek weakness and Turkish avarice had wrought a terrible cost to the Church.[30] Even among the better-placed clergy in Constantinople he found a 'love of ease and quietness' which was quite debilitating.[31] The senior bishops were very amenable to the blandishments of Western ambassadors. He singled out for special mention the way in which Parthenios and Dositheos crawled to Nointel, and (the deposed) Joachim of Alexandria to Sir Daniel Harvey. When Parthenios was turned out of the Patriarchate by a 'junto' of bishops in 1671, some of the conspirators, who coveted the throne for themselves, nevertheless stood down in favour of Dionysios of Larissa in return for a bribe of £3,000. The Vizir Kuprioglu (himself a former Albanian Christian) characterized them as a 'Company of Dogs'.[32]

As far as Covel could see, the whole structure of independent church government had collapsed under this weight of corruption. There were 'Mercenary patriarchs' and 'pretended Councils' (little more, he thought, than 'Conventicles') but 'very little or no' real authority. Gold, not God, determined the patriarchal succession. He stood aghast at the way in which one bishop could buy out another or even get him banished by the Turks so that he might have his place. On one occasion he witnessed several bishops issuing a diatribe against Patriarch Parthenios simply in order to justify their envious moves against him, making him appear 'the veryest Rogue', a *diabolos*. The French ambassador and other 'Franks' present 'could not but smile'. He was assured by his guide that they would do as much the other way round if there was a change of fortune. In the matter of Bishop Arsenios, which we shall discuss in the next chapter, the Reverend Geoffrey Wheler was telling him nothing that he had not been persuaded was true in more than thirty years, that the Greeks were vulnerable to Rome principally because of their ignorance wedded to an extraordinarily mercenary nature.[33]

Dositheos of Jerusalem puzzled Covel greatly. On one occasion the Chaplain characterized him as 'a very perfidious, crafty, true Greek' and 'notorious Prevaricator'. At another time he could view him as a 'Great Man' among pigmies, a man 'imposed upon' by the system and 'wrought off from the Truth' to half-say what he had not believed, thus acquiring by degrees an erroneous conscience.[34]

In describing the Greeks, Covel readily resorted to animal imagery, for he truly despised animals, particularly dogs. When talking of the way in which the Fathers of the Second Council of Nicaea described the reverencing of ikons, he likened it to the way dogs greeted one another, or humans, by crouching and touching nose-to-nose or nose-to-hand. The image was clearly not meant as a respectful one, certainly not to accord any spiritual value to the act. Before he left England Covel had been fed similarly contemptuous accounts of 'credulous votaries' of saints. His mental horizons did not equip him to revise these estimates when brought face to face with what had been reviled. It was not that he was anything less than meticulous in his observation of detail. Just as he made accurate drawings of flora and fauna, he put himself in the way of doing the same with the Greeks at prayer and contemplation. He was present at the consecration of Dionysios of Larissa as Ecumenical Patriarch in 1672 and described it precisely. On one occasion he was allowed in the sanctuary throughout the Liturgy. He therefore had plenty of opportunity to record the exactitude of vestments. Travelling in Anatolia, he made similar meticulous note of which volumes of the Fathers particular monasteries had. But it was a bit like stamp collecting or train spotting. He sought no deeper meaning in these discoveries (unlike Smith at his best). His account of Mount Athos has rightly been praised in modern times as not only the first English account of the Holy Mountain but also one of the best in the sense of the most vivid. In it he pays simple tribute. Indeed, his relatively positive impression of Athos was passed on to Rycaut before Rycaut made his own visit. Expecting the best, Rycaut then found the best, seeing the monks as 'for the most part good simple men of godly lives ..., real and moral good men' and 'somewhat touched with the Spirit of God', whose discipline of life carried them further to Heaven than the wisdom of the philosophers. In this rare context Covel saw things he did not expect or admit in his general observation of Greek Orthodox. For instance, he began to see the value of making the sign of the Cross. It would never occur to those in Christian England, but in an Islamic state it was a profession of faith.[35]

Back in the 'real world', Covel's rationalism told him that the Turks were encouraging the growth of monasteries because the more single Greeks there were the sooner the Greek Church would die out; for the main body of the Church seemed to him so feeble that it would not frustrate such a prediction. The village 'Papas' had clearly lost all command of Greek except what they had memorized for the purpose of liturgy: for all practical purposes they had become Turks and so had their people. Hence the carelessness of their funeral habits in the village communities, as distinct from the provision for great men. Hence their devotion to imagined saints who were not found in the calendar of Maximus's *Lives of the Saints*. It did not seem to matter to the devotees, who happily dedicated streams to unreal saints without any evidence of a connection, except perhaps as a transmutation of a pagan cult. Hence fables about the translation of ikons from one place to another (which he found even on Mount Athos). Hence the obsession of Greeks and Armenians with hobgoblins into which children were thought to change if not baptized by a priest within twelve days of death. Hence the obsessive fear of 'waking the dead'. He saw all such things as evidence of lightheadedness. He marvelled at how an elderly man could carry the enormous silver cross of St Athanasios throughout his monastic profession. If such a thing were done in England people would rightly think the individual fit only for Bedlam.[36]

Contemplation of such things led Covel to a remarkable statement of personal faith in his travel journals. It is the only instance of depth which he has left us, and, given all his worldly failings, it is right that this statement should be placed on record. 'In general', he said, 'I shall now tell you that I have found all religions as to the outward practice and profession the same; they have Saints and Fathers or Doctors whom the body followeth; they all have strange fancyes and humaine conceits of the stations in eternity; they all have factions and furiously persecute, censure, damn one the other . . .; they all strictly persist in their own way; yet I am so fully persuaded of the excellency of my saviour Jesus Christ, his doctrine above whatever was yet in the world, as I am ready to seal to it in this very place with my dearest blood, and will undertake to demonstrate what is of good doctrine throughout the world have come from him. It is we that have so changed, and corrupted and abused his divine precepts as certainly we may fancy that those words (Luke 18:8) *when the Son of Man cometh shall we find faith on the earth?* were spoken of our times.' He admitted to some discomfort that in certain ways he found the Muslims closest to his ideal.[37]

Our chaplain approached the Greek Liturgy and Sacraments with some background textual knowledge, although probably not as much as Basire or Smith had had. It is highly unlikely that he knew of Jeremy Taylor's revised St James, and even when he wrote up his book in 1722 he probably knew nothing of John Ernest Grabbe's version of St James which was still in manuscript, although he may have seen Thomas Brett's St James-indebted Nonjuror Liturgy of 1718. As his title page indicates, he had read Jacques Goar's commentary on the Eastern liturgies, but he was contemptuous throughout the book of Goar's popish intelligence and thought him fanciful and slipshod as an editor.[38] One practical advantage he did have was that he was permitted to stand within the royal doors and observe closely the celebrant's actions at the altar.[39] Unfortunately, this closeness to the 'engine room' only had the effect of making him more cynical. He derived no sense of reverence from the gestures. In fact he made no effort to conceal that he found them 'amusing'.[40]

To be fair to him, *ritual*, in the crude colloquial sense, was not the only factor which made him feel this way. He found the liturgical texts themselves a jumble, and this for two reasons (a) what he had read of commentary and textual criticism led him to conclude that in both the Greek and Latin rites prayers had become displaced over the centuries and so no longer served an intelligible function; (b) even if the Liturgy was to be seen as a 'shadow play' of the life of Christ (an idea which he found in any case distasteful), many of the prayers did not respect the order of events in the Gospel narratives. The Greeks, he said, had 'quite lost the Kabala' and were 'wonderfully perplext in their new inventions to make it out.' If the commentators were perplexed, pity the 'poor Ignorant Common People, who only gape on'. He really wondered how the plebs could be at all 'better for it'. As to those ritual acts which he saw in the sanctuary, he could make no sense of them at all, especially the priest's acts with the *asterisk*.[41]

Covel found 'secret' prayers particularly obnoxious. He suspected that they were *sotto voce* because they made no sense and so would sound ridiculous if said aloud. He singled out the celebrant's prayer during the singing of the Cherubic Hymn containing the words, 'For Thou, O Christ our God, art he who offerest and art offered, who receivest and art distributed and received'. He believed that learned men in Manuel Comnenus' time had not been able to agree on what it meant and had left it to the Emperor to determine.[42]

Like the English Reformers justifying the overthrow of the Latin Mass, he suggested an element of 'numpsimus' behind the screen. The fact that the people could not hear (for instance the *prothesis*) made him suspicious.[43] He did not like the comings and goings during the Anaphora, preferring to think that 'primitively there was only one long continuous prayer' as implied in the *Apostolic Constitutions*, which later Greeks ignorantly cut into pieces and interlarded with other matter, apportioned between the priest and the deacon. The rubric 'The Priest goes on praying' seemed to him to confirm his theory.[44] Although like other Anglican scholars of his day, he was contemptuous of the ascription of *St James* to the Apostle, he was impressed by the provision in that Liturgy for several loaves and cups to be administered separately. He thought this to be obviously the 'Primitive Way' and liked especially the idea of each loaf being broken clean and not hacked with a knife. He also tried to make a positive and quite erudite suggestion for the origin of the Particles in the chalice in the main Byzantine rite.[45]

Like Rycaut, Covel was deeply unhappy about the attitude of the Faithful to the *Antidoron* distributed at the end of the Liturgy. Patently it was not being received solely as the 'bread of blessing' but in the superstitious hope that its contact with the 'Holy Portion' had made it a remedy for diseases and an amulet against all mischief, whether it be by bugs, vermin or 'Pismires'. He scorned such charms as he scorned repeated *Kyries*, which he saw as no better than the Muslim 'Sabanallas'. He had not the slightest inkling of an alternative and coherent explanation of both of these things because he lacked an Orthodox sense of reverence.[46]

The role in prayer of the Mother of God provoked Covel to more open misgiving than we find in either Rycaut or Smith. His youthful Puritanism rebelled against it. The Greeks seemed to ascribe to her 'almost as great a Providence as to God Himself'. The familiarity and almost reflex action towards her particularly riled him. He noted the monastic farewell, 'May God keep you and the all-holy Lady'. The Greeks seemed to make altogether more prayer to her than they made to her Son, not only in private devotion but in the very *Euchologion* itself. He easily convinced himself that it was a very early practice but one transferred by ignorant converts from their worship of Isis, Minerva or Festa, all of whom had been thought to lead benighted and besotted humans into the underworld. Hence the common description of the Virgin as 'guide'; hence her ikon being taken to war by Manuel Comnenus. He viewed the cult as part of the warp and weft of Greek life: the Virgin was the object of 'diurnal reverence'. Clearly there were even more yawning 'Idiots' among the Greeks than among the Latins. Perhaps whoever had set the system rolling had had some 'Inward Reflection upon it' but he thought it unlikely that those who came later had any idea at all what they were doing. In his view, whoever unthinkingly used such an amulet invited the remark of the Devil, 'The Crucified Jesus I know, and his victory over me I know, but who art thou?'[47]

Yet Covel's attitude to ikons was ambivalent and not quite what one might expect from a rationalist Protestant. He tells us that he discussed the matter with Dositheos of Jerusalem and obtained from him some lengthy quotations from St John Damascene which he made no direct attempt to refute although he wanted to query John's argument that if God the Father per se might not be represented, God walking in the Garden of Eden might.

However, in the matter of representation Covel's chief ire was reserved for the Latins, whose schoolmen had made fools of themselves by trying to justify representations of the Divine intellectually. To this extent he sympathized with the iconoclasts who were decent rationalists like himself. But when faced with an ikon of the Old Testament Trinity he began to lose his self-confidence, and when he tried to intellectualize his own intuitions he tied himself in knots. A good example was when he argued over whether a temporary apparition of God or an angel could constitute an 'emanent prototype' which could receive 'any future adoration'. The Thrones and many-eyed, many-winged Cherubim and Seraphim in the Liturgy were a puzzle for him. He could not deny that they were in Scripture but he wanted to deny that they could be 'anchored' by worshippers in any kind of representation. Insofar as such representations were 'Inventions' of the imagination they were 'dishonourable'. He could not see them as St John of Damascus did, as having God as their author. Despite all this, he could not resist the force of Patriarch Dositheos' argument that ikons were truly 'the Books of the Unlearned', although he doubted the precise value which could be derived from them by the unlearned and had a niggling fear that embodiments of Scriptural narrative might make sublime truth look a little ridiculous even to the ignorant. He could not, in spite of his Puritan background, simply call ikons 'idols', preferring to keep a reservation in his mind that the justification offered for them by the Orthodox was 'at best but a disputable and very doubtful Point'.[48]

If we move on from this metaphysical question of the licitness of representation to that of whether it is right to reverence such representations and seek the intercession of angels and saints depicted in them, we come up with a more conventional Protestant response, namely that the very idea brought God down to the level of a mortal tyrant who could only be addressed through a favourite or favourite's favourite, and that in any case the majority of those called 'saints' in church history were of an altogether lower level of sanctity from Peter and Paul so that the Church which honoured them with ikons was of very little discernment.[49] He would have us believe that his problem was not with reverencing *as such*, for he was no Quaker and recognized reverencing in the civil sphere as the proper acceptance of order and priority.[50]

We may now turn to the subject of the *rituale*. Covel was by no means entirely dismissive of the Orthodox canons regulating the unction of the sick. He accepted that the requirement of multiple 'elders' to lay hands on the sick was in line with St James and as such superior to the Roman practice, although he thought it must often be rather impractical except in the case of wealthy households with several chaplains. He agreed that it was more biblical to give the sacrament to the sick as well as the dying and that therefore Orthodox practice was superior to that of Rome. (It was, after all, in James's view, for the body as well as for the soul.) But he thought the Orthodox rite deficient in not allowing people to pray for one another and reserving prayer to the priest. Also he remained convinced that a 'plain Visitation', like that provided in the Prayer Book, was superior to many and 'mysterious' prayers.[51]

As regards confession, he began from the principle that his own Church was 'most exact and Conspicuous' in making it possible for a believer to open to a ghostly father 'in difficult or doubtfull matters of Conscience, or for Direction in our Practice of a Holy Life'. He therefore praised St John Chrysostom for his teaching on this.[52] Further, he was satisfied by Patriarch Jeremias's presentation of the concept of satisfaction to the Wittenberg divines, which stressed not canonical requirement but inward repentance as essential to the covenant of grace, and outward works as 'true signs' of a change of life exhibiting trustworthiness. He found in Jeremias's testimony a 'franchise' quite different from the mechanical requirements of the Roman Church, for it made clear that the penitent must 'enquire after' the penitential canon by a voluntary act. He gave due credit to St Basil for this.[53] However, he still insisted in Reformation fashion that individual absolution was not necessary where true contrition existed and asserted that in the time of the Cappadocian Fathers auricular confession and absolution were 'a meer speculative Conception' because corporate public confession was still then the norm. He therefore could not see the point in citing the Fathers in defence of the modern practice.[54] Covel was pleased that the Greek Church did not claim, as he thought the Roman did, the power to absolve the dead but simply prayed God that they might be absolved. Indeed he was deeply impressed by the generally deprecatory nature of Greek absolutions, not only in Basil and John Chrysostom but in more modern prayers. He was equally impressed by the passive form of Orthodox baptism. He was well satisfied that neither Arcudius nor any other Roman apologist could fault it.[55]

However, he was alarmed at the inadequacy of the provision for the confession of the common people by itinerant monastic confessors and its limitation to the seasons of fasting. There seemed to him to be no equation between the supply of confessors (required by the canons to be not less than forty years old) and the potential number of penitents. He knew of many in the villages outside Constantinople who never went to the itinerant, although several of the super-sophisticated devout did so frequently, giving substantial presents to their confessors and thus rendering it something of a business. Because of this imbalance between the minority shriven before communion and the majority unshriven and uncommunicated, the nature of the Eucharist had changed. Very little of the bread offered in it was now used for communion, even allowing that the *margarita* or 'pearls' dropped in the chalice had always been very small. A ban had been placed on priests taking away the 'overplus' to consume as food, so it went in the antidoron, which many non-communicants carried around with them as 'amulets'. The common people had thereby lost all sense of the true significance of the eucharistic bread. The failure to increase the number of confessions was, Covel understood, linked to the strict limits of authorization to bishops from the patriarch and that, at root, was due to the notorious unworthiness of many village priests. He wondered what would happen if a common person in desperation went to an 'ordinary' priest to make his confession. Would it be 'valid'?[56]

The nub of Covel's concern with Orthodox sacramentology was the understanding of the Real Presence, for this is what he specifically promised to find out about and it had contemporary polemical importance. He was aware that the Muslims regarded the Latins contemptuously as 'Devourers of God'. The question which niggled him was whether the Greeks had the same reputation and, if so, whether rightly so. A study of methods of Reservation did not help. He could see little to choose between shutting the 'Invisible, Glorified Christ' (if that was how the Elements were seen) in boxes and secreting Him 'in a miserable musty Bag hung up in a wall'.[57] As we have already seen, Covel had no respect for scholastic reasoning. He therefore scorned the suggestion that he should discard the evidence of his 'unjust', or unfaithful, senses' in order to believe that the elements transubstantiated. He regarded Aquinas as one who tied 'a Knot upon a Ray of Moonshine' by making an *accident* into 'a Nothing, neither in nor out of a subject'. This surely annihilated substance, making both accidents and substance mere intellectual notions of potential things – a mere 'rope of sand'. If the whole Romish idea were true and the sacrifices of the Old Law were types of Christ, then it would surely follow that the goats, kids, pigeons and other animals sacrificed in the Temple were 'verily and indeed Christ himself' an idea particularly nauseous to Covel as he loathed animals.[58]

Covel had just as little time for the theories of modern scientists about the generic nature of things – 'imperceptible Motions or very minute insensible particles of Matter' which were 'an Hypothesis or Meer Guess still'. 'Outward Appearances, Affections, Effects and Circumstances' were all that he had for 'trueness'.[59] One wonders what he would have made of quantum physics if anything other than what he could see or touch was 'one continued Dream'.

Finding himself in this line of logic, Covel was impaled on metaphysical uncertainty. He felt forced to argue that to have by *liturgical* means a true substantial presence of Christ's Body, it would require not one but two miracles, because the bread transformed alone would be but a 'dry body' and the wine 'disembodied blood'. So the elements must even then be united again by a special act. At least the Greeks were consistent, he thought, by suggesting such 'vivification' in their warm water mixed with the wine, feeble though that idea was to his sophisticated mind. The Latins with their *cold* water could make nothing intelligible of *their* 'concomitance', for it made not one reality but a mere mixture, like oils in chrism or water and salt in baptism. So far so good; but if transubstantiation was true, what meaning could there be in the Orthodox expression 'unbloody Sacrifice'?

The adding of water after the *epiclesis* posed further problems to Covel. He was aware that it had been a problem for Aquinas also. In his philosophy, the resultant mixture would not be the 'same Numerical or Individual Wine' but of another kind. Covel's scientific scepticism concealed a deep anxiety. The longer the time he spent in Constantinople and the more people he spoke to, and the greater his efforts to disentangle the 'Latinizing' influence in the Arnauld testimonials from more primitive strata, the more confused he became about what the Greeks actually believed. And so, in the process of collating the material, he allowed himself to digress more and more into a pure diatribe against popery and looked less and less closely at the reality of Orthodox liturgical experience. His frustration is glimpsed in his impatience that John Damascene – that 'Dad of the Greek Schoolmen' – sowed the seed of the 'conceit' which led eventually to transubstantiation in Latin hands, by diverging ever so marginally from the testimony of the earlier Fathers.[60]

Covel's personal preference – which was scarcely that of the Caroline Anglicans – was to rest content with the idea of 'This is My Body' as a 'Hebraism', like 'Christ is the Door of the Sheepfold', 'The Lamb is the Lord's Passover', 'God's Word is a Lamp' or even 'The Plague of Lice is the Finger of God'.[61] Not that this prevented him from trying to teach the Greeks how they should better order their own perceptions! Like other observers, he took them up on the illogicality of reverencing the elements in procession *before* they were consecrated or the Spirit invoked. He called in aid those who would explain the reverencing at the Great Entrance as a mistaken transference from the Liturgy of the Pre-sanctified where the elements were already consecrated at that point, indeed before the rite began. He raised also the idea – an idea consonant with his love of degree – that it signified really a 'civil' honour to the priest carrying the elements. Either way, the Greek commentaries at this point were, he thought, perverse. Even Nicolas Cabasilas, for whom he harboured a sneaking respect, was perverse on the Great Entrance.[62]

Occasionally Covel reveals some awareness that the later Fathers saw the whole eucharistic action as one image reflecting one economy of Christ.[63] But he failed to consistently apply this understanding and so was doomed to seeing Orthodox eucharistic liturgy as discontinuous and disordered. Finding discontinuity all the way through church history right up to the Reformation, he could not see why, in purely intellectual terms, he should not prefer 'even John Calvin's exposition of any Text ... if it hath more Reason to back it' and if the truly primitive faith and practice of the Church was silent.[64] And since St John Chrysostom in his letter to Caesarius spoke of the continuing structure of the bread and wine throughout the action, he was sure he could not be far wrong if he affirmed a spiritual presence.[65] His conversations with Jeremias Germanos when he visited England in 1668 and 1669 settled him in this view before he even went to Greek lands and witnessed the Liturgy.[66] He interpreted the repeated prayers for God to receive the Gifts as further confirmation that Christ was not substantially present and as proof of the validity of the Prayer Book's teaching of 'spiritual Sacrifice'.[67] Whether Covel should be seen as a receptionist or a virtualist is not clear: sometimes his expressions suggest the one, at other times they suggest the other. One would expect him to be a receptionist, if only because of his sceptical temperament, but he did seem to make an effort to persuade the Greeks that on the basis of their Liturgy they should be virtualists.[68]

The main weakness of Covel's presentation of Orthodox Liturgy was that he assumed throughout a teaching of an omnipotent Christ present by His own sole power. Orthodox tradition has rather seen His presence as not so much discreetly omnipotent as a presence in and through the gracious ever-presence of the Holy Spirit. He therefore wastes pages on logical-linguistic analysis of a chimera. The Orthodox notion of type and antitype stands in spite of his polemic.[69]

There is one other element in Covel's attitude to Orthodoxy which deserves attention: his view of the authority of Tradition. Clearly this colours everything else as it determines what in his view can be received with respect and what cannot. He scorned both Latin and Greek claims to receive the most minute details of usage from Christ and His Apostles, whether it be the type of bread to be used in the Eucharist, the temperature of the water to be used in the chalice, the form of ordination, the dating of Easter or the use of images. The very prodigality of traditions to his mind disproved all their inclusive claims. He scorned attempts to lend them significance by means of spurious mystical arguments.[70] The common people had no comprehension of these layers of interpretation and even the wisest priests could not bear the hundredth part in their memories: hence the contradictions which arose whenever they tried to explain them. If the celebration of the Eucharist was the image of the body, polity and history of the

Saviour, how was it that it had changed so much over the centuries, even to the placing of the *epiklesis*? What the Greeks had now therefore could not possibly be 'The entire and certain Traditions of Christ Himself ...' It had been imposed by patriarchs just as they pleased and passively received by the ignorant multitude.[71] In reality the Greeks played fast and loose with their traditions to an extent that made him wonder if they were capable of an 'honest and sincere search after plain Truth'.[72] Councils, of which much was made as a talisman of permanent truth, were corrupt. Dismissing therefore all idea of inerrancy, Covel suggested that 'one Fool' might raise a 'Devil' which 'forty Wise Men' could not 'lay again'.[73] He could not accept the idea of providential *koinonia* as the basis of truth in the face of what he believed he saw working itself out. All the People of God were doing in fact was following 'the Great and Leading Men'. The idea that they were 'believing what the Church believed' was just so much sophistry.[74]

Covel prided himself on his objective analysis of historical documents, declaring himself a disciple of the liberal Catholic scholar Richard Simon, who was the first to bring modern historico-critical scholarship to bear on the Liturgy. Simon is repeatedly acclaimed by Covel as the 'Learned R. Simon'. On one occasion Covel even refers to him as a 'wellbred Gentleman' – which is very revealing.[75] Covel was astounded that so distinguished a scholar as Allatius should not think it mattered if the ascribed Liturgies were genuinely from the hands of St John Chrysostom, St Basil or St James. 'Would a man', he asked, 'who loves Wine and hath any care of himself, if he was assured that his Vintner sold nothing but balderdash stuff, and mixt only with a very little good wine, or perhaps none at all with it, would such a one say, It is no matter, it is sold by public Authority of this City ...'[76]

In truth, however, Covel was not as objective in this matter as he claimed. He all too eagerly seized on the acclamation 'Mercy of Peace, Sacrifice of Praise' as the oldest part of the existing Eastern liturgies, not because he had proof that this was so but because it fitted with his preconceptions. Here

historico-critical method 'went out of the window'. Similarly
with 'Thine of Thine own, in all and for all': this he reduced
to his convoluted cerebral equations – 'we depute these Creatures of Thine to Thy Worship, and we pray that (by the Holy
Spirit) they may be made Promptuaries of Store-houses of thy
Grace and that (by partaking of them) we may be rendered
more Holy thereby'![77] Indeed, Covel was not as good a
textual critic as he flattered himself to be. He was all too
ready to argue from silence, especially where it was convenient to establish his own preconceptions of what was appropriate. To give one example, because there are no manual acts
or materials such as chrism mentioned in the liturgical fragments of *The Clementine Constitutions* but only prayers, he
concludes that at the date of writing Christian worship
consisted only of prayers with no ritual. This judgement not
only mistakes the character of the writing but also undermines
what he concedes elsewhere about the antiquity of the laying
on of hands.[78] His main agenda – to demonstrate beyond
peradventure the unwisdom of the Greeks' assumptions about
fixity of rite as being of divine institution – came before
everything else.

One by-product of Covel's attitude to Tradition was his
suspicion about the dignity claimed for and accorded to the
priestly office in the Greek Church. He had seen 'nasty,
slovenly, beggarly priests', scarcely above the level of their
parishioners in their lifestyle and 'mean offices', who, when
clothed with the sacred vestments, were revered for the power
to bless heads with the Book of the Gospels or pray for the
living and the dead on request.[79] He thought this to be the
route by which generations could 'hook in a Power to the
Church' which permitted any kind of abuse, and all could be
excused by appeal to 'Christ's general authority'. For this
reason he thought it dangerous to call ordination a sacrament
rather than a 'Recommendation' to 'God's peculiar service
. . .'[80]

Although Covel shows occasional awareness of the principle of *oeconomia*, which he quite fairly translates, or rather
paraphrases, as 'gentleness', it is not clear that he fully appre-

ciated its importance in the Orthodox concept of the Church and its workings.[81] He had but a theoretical understanding of *koinonia* in relation to the Eucharist and so little or no sense of eucharistic community. To his mind, *koinonia* could not do what the Greeks claimed for it unless there was a literal gathering together by 'nothing less' than Christ's direct 'authority and power' juridically and visibly manifest. A mere desire to be united with Christ, whether on the part of isolated individuals or groups, would not necessarily result in the end desired. The conditions he required were clearly impossible and he knew it.[82]

Covel's discussion of the 'Seven Mysteries or Sacraments' which constitutes the whole of Book II, Chapter 1, reveals an impoverished idea of the ongoing abiding of the Spirit within the Church. His approach is purely archaeological and external. In fact it bears a curious resemblance to nineteenth-century Anglo-Catholic attempts to demolish the Catholic Apostolic ('Irvingite') rite of Sealing. He was made uneasy by the frequent appeals by his Greek hosts to a 'secret tradition' from Christ and His Apostles, which he likened to the spurious apologetic of the Latin schoolmen. Covel disliked and suspected secret traditions and saw the claim as a disreputable cover for confusion and error. He was sure that in reality the Churches of the Latin West and Greek East had just been making things up as they went along.[83]

Furthermore, Covel detected and profoundly disliked what he thought was a process of gross mechanics being dressed up as mystical and eternal reality. For him this was not true *mysterion*. He could not see the Church as proto-sacrament within which all kinds of gracious sacramental presences were disclosed. There may have been a deficiency in his idea of grace which led him to think the worst. Wherever he uses the word 'grace', it seems to mean for him 'Comfortable Assistance'. Nowhere does he seem to see it as the *power of eternal life*. Hence, perhaps, his inability to see the difference between Christian and secular marriage. He was right, of course, to castigate the hypocrisy of the Greek clergy in allowing so many divorces without asking themselves whether a great many partners so put asunder as a matter almost of routine had ever grasped the meaning of marriage in the Kingdom or felt its power. But Covel himself does not appear to have understood the abyss of meaning beneath his own criticism.[84]

At the beginning of this chapter we touched upon Covel's analysis of the vulnerability of the Greek Church to Roman subversion. To this we must return in conclusion but in somewhat more detail.

Although he realized the enfeebling effect of Turkish rule, he realized that the Roman threat to the inner fabric (as distinct from the outward polity) of the Church did not follow immediately from the fall of Constantinople in 1453. In some senses it was much older, in others much later. He found seeds of subversion in the Frankish conquest of Constantinople in 1204, even though that conquest lasted only two generations. While the Latin occupation was in progress, Pope Innocent III held his Lateran Council (1215) at which Transubstantiation was made *de rigueur* in the Western Church. The intruded Latin patriarchs attended the Council and took back East with them various glosses on the Greek Liturgy designed to bring it in line with papal teaching. Some Greeks were won over to the glosses 'by degrees', while those who stood firm against them tended to take themselves off to the exiled court of the Greek Emperor at Nicaea. When the Palaeologi were restored to Constantinople in 1261, the theological rift continued and was raised to 'a prodigious Height', fanned by Latin offers of aid against the Turks. By the time of the Council of Florence (1439) the Greeks were already confused and demoralized.[85] When the City fell to the Turks, Patriarch Gennadios's digest of doctrine prepared for Sultan Mehmet II contained no sign of Latin influence.[86] Neither, more than a century later, did Patriarch Jeremias's replies to the questions of the Lutheran divines. Jeremias did not even use the compromise formula signed by the Greeks at Florence.[87] Nevertheless, in Covel's view a softening up process had already taken place and there were enough Greek clergy ripe for a new wave of Romish blandishments. Romish influence continued on the Maronites, Armenians and Ethiopians. He had seen the Ethiopian 'Mass Book' published in Rome in 1649 and an Armenian equivalent published in 1642 and these convinced him that Latin tendrils were wound tight around many of the lesser Eastern Churches.[88] Throughout the sixteenth century, said Covel, Rome was drawing ambitious Greeks to her educational bosom and thus 'by degrees the Latins everywhere insinuated their Doctrines'. He singled out Gabriel Severus, the Padua-educated Metropolitan of Philadelphia and Metrophanes, Metropolitan of Caesarea, as examples of how far the rot had spread. Metrophanes ultimately became Patriarch. Covel contrasts him unfavourably with his predecessor Josaphat who had set up schools to combat Latin influence and tried to stop Greek students going to Italy, yet was deposed.[89]

Covel thought that the Greeks who studied in Italy degenerated from their 'Antient simplicity' and took easily to copying out Latin texts books instead of thinking things through for themselves.[90] He believed that Cardinal Barberini had been advised to send back Italian-educated Greeks to their own lands with specially revised office books in order, 'under that subtle disguise', to 'trepan their ignorant Countrymen and wheedle them into the Roman Pen', imitating 'cunning Fowlers who breed up and send forth Coy ducks to allure other wild ones and bring them into their nets'. He detected in Goar, the Roman liturgist, a contempt for the 'Rusticity and Clownery of the Greeks' and assumed that this was general among papists who knew anything of the matter.[91] But he visualized great difficulty for the Latins or their recruits to lodge alien ideas in minds so unprepared. Convinced that most of the monks and clergy were incapable of handling theological concepts, he feared that the Huguenot Claude had gravely misunderstood the situation when he did his study of Greek eucharistic doctrine on the assumption that the 'Greeks and the Easterlings' were 'learned and well-versed in this Controversy'. On the controversy, said Covel, none of them 'ever pretended fully to understand, much less ever offer'd clearly to answer any of them'. Even those educated at the Propa-

ganda in Rome had only a scrappy knowledge of Latin dialec-
tical method, and those with no training tried to avoid getting
into theological disputes for fear of revealing the depths of
their ignorance, feebly pleading 'dreadfull or hidden Mysteries' which must not be probed. The ordinary *papa*, he said,
scarcely read a book apart from the office books and these
they tended to memorize so that they were unable to quote
without stumbling into 'strange variety and confusion'.[92] He
assured Ambassador Nointel that even the libraries on Mount
Athos were not carefully looked after as they would be if the
monks could read the books intelligently. He was sure that the
wily Latins realized this all too well and only exploited the
Arnauld/Claude controversy in order to see 'what Crop they
might reap thereby', rather than out of any desire to advance
the cause of truth.[93]

Covel's diagnosis was dire. Yet for all that, he would not
have his English readers, even in 1722, think that the Greek
church leaders were a complete walkover. He knew that some
'Great Men' had been very cautious when approached for their
signatures to testimonials, suspecting a trap. They did not like
'private Letters or personal Demands' on matters of faith.
Their initial response had therefore been 'very cold or
insignificant'. Nectarios advised Paisios to give wide berth to
the Franciscan Lazarus and to let him have not 'so much as
the very Lord's Prayer in writing', because Lazarus and his
associates had come to 'traduce and disturb our affairs' by
craft. Covel's chief fear was that the well-funded French espi-
onage machine would overbear even such astute opponents if
it was allowed free reign.

The Marquis de Nointel came to play an increasing part in
efforts to obtain signatures to the testimonials during the chaplain's tour of duty because it was thought in Latin circles that
such a 'Man of Address and great Devotion' would penetrate
reserve and, through his status, put Greeks at their ease. For
good measure, he was a Jansenist and so could argue plausi-
bly that he was no friend of the hated Jesuits. The ambassador
first tried his persuasion on Patriarch Parthenios II. When he
found that he could not budge him he bought Parthenios out

of the Patriarchy and brought in Dionysios of Larissa. Dionysios thereupon, with 'several others of his Party'; subscribed
to a declaration but carefully did not write it on the paper
offered to him. About forty other bishops, whom Covel understood to be all in Dionysios's interest, thereupon anathematized Parthenios in the hope that this would secure the favour
of Nointel without further perjury. This, declared Covel, was
all that the boasted Synod of Bethlehem/Jerusalem amounted
to – the signing of one piece of paper. Given the importance
claimed for it and the very large number of clergy who
attended, he thought it significant that so relatively few signed
the document.[94] But it was good enough for Nointel's
purpose. Covel understood that one of the ploys used to get
signatures for Dionysius's 'paper' on transubstantiation was
the threat that those who did not sign might be thought Calvinist.[95]

In view of Nointel's intense activity, Covel assumed that
the campaign for signatures must have huge diplomatic and
military ramifications. It was widely argued in England during
the Popish Plot scare that the French had their own reasons
for colluding with Rome to subvert both Protestant Europe and
the poor little Church of England.[96] Ever since the time of
Henry IV, if not indeed that of Francis I a century earlier, the
French had been pushing their luck in the Near and Middle
East, especially in relation to the custody of the Holy Places.[97]
The honour and dignity of the French King had been trum-
peted abroad as the protection of 'all who ... profess and
Worship the Blessed Jesus' in order to cast a veil of 'Immense
Glory' over His Most Christian Majesty.[98] Nointel went on a
great progress to Athens, the Greek Archipelago and
Jerusalem, dazzling all eyes with his 'Majestic Appearance'.[99]

Other Western interest in the Greek islands was of even
longer standing. The Venetians and the Genoese had long held
power and influence there. The Venetians had had the advantage of controlling Crete. In that one area there were so many
Greek bishops that if they could be won over it would look at
least numerically impressive. But under the Vizirship of
Kuprioglu Mehmed Pasha the Turks had waged a sustained

campaign against the Venetians in Crete, culminating in its final conquest in 1669. The French sought quickly to fill the vacuum. By the time of Parthenios there was, reported Covel, a tight and sizeable knot of bishops in French pay and Parthenios himself (though not ultimately to his own advantage) did 'fair Homage'.[100]

When Covel arrived in Constantinople in 1670 he found widespread demoralization at this foreign influence. A young monk of Venetian origin called Hilarion Bubuli (already mentioned in Chapter 3) visited his lodgings, giving the name of Father Jeremias Germanos, whom Covel had met in England the previous year, as his introduction. Ostensibly Bubuli's purpose was to ask if there were any English ambassadorial letters which he could take with him to Venice. He had not, apparently, been briefed by Father Jeremias and at first Covel suspected that he was a Romanist because of his second name. The young man gabbled indiscreetly about many 'Metropolites' being 'Roman in their Hearts'. Since money would 'do anything among them', he doubted not that many more bishops could be persuaded in the same way. Bubuli also made some derogatory remarks about the Patriarch, but Covel's notes of the interview are so strangely garbled that it is not easy to make much sense of them. Bubuli claimed that the French ambassador, the Imperial (Habsburg) Resident at Adrianople and the Venetian Resident were all seeking to unseat the Patriarch (Parthenios) and advance their own man, Metropolitan Panagiotes of Paros and Nixia, in his place.[101] The Jesuits and Capuchins, he claimed, were deeply involved.[102] When Covel spoke to Jeremias Germanos, the priest professed to be completely in the dark about it. Bubuli urged the chaplain to keep the secret. He never visited again, and – try as he would – Covel could never trace him.

Nointel harboured in his embassy a whole string of deposed patriarchs who might come in useful to him, including at various times Methodios and Parthenios. They had his diplomatic protection. Covel called them his 'junto'. Their signatures to the eucharistic document were extracted while they were house guests. Another Patriarch, Joachim of Alexandria, having been bought out by his nephew and become a refugee from debt, was also constrained to sign when he arrived in Constantinople. How could he resist? Covel half-regretted that his master, Sir Daniel, did not get to him first, though had he done so it would have cost a pretty penny! In due course, Covel uncovered what he claimed were the details of how the Nointel plot was devised. Those who thought it up did so before Nointel himself was involved – Cabova, the Venetian consul in Ragusa, Fieschi the ambassador of Genoa, Quirini, the 'Bailo' of Venice, Andreas Ridolphi, the Franciscan bishop of Calamina, and Casimir, the Polish ambassador. They drafted the document which was then taken by the Jesuit Michel Nau to Nointel.[103]

Covel made no effort to conceal from Nointel his feeling of fatuity regarding the plan. Since the Marquis had given him 'a fair and generous Liberty of speech', he told him, with what he called 'Humility and Deference', that there could not be any semblance of synodical authority in the subscriptions. 'Did the most ignorant Subscribers, Armenians, Cophtes [sic], Mengrelians', the 'miserable Ignorant Easterlings', and 'the rest, Deliberate, Examine, and Debate the Articles contain'd in them? Or were they in the least capable of doing it?' He even begged to question whether some of them were capable of writing coherently, apart from some 'affected Scrol [sic], or Cypher'. He put the subscriptions down to 'Reverence and Fear; private Interest, compliance and easieness of Tempers; plain Ignorance of the whole matter; Stupidity, or Inadvertence, or want of Judgement . . .'[104]

Our chaplain realized, however, that the 'Testimonials' were not the only weapon in the Latin armoury; there was also the Confession of Peter Moghila, Metropolitan of Kiev, which had been in circulation in various forms since 1640. Covel had been interested in this document because of the part played by the Jesuits earlier in bringing parts of the Ukrainian Church into Uniate status with Rome through the Union of Brest-Litovsk (1596). The process parallelled to his mind the way in which the Latins, by means of the Jesuits for the most part, were now trying to entrap the Greek Church from Jesuit bases in the Ukraine and Moldavia. The Ukrainian bishops were, according to Covel, compromised in their succession, Moghila and his three suffragans all being consecrated by Theophanes of Jerusalem, a 'meer ... Slave' of Cyril of Berrhoea, who was himself in the pocket of the Latins. When Moghila's Confession was sent to Constantinople in 1661, having already been published in Russia in 1643, the text, in Covel's view, was adulterated with 'many new Disquisitions' and much 'sifting', the sifting having been done by Meletios Syrigos, Patriarch Nectarios's chief go-between with the Latins, and himself a former student in Italy. The resultant Greek text, translated from the Russian, was therefore 'gaged or Siz'd from the Original and Infallible Standard in the Council of Trent'. Nectarios gave it a prefatory letter. A Latin translation came out simultaneously. The publisher, Panagiota, was Greek interpreter to the Sultan but also, Covel believed, in the pay of the Holy Roman Emperors Ferdinand and Leopold, who were patrons of the Jesuits.[105]

The political ramifications were wider even than Covel, with his sharp acumen and fertile imagination, suspected. As well as serving the political objectives of Louis XIV in his competition with the Habsburgs, the Arnauld testimonials were seen as a possible way of winning the great Huguenot general Turenne to the Roman Church. Once done, this paved the way for the revocation of the Edict of Nantes, Henry IV's guarantee of civil liberties to the French Protestants, which in the event did take place in 1685.[106] It was in the interests of the English and the English Church to spike the plan; so Covel was appealing behind the scenes to the 'true Patrons and Sons of our English Church' to support the Claude counter-campaign. He made sure that Sir John Finch, Harvey's successor as ambassador, met as many of the senior Greek bishops as possible in the hope that this would cast doubt on the French campaign and partly to head off the Turks' threat-ened expulsion of the Greeks from the Holy Places, which had been discreetly suggested to the Porte by the French and was clearly in their interests.[107] For the benefit of his later readers, however, Covel was at pains to stress that he would in no way have descended to the 'bargaining and trucking' in which the French were engaged.[108]

In his efforts to head off the Marquis de Nointel, Covel used two arguments, one ecclesiastical and the other political. He pointed out that collecting a mass of individual subscriptions was contrary to the Greek idea of church and consensus and that it was for this reason that many Greek clergy had refused to sign, quite apart from the wording of the document. Therefore, however large a volume was assembled, it would not be seen in Greek lands to 'signify anything to the end for which it was by the Latins designed'.[109] As to what was politic, Covel deftly used his experience of parliamentary lobbying in England. Even in such a relatively well-educated country votes and subscriptions were all 'managed' by the 'Authority and Countenance of great Men' and the 'active warmth and Noise of zealous Sticklers' who played upon the 'Easiness and Indifferency of the middle sort of People'. For that reason he could not think that any man's public subscription was 'really and steadily the sincere studied Opinion of his Heart'. Influence and management determined all, whether in Byzantium or in Albion. Men, after all, were 'meer Men'. In Greek lands the Marquis must realize that the *hoi polloi*, followed their prelates 'as the common Shepherd's pipe or Whistle' and the bishops themselves were, of course, bought.[110]

In Covel's view, the Bethlehem-Jerusalem Synod (so-called) was framed by Dositheos on Nointel's advice, as the ambassador himself had admitted before witnesses in his own hand. So although there may have been a *document*, there had not been – nor was there intended to be – synodal deliberation and free choice. In any case, the Turks would never have allowed Synod to go on long enough to deliberate without monetary penalties.[111] Dositheos was therefore the sole author of the document and he, Nointel, had said in writing that the Patriarch had 'fully satisfied that which we had desired of him'. The fact that Dositheos had had to take responsibility for the textual details because the Ambassador understood no Greek nor Dositheos Latin or French was beside the point. Covel was convinced that the whole thing was a French stitch-up in collusion with sympathetic Catholic diplomats. The Jesuits in the Ambassador's train had done all the preparation and supplied Dositheos with statements to make about Claude and Bellarmine which were quite beyond him to judge.[112] He, Covel, had obtained confirmation of this from Dionysios when the Patriarch was sick and in prison. Covel saw Dionysios as an unwilling accessory in a process which ran counter to Orthodox canonical procedures. Modern scholars keep an open mind as to whether the synod was wholly 'synthetic'; but it is easy to see how Covel, knowing the principals as he did, could have come to this conclusion, given his general estimate of Greek ecclesiastical character and the capacity for influence which the western diplomats possessed.[113]

Covel was satisfied that, despite their very best endeavours, the Latins could not quite make their sophistries pass into the centre of the Greek mind. At best they floated on the surface. Neither the noble Marquis and his 'Conclave of Loyolans', nor the Pope, the Emperor, Spain or the other Catholic princes and republics could transubstantiate even the slippery Dositheos into 'pure Bellarmine and Trentins'. Looking back on these events from his old age, he was pleased to find that when the Greeks repossessed the Holy Places from the Latins, they ceremonially cleansed the altars with soap and water. They would surely not have done so if they had really believed the same things as Rome.[114]

In all this Covel had been an exceedingly sharp observer, but he did make one potentially dangerous error of judgement. He sent to England, so that Sancroft, Gunning and Pearson might see that he had not been inactive, a copy of the Jerusalem statement of 10 January 1672, signed by Patriarch Dionysios, four ex-Patriarchs of Constantinople, the Patriarch of Jerusalem, and thirty-one metropolitans. Perhaps he thought the three divines would keep it to themselves as a mere matter of reference in their studies. In fact it was printed in English as '*A Synodical Answer to the Question, What are the Sentiments of the Oriental Church of the Grecian Orthodox, sent to the Lovers of the Greek Church in Britain in the Year of Our Lord 1672.*[115]

Although linked to the Bethlehem-Jerusalem Declaration, this document, as sent by Covel, was in no way at all synodical, even by the standards of that Declaration. Its preamble is unpolemical. It claims seven sacraments coeval with the Gospel, each necessary to the salvation of 'all the Faithful'. It stresses their conveying of spiritual power. It affirms the presence of the 'Living Body of our Lord Jesus Christ . . . changed by the Holy Spirit' and declares that what was changed was 'truly and properly changed', the 'intire Christ' who both offered and was offered. Furthermore it insists that the worship given to the consecrated elements in the Eucharist was *latria*, namely 'divine worship'. The document deals in detail with the meaning and effect of baptism and the Orthodox understanding of Justification. It makes a moderate reference to holy orders in terms of high-priesthood and the placing by Christ in the Church of pastors and teachers. It says that the Church acclaims the saints as mediators because they have suffered for Christ and are 'friends of God'. It insists that the worship offered to them is of a wholly different kind from that offered to Christ. Reverence to images is referred back to the 'Apostolic age' and is described as 'relative' inasmuch as the thoughts of the worshipper are not fixed upon wood or paint. The other points covered are dealt with in an equally measured fashion.[116]

This moderate document, so remote from manipulated statements about transubstantiation, was nonetheless liable to be used in ways which were not helpful to understanding between the Anglicans and the Orthodox, given that two years later the process began with the conversion Duke of York to Rome which led to the anti-Popish hysteria of 1679–80 and the intimidation of Metropolitan Joseph of Samos when he visited England. Covel continued to ferret out Greek eucharistic belief for his own satisfaction for the rest of his life, asking Humfrey Wanley in 1714 to enquire with Arsenios of Thebais and Archimandrite Gennadios while they were in England what meaning they gave to *metamorphosis*. These two clerics resisted all blandishments, to Wanley's evident discomforture, referring him simply to the Liturgies of St Basil and St John Chrysostom. Wanley found their response 'craftily worded'.[117]

Covel flattered himself that by distributing copies of the Prayer Book in Greek he left behind him a better image of the Church of England which freed its adherents from being seen in the East as mere Lutherans or Calvinists or whatever 'kind of Mongrel Christian'. But he had no great optimism about the future of the Greek Church. He did not expect there to be any more like Cyril Lucaris, because the Greeks were too ignorant, cowardly and lazy to throw up such heroes very often. 'I really expect', he wrote, 'that in a few years, not only the Greeks, but all the East, will be forced to own all that the Conclave [of Rome] shall dictate.' The only hope was for a brief respite, while Rome, having made so great a progress, might for a while rest content. 'For should they attempt to settle that chief Point, the Pope's Supremacy, in Turkey, as they have done it in the Church of Malabar, I believe neither the known pride of the Greeks, nor the Grand Seignor himself (who would be jealous of such a Monarch) would ever bear it'. In which case, the Greeks, weary and sadly pressed between the upper and nether millstones as they were, might be left alone for a little while though not for ever. 'It is an inexpressible Grief to me, and I pity them with all my Soul; the Turk hath robbed them of their Empire and, I fear, the Pope will soon strip them of their Faith'.[118]

Come what may, he comforted himself with the thought that his own hierarchy was quite unlike either the Latin or the Greek because it had apostolic authority without adventitious tricks; and so he reverenced, 'with all humble obedience ... the true Primitive Hierarchy in the Church ...'[119]

Notes

1. Southwell to Sir William Petty, 5 October 1687, *The Petty-Southwell Correspondence* (ed. The Marquis of Lansdowne), (New York, 1967), p. 289; Sir Paul Rycaut to Thomas Smith, 10 December 1670, Smith MS 53, f.155, Bodleian Library. There are occasional incongruous uses of tense which suggest that a much earlier draft was being used unaltered and in a hurry, possibly by an editor after Covel's death; for example his present tense reference to Dositheos of Jerusalem. *Some Account of the Present Greek Church, with Reflections on their*

*Present Doctrine and Discipline, Particularly in the Eucharist
and the Rest of their Seven Pretended Sacraments, compared
with Jac.Goar's Notes upon the Greek Ritual, or Euchologion*
(Cambridge, 1722), p. 157.

2. Covel's profusely illustrated botanical notebooks may be found
in BL Add. MS 57495, British Library. The travel journals,
covering the period 1670 to 1680, are also full of botanical
information and illustration. These may be found in Add. MSS
22912-4. For Covel's relations with William of Orange, see
Covel to William, 14-24 October 1685, Add. MS 22910,
ff.241-2v. For Covel's motive in going to Constantinople, see
Covel to James Crauford, 17 November 1674, Add. MS
22910, f.80. 'Meer curiosity of learning some things abroad
whereof I thought we had but a slight account at home . . .' For
his superficial curiosity about Roman and Greek Churches, see
Covel to George Davies, 5 July 1678 and Davies to Covel, 12
July 1678, Add. MS 22919, ff.164-5. Covel was irritated to
hear while still abroad that he was whispered against at home
because he was seen entering churches in Rome. He protested
that he would be willing even to enter a mosque for the
purpose of seeing what was in it. '. . . and yet I am neither
Greek nor Roman Catholick (God is my witness), no more
than I am Venetian or Neapolitan'. See also his travel journal
for 1677-78, Add. MS 22913, f.16v. For his later cantanker-
ous manner regarding the expenses incurred by construction
work at Christ's College and his ambiguous relations with the
fellows, see his letters to the Rev. Alexander Young, Add. MS
255, ff.2213-3, 264; Thomas Lynford to unidentified correspondent, 9 April 1684, Add. MS 22910, f.229.

3. Sir Steven Runciman, *The Great Church in Captivity*
(Cambridge, 1968), p. 293. He also spent some time in
Holland before returning to England, leading a 'Kind of Itin-
erant Life'. *Some Account*, op. cit., Dedication.

4. Edward Carpenter, *The Protestant Bishop, Being the Life of
Henry Compton, 1632-1713, Bishop of London* (London,
1956), p. 363.

5. Runciman, op. cit.

6. Covel, *Some Account*, op. cit., p. vi; Sir Paul Rycaut, *The
Present State of the Greek and Armenian Churches* (London,
1679), p. 216. It was Rycaut who called Covel an 'ingenious
Person', ibid.

7. A prime instance was when, in his zeal to put down the ubiq-
uity of the sign of the Cross, he said – like any modern
Jehovah's Witness – that the Greek term meant only 'a plain
stake' or fork. *Some Account*, op. cit., pp. 387-91. Ironically,

when travelling alone in Anatolia in 'Turkish Habit', he himself made the sign of the Cross, with an invocation of the Trinity, to make it clear that, despite his garb, he was a Christian and thereby excuse the fact he was carrying wine with him! (p. 399).

8. Cf. ibid., pp. iv–v, xl.
9. Ibid., pp. iv–v.
10. Ibid., *Some Account*, p. 51.
11. Ibid., p. 1.
12. See Stone's article on Pearson in S. L. Ollard, Gordon Close Crosse and Maurice F. Bond, *A Dictionary of English Church History* (3rd edn, London, 1948), p. 464; Gilbert Burnet, *History of His Own Times*, abridged Thomas Stackhouse, op. cit., p. 157. Cf. Middleton, op. cit., p. 181.
13. Covel to the Reverend James Crauford, 17 November 1674, cited ibid., p. iii.
14. He mentioned that the Consul at Smyrna, Sir Paul Rycaut, had been 'many years about a Book concerning the Greek Church and for certain cannot be wanting in his search after this point'. Covel to Crauford, ibid.
15. Ibid., p. i; Runciman outlines the context of this controversy, starting about 1660, in *The Great Church in Captivity*, op. cit., pp. 306–7.
16. Cf. James Covel to Crauford, 17 November 1674, BL Add. MS 22910, f.80; Crauford to Covel, 2 March 1675, ibid., f.89; Crauford to Covel, c.10 August 1674, ibid, ff.74–75; Crauford to Covel, 22 August 1674, ibid., ff.76–77; see also ibid., f.76v. For Arnauld's Jansenism, see Sir Robert Southwell to ?, 22 November 1682, Add. MS 22911, f.279. Cf. 9 January 1682–3, ibid., ff.280–4.
17. *Some Account*, pp. ii–iv.
18. Covel to the Earl of Arlington (Henry Bennett), 30 April 1672, PRO SP97/19, f.182–3; Covel to Joseph Williamson, 8 January 1674–5, ibid., John Newman (ambassador's secretary) to Arlington, 27 August 1672, SP97/19, ff.189–91. For Covel's command of Italian, see his travel journals 1677–80, Add. MS 22914, ff.154–98. For ambassadorial duties (Winchelsea and Harvey), see Winchelsea to Henry Bennett, 22 July–11 August 1666, SP97/108, ff.199–200v; Sir Daniel Harvey to Bennett, 19 April 1669, SP99/19, f.96; also Instructions to Sir Daniel Harvey, 9 August 1668, SP97/19, f.27v; Winchelsea to Bennett, 9 June 1663, SP108/08, f.27. Cf. ibid., f.35. For Winchelsea's estimate of the Turks, see Winchelsea to Bennett, 28 October 1663, SP97/108, f.55v; cipher message, SP97/108, f.159. For Turkish flattery of western powers, see Sultan Mehmet IV to

Charles II, n.d., 1669, SP97/19, f.134. For the destabilizing
behaviour of the Venetian and Imperial residents, see SP97/118,
f.26 (June 1662); Winchelsea to Bennett, 8–19 January 1664,
SP97/108, f.66; comment by Covel, in Add. MS 22910, f.95.
For Winchelsea's attitude to the Jesuits, see Winchelsea to Sir
Edward Nicholas, 4 August 1668, BL Egerton M52539, f.246v.
19. Winchelsea to Bennett, with report, 15 September 1664,
SP97/108, ff.98–100 and 102v; Winchelsea to Bennett, 3–13
January 1665–6, SP97/108, ff.157v, 159; Winchelsea to
Bennett, 15 December 1665, ibid., f.48; memorandum on
Nointel, Add. MS 22911, f.217; Cf. Add. MS 22910, f.95.
The 'French' problem was strangely affected by the conversion
of a French Dominican Friar to Islam and his appointment as
Governor of Smyrna from where he made difficulties for all
the western embassies. See Arthur Barnardiston, James Hoder-
ley and Nathaniel Thraston (English factors) to Thomas
Dethick (Levant Company) 26 April 1667, SP97/108, f.248.
This is not an isolated instance but part of a pattern. In 1725,
the Greek bishops and clergy laid charges against the Roman
Archbishop of Sofia. The Vizir ordered the arrest of the Archbishop and his priests. Keleman Mikes to Princess Amalia
Rakoczi, 7 December 1725; Keleman Mikes, *Letters from
Turkey* (London, 2000), pp. 100–1.
20. Crauford to Covel, 2 March 1675, ibid., p. iv; memorandum
by Winchelsea, PRO SP97/108, f.315; Winchelsea to Charles
II, 8–18 January 1668, SP97/19, f.55; Harley to Arlington,
n.d. (1668), ibid., f.94; Harvey to ? Williamson, 20 October
1671, ibid., f.170v; Sir John Finch to Arlington, 23 December 1672, ibid., ff.200–v; Finch to Arlington, 25 May
1674, ibid., f.207; Finch to Williamson, 12–22 January
1674–5, ibid., f.116v; Finch to Lyonell Jenkins, 8–18 October
1680, ibid., ff.258–9; Finch to the Earl of Sunderland (Secretary of State), 8–18 October 1680, ibid., ff.262–3. See also
ibid., ff.264–5v. Lord Chandos inherited the same attitude and
policy towards the Turks: '. . . pray God defend all Christians
from the violence of the Turks', Chandos to Jenkins, 4–14
January 1682, ibid., f.308; Chandos's official report of the
same year, SP105/109, f.136–v; Charles II's letter to the
Sultan, ibid., f.140. For the Government's supply of ecclesiastical goods through the Embassy, see Memorandum of the
Earl of Carlile (sic), n.d. (1668), SP97/19, f.78. For the struggle for protection of the Holy Places, see Mr ? Carpenter to
Covel, 16–26 May 1679, BL Add. MS 22910, f.198.
21. *Some Account*, p. xli.
22. Diary, (ed.) T. T. Bent (Hakluyt Society, Series I, LXXXVII

(London, 1893), p. 133. Cf. Add. MS 22910, f.84; Covel's *Travel Journal*, 1677–80, Add. MS 22914, f.6, also Add. MS 22912. For Turnbull's estimate of Cordato, see *Travel Journal*, Add. MS 34799, ff.28–30v, 32, 37.

23. *Some Account*, op. cit., p. lv. He disliked the way in which the Greeks habitually put the Latin clergy's lack of beards and the legend of Pope Joan on the same level as what he thought really major issues. Ibid., pp. x–xi. However, he did take their point about unleavened bread, seeing its appearance in the Liturgy in the same time as the Lateran definition of transubstantiation as sinister. Little did the Greeks know then, when they made a fuss about the Bread, what a 'Monster' was 'hatching under it'. Ibid., p. 179.
24. Ibid., p. xl.
25. Ibid., p. 105.
26. Ibid., p. viii.
27. Ibid., p. 86.
28. Ibid., pp. xvii–xviii.
29. Ibid., pp. 156–7.
30. Ibid., p. 121.
31. Ibid., p. xxi.
32. Ibid., p. xxi.
33. Ibid., pp. xxiii, *Travel Journal* 1670–78, BL Add. MS 22912, ff.147, 198; Geoffrey Wheler to Covel, 23 May 1717, Add. MS 22911, Add. MS 22911, f.217.
34. Cf. Ibid., pp. lii, 155.
35. Ibid., p. 344. Cf. fragment of a letter, Add. MS 22910, f.128 [73]; *Travel Journal* 1678–80, Add. MS 22912, ff.65v–66, 147; *Travel Journal* 1670–78, ibid., ff.105–7, 33015lv; *Travel Journal* 1677–81, Add. MS 22914, ff.21–22v, 37–47v. Cf. Michael Llewellyn Smith, 'Perceptions of the Holy Mountain', in *Friends of Mount Athos Annual Report for 1999* (Oxford, 1999), pp. 24–42. Also an extract from a letter, Add. MS 22910, f.115.
36. Covel's *Travel Journal* 1677–80, Add. MS 22914, f.20; *Travel Journal* 1667–8, ibid., f.15v. For careless funeral habits see Covel's letter to his father, 4 April 1674, Add. MS 212910, f.129; for Covel on non-existent saints, see *Travel Journal* 1670–78, Add. MS 22912, f.68; Also *Travel Journal* 1670–78, ibid., Add. MS 22914, ff.6, 108; for Covel on the translation of ikons, *Travel Journal* 1670–78, Add. MS 22912, f.344. For Covel on goblins, see *Travel Journal* 1677–78, ibid., ff.158v–159, 227. For the Cross of St Athanasios, *Travel Journal* 1677–80, Add. MS 22914.
37. *Travel Journals* 1670–78, Add. MS 22912, f.236v–237v.

38. *Some Account*, ibid., pp. 94ff.
39. Ibid., p. 76.
40. Ibid., pp. xiv–xv.
41. Ibid., pp. 35–37. His wildest comment was 'Farragos or plain Huispots of wild Rites and Bits and Scraps of a mangled devotion'. Ibid., p. 11.
42. Ibid., p. 20.
43. Ibid., p. 37.
44. Ibid., p. 36. On this at least modern liturgical research seems to support him. But Covel's only hard evidence then was the *Apostolic Constitutions* and he was aware that Goar and others questioned its authenticity. Ibid., p. 50.
45. Ibid., pp. 78, 80, 87, 93–94.
46. His theory was that it had started with 'vicarious entertainment' of guests in monastic liturgies which subsequently became transposed into the idea of the 'vicarious Communion' of Saints. He even cited a medieval English MS account of usages in Barnwell Priory, in which a 'Portion' of food was set aside for the departed benefactor, Sir Pain Peverell. There is, however, in this lateral thinking just a suggestion of mockery! See ibid., Chapter IV, passim.
47. Ibid., pp. 89–90, 100. Rycaut's additional thought that the discipline of receiving the Antidoron took the place of communion does not seem to have occurred to him, or – if he had seen it in Rycaut or even discussed it with him – it did not seem to him to be likely.
48. Ibid., pp. 376–8, 380–1, 383, 400.
49. Ibid., pp. 348–9. He does not seem to have learned anything of the ascetic context of ikon painting, but he was eloquent about the use of 'unhallowed' models by Renaissance artists when they painted Christ, the Virgin or the saints. Ibid., pp. 365–6.
50. Ibid., pp. 358–64.
51. Ibid., pp. 84, 103–4. Perhaps just as a debating point, since it leads nowhere, he faults Patriarch Jeremias for not using in his rely to the Lutheran divines what he called the 'best' argument for invocation, namely beatific vision or intuitive contemplation. Perhaps this was suggested to him by Rycaut or Smith and he had not properly digested it. Ibid., p. 363.
52. Ibid., pp. 333, 336, 338.
53. Ibid., pp. 258, 294.
54. Ibid., pp. 286–90, 299.
55. Ibid., pp. 231ff.
56. Ibid., pp. 297–8, 300.
57. Ibid., pp. 249–50, 252, 255. He was aware that the Latins had

been contemptuous of Greek confession practice as far back as the Council of Florence. So he could not see it simply as a by-product of Turkish oppression. He was also aware, from a fifteenth-century MS canonarion in his possession, of some Latin modification of Greek penance practice in certain parts of the Greek lands – for instance, the introduction of the rosary as a penance in Thessalonica, which was at one time occupied by the Venetians. Ibid., pp. 251, 259.

58. Ibid., pp. xvii, xxxi, 143–5.
59. Ibid., pp. 133, 143–5. He saw no more credibility in the idea of Christ transubstantiated into bread and wine than he would thinking of Christ transubstantiated into cats and dogs. Ibid., pp. 65–68.
60. Ibid., pp. 81–82.
61. Ibid., p. xxxiii.
62. Ibid., p. xvii. He produced a catena of Fathers to uphold his way of looking at the Eucharist – the Pseudo-Dionysius ('eikones'), Tertullian ('figura'), Augustine ('signum'), Cyril of Jerusalem, Gregory Nazianzen, Theodorel and Macarios ('antitypes'), Maximos the Confessor ('symbolon'). He also offered as collateral evidence the story of how Nazianzen's sister, Gorgonia, mixed the reserved sacrament with her tears. Ibid., pp. 152–61.
63. Cf. Ibid., p. 158. On another occasion he agrees with Maximus the Confessor and Cyril of Jerusalem that it was the *whole* liturgy which consecrated and neither simply the words of Institution nor the *epiclesis*.
64. Ibid., p. 258.
65. Ibid., p. 141.
66. Ibid., p. i. But see Runciman, op. cit., p. 308.
67. *Account*, pp. 74–76. He took the elevation of only part of the 'Crumbs' before communion as further evidence of this.
68. Cf. Ibid., p. 61. He quotes approvingly the pseudo-Erasmian couplet:

'That Man the Mysteries of God doth see,
Who shuts his Eyes believing them to be.'
Ibid., p. xxviii.

69. Ibid., pp. 58, 63.
70. Ibid., p. xxx.
71. Ibid., p. 105. He gleefully quotes Bessarion of Nicaea's admission that words in the Liturgy had sometimes been transposed 'cart-before-the-horse' and yet in this state been made sacrosanct and explained away 'by a Rhetorical Figure'. Ibid., p. 50.
72. Ibid., p. 154. The greater part of the bishops at II Nicaea, he

said, quoting Tarasius, 'came in by Simony', starting at the top with Neophytos who went straight from layman to Patriarch by that means.

73. Ibid., p. xxxii.
74. Ibid., p. 180.
75. Cf. Ibid., p. 107.
76. Ibid., p. 12.
77. Ibid., pp. 36, 41.
78. Ibid., pp. 197–9, 200–3.
79. Ibid., p. xli.
80. Ibid., p. 206.
81. Ibid., p. 256. He missed the significance of Jeremias's 'Truth of the Body' stress on the integrity of the sacred action. Ibid., pp. 123–5.
82. Cf. Ibid., pp. xxv–xxvi, xxviii–ix.
83. Ibid., pp. 184, 188. For Covel's destructive analysis of the evolution of major and minor orders in the various traditions, see pp. 189–92, where he argues his case for the complete lack of correspondence and therefore the impossibility of claiming dominical or primitive authority for any.
84. Cf. Ibid., pp. 105–8, 119, 209–18.
85. Ibid. He notes that there was no open debate on transubstantiation at the Council of Florence and that the four Greek delegates who approached the Pope affirmed only that the bread and wine were consecrated as the Body and Blood. Ibid., pp. 91, 120–1. They 'shuffled off the point ... by a Tacit Meaning'. Covel viewed Bessarion as a traitor to his Church and thought he tried to make the Greek statement 'firmer'. He commented on the *nemesis* of Bessarion's acceptance of a cardinalate that he 'juggled (after his Greek way)' with western politics and ended by dying an ignominious death 'far from his own Country'.
86. Ibid., pp. xxxvi–viii.
87. Ibid., pp. xxxix, 106–7, 181.
88. Ibid., pp. 106–7.
89. Ibid., pp. 121–2, 126.
90. Ibid., p. 127.
91. Ibid., p. 260.
92. Cf. Ibid., pp. vii–viii.
93. Ibid., p. 136.
94. Ibid., pp. 136–8. Cf. Runciman, op. cit., p. 308.
95. Ibid., p. xvii.
96. Cf. [M.D.], *A Seasonable Advice to all True Protestants in England* (London, 1679), pp. 11–12, 21.
97. *Some Account*, op. cit., p. xx.

98. Ibid., pp. xix.
99. Ibid., pp. xiv–xx.
100. Ibid., pp. 128–31. Covel recalled the 'infinite' number of Latin 'myrmidons' running around in Greek lands in the 1660s and 70s. They were especially numerous in Galata. He quoted the Jesuit Michael Nau as saying that the object was to 'put a Firebrand into a barrel of Gunpowder'. Ibid., pp. xxii, 105–7.
101. Ibid., pp. i, xviii, xx; Add. MS 22912, f.148.
102. Ibid., pp. xvi. To Covel the Jesuits seemed for the most part 'subtle, cunning, intreaguing Persons', prying into 'every Man and every Matter'. He claimed to have seen a copy of their instructions for dealings with the Greeks. He feared the effect of their prolific publications from the presses in Moldavia and Walachia. Ibid., pp. viii–ix.
103. Ibid., pp. xx–xxii. Covel also mentioned as important Carnizaras, the Latin Commissary in Jerusalem. He knew that Nointel thought Carnizaras 'mad'.
104. Ibid., pp. 131–2.
105. Ibid., pp. 131ff.
106. Rycaut, *Greek and Armenian Churches*, op. cit. pp. 447, 450.
107. *Some Account*, op. cit., p. xxi.
108. Ibid., p. vi.
109. Ibid., pp. xii–iii. He knew, and probably told Nointel, what Patriarch Nectarios of Jerusalem had said to Patriarch Paisios of Alexandria: 'For God's sake, do not give any Declaration, for the emissaries do not come sincerely but knavishly ...' Nectarios declared that true Orthodox doctrine was sufficiently and manifestly seen in the Fathers.
110. Ibid., p. xxi.
111. Ibid., pp. xx–xxi, 147–8.
112. Ibid., pp. 146, 159.
113. Ibid., p. 140. Even in his preface to the Declaration, Dionysios showed, in Covel's opinion, an ill-conceived contempt for those who had so heavily solicited his statements – their 'vain meddling'. Covel gave him the credit for trying hard *not* to suggest in his response a gross material presence. The author is indebted to cautionary conversations with Professor David Melling on the credit that can be given to Covel's interpretation of Jerusalem/Bethlehem.
114. Ibid., p. 147. Covel thought Dionysios's expressions in the Bethlehem-Jerusalem Declaration could be construed as nearer to the Roman position that what the Greek delegates said at Florence, notwithstanding the conscious attempt to avoid transubstantiation. The delegates to Florence had added the phrase 'in us' (*en amin*) which Covel thought avoided gross material

presence, but he suspected that Dionysios's 'proper Body' might be seen as a shift away from this in a Roman direction. Ibid., p. 138. For the full text, see George Williams (ed.), *The Orthodox Church of the East in the Eighteenth Century*, (London, Oxford and Cambridge, 1868), pp. 67–76. Williams gives a list of the signatories.

115. Runciman, op. cit., p. 308, refers briefly to the document, but his comment on its significance is not very perceptive and could mislead the non-specialist.

116. For the quizzing of Arsenios, see Humfrey Wanley to Covel, 21 December 1714, Add. MS 22911, f.163, also ibid., ff.4–7.

117. *Some Account*, op. cit., p. 147.

118. Ibid., pp. xlii, 147, 157, 343. After his return to England, Covel continued to follow the Roman propaganda campaign from a distance, including the publicity given to the pseudo-official declaration of 1691 against Joannes Cariophilles, a statement which he thought manufactured by the Latins. By 1705 there was a heavily-funded Latin college at Bucharest, tempting Greeks, Armenians and 'Persians' to study at little expense and drink in the 'Latins Potions'. Against this, only Dositheos was able to respond in print. He reproduced various documents concerning Patriarch Photius and Rome, the apostate Bessarion and the devilish Union of Brest-Litovsk. Covel relished Dositheos's pungent comments on the headship, universal pastorate and monarchy of the papacy, on purgatory and other 'sophistries' and 'blasphemies' which, said Covel, he 'dissolved and shattered to pieces like Cobwebs', declaring the whole papal system to be 'nothing else but a separation from the true God'. Nevertheless, Covel feared that even Greeks who denounced the Pope as Antichrist would still be happy to receive retainers from Rome for 'dark and secret Services ...' Ibid., pp. ix–xi. One can find an echo of Covel's view in a letter from one S. Hayward in Zante to the S.P.C.K. in 1708: 'I am mightily tormented by these bearded ignorant priests' – presumably begging for subsidies! Cf. W. K. Lowther Clarke, *A History of the S.P.C.K.* (London, 1959), pp. 110–11.

119. *Some Account*, op. cit., ibid., p. xli.

CHAPTER FIVE

IN SEARCH OF A HOME: THE REMNANT DILEMMA AFTER 1688

We have seen already that in 1672 a question was sent to Constantinople 'What are the sentiments of the Oriental Church of the Grecian Orthodox?' The Greeks, ever inclined to see themselves as the centre of attention, designated the senders as 'the Lovers of the Greek Church in Britain', but modestly professed not to know the precise motives behind the enquiry.

Their reply bore the names not only of Dionysios, the current Patriarch of Constantinople, but also those of Paisios, Methodios, Neophytos and Gerasimos, former Patriarchs, plus the names of thirty-two other bishops. The document looked very impressive.[1]

Some of the expressions used in the reply concerning the Eucharist would have caused no problems to Andrewes, Cosin, Thorndike or Taylor such as 'the holy Participation', presence by way of the 'parousia of the Intire Christ', &c. Yet we have seen in our discussion of Thomas Smith and John Covel how selectively this document could be quoted during the Popish Plot hysteria to the detriment of the Greeks in London.

The Greeks, believing that the request had emanated from Bishop Compton of London, kept copies of their reply and sent them with their response to the Nonjurors in 1711. They obviously felt the 1672 statement to be definitive. And well they might have done because they wrote it in the same year as the Confession of Patriarch Dositheos of Jerusalem was ratified by the Council of Jerusalem-Bethlehem. But there was an ambiguity hidden from the Anglicans, for Dositheos's Confession, like the earlier one of Peter Moghila, was tinged with Roman sacramental notions of substance, accidents and transubstantiation as well as ideas of purgatory, all which Anglicans would have repudiated outright. Bishop Kallistos of Diokleia judiciously says of Dositheos's Confession that it demonstrates the 'limitations of Greek theology in this period' and that one does not find it in 'the Orthodox tradition in its *fullness*'.[2] This chapter will be, among other things, an extended gloss on Bishop Kallistos's judgement.

There is a curious successor document dated 1691 and seemingly intended for western eyes. It bore the signatures of Kallinicos of Constantinople, Dositheos of Jerusalem and fifteen other bishops, attested later as genuine by Samuel, 'Judge of the Universe', Patriarch of Alexandria. To the extent that it was known in England, this 1691 document would also have caused qualms, declaring as it did (at least in English translation) that the substance of bread and wine no longer remained after consecration as they were 'converted and changed', although not in such a manner that there were 'many Christs and many Bodies of Christ'. This was clearly designed, as the Dositheos Confession was not, to counter the philosophical implications of *consubstantiation*. The Holy Orthodox Church, it said, through the Holy Spirit hit upon the word *metamorphosis*, 'intending no more thereby than that there was a *metabole* in the Sacrament'. This word was not borrowed from the Latins because it was 'stored with [the true Church] from her own proper and orthodox Doctors, many ages before ...' It had been extensively expounded by Patriarch Gennadios of Constantinople (458–71) who had maintained that even then it was central to the Tradition and both 'settled and received'. From Gennadios's time – 'Hereticks only excepted' – it had been taken with 'a sincere and pure Conscience' and expounded on numerous occasions by Maximus of Cytheri, Meletios Pega of Alexandria, Gabriel of Philadelphia, George Koressios and Nectarios of Jerusalem among many others. Most recently it had been used by

Meletius Syrigus 'of happy memory' in his controversy with the 'Luthero-Calvinists'. Nevertheless despite this carefulness, the document's insistence that the bread and wine 'disappeared' and the way it interpreted the Protestant obsession with transubstantiation as no more than a covert way of rejecting entirely the real presence were calculated to alienate many sincere Anglicans who might encounter the document.[3] It therefore provided no great encouragement to the Anglican Establishment to enter into ecumenical dialogue.

There was no further contact until, shortly before July 1716, Arsenios, Bishop of Thebais in The Greek Patriarchate of Alexandria, while visiting England on a 'begging' mission on behalf of Patriarch Samuel, was approached by the Nonjuring Bishop Alexander Campbell, with a view to communicating with the Greek patriarchs. It was a risky business for Campbell as a representative of the 'faithful remnant' of the Church of England who had separated themselves from the perjuring establishment after the Revolution of 1688. The fund-raising was, as usual, not for the benefit of the Orthodox faithful but to pay off a huge debt, incurred on this occasion by Samuel (Patriarch since 1710) to buy off the Turkish intrusion of Cosmo of Sinai in his place.[4] Arsenios, all Greek diplomats smiles, would be inclined to say 'yes' to anyone if there was a chance of donations and snub those, like the Nonjurors, who were penniless – Covel suspected that Arsenios also had a hidden agenda – to collect what money he could and then buy the Patriarchate from the Turks for himself. This, if true, would have made him even more slippery. Arsenios was snubbed by the 'official' Church of England. Humfrey Wanley, the Bishop of London's chaplain, warned John Covel as an officer of the University of Cambridge, 'We are against a Brief, or any General Collection for them, and we do not like that the Universities should be pestered with them. The Poor Archbishop cried out like a Child, when my Lord of London told him he must Depart.'[5]

Campbell, a 'College-bishop' of the Scots Nonjuring Church (i.e. one without diocesan responsibility) and living in London, boldly suggested a union between the Remnant of the

'British Church' (i.e. both English and Scottish) and the Greeks. Arsenios, for whatever reason – perhaps idle curiosity – listened. Campbell's fellow Episcopalians were not all equally enthusiastic about what he was trying to do, and in the end the substantive negotiation came down to a volunteer group consisting of Campbell, Jeremy Collier and Nathaniel Spincks – a judicious mix of Scottish and English Nonjurors. Of the three, Collier was the best scholar and a noted liturgist. One English presbyter (later bishop), Roger Laurence, stood on the sidelines bewailing that the Greeks were 'more corrupt and more bigoted than the Romanists'. Perhaps he got *that* from Covel.[6]

It is important to understand the background of this high risk venture, and the psychology of the Nonjurors is crucial to any such understanding. Embittered by two political 'boulversements' in one century – one of which, the Commonwealth, nearly extinguished classical Anglicanism altogether and humiliated its surviving champions, now bound by their consciences to meeting for worship in private rooms and oratories of stately homes as the Catholic recusants had done for a century past and liable to sudden raids by the magistrates or the mob,[7] they were inclined to take an abstract purist line concerning the 'Christian state' which has no parallel in western Catholic tradition or indeed in Orthodoxy which, in its Babylonian captivity, still hankered after the Byzantine commonwealth. The question could be put starkly as how to obey the 'Laws of the Catholick Church' and also the laws of the country.[8]

Edmund Chishull, one of those who conformed to the 'Williamite' settlement of 1689, was scathing about the way in which the Nonjurors were 'very free in determining how far this [his own] and all other Establish'd Churches in the World, are in a state of Heathenism'. Chishull even charged Henry Dodwell, a paragon of Nonjuring rectitude, with denying 'the Church of which he was once a member the ordinary Methods of Salvation' and thus with being nothing but a Donatist. Chishull may have been generalizing wildly but he was not a million miles from the truth as some of the Nonjurors saw it.

George Hickes said of the Establishment clergy, 'They can perform no valid acts of Priesthood' their very Prayers are Sin, their Sacraments are no Sacraments; their Absolutions are null and of no force; God ratifies nothing in Heaven, which they do in his Name upon Earth . . .' The horror of sacrilege had been recently rekindled in the minds of High Churchmen by Sir Henry Spelman's *History and Fate of Sacrilege*, published in 1698 fifty-one years after the author's death but known of throughout the Restoration period in manuscript. Thomas Smith was just one among many later Caroline divines for whom the double desecration of Commonwealth and Revolution were psychologically almost too much to bear. His extensive correspondence with George Hickes in the 1690s is full of bitterness on this score. He harboured a special revulsion at the way in which the Scottish Bishops were abandoned by the state 'as a prey to Sacrilegious Covenanters' and he prayed that the Church of England might yet be preserved from the machinations of 'Schismatical Republicans' who sought to 'blow it up'. The sacramental inferences from this were not hard to see for a Nonjuror who had lost everything for the sake of obedience. If everything for the Nonjurors seemed to hinge on the episcopate, this was not merely a legalism concerning sources of jurisdiction but, as Arthur Middleton reminds us, primarily a question of *charisma* touching upon the true spiritual power of excommunication, absolution, ordination and confirmation. Roger Laurence's pugnatiously argued tract *Lay-baptism Invalid* of 1712 in its anxiety to stand up for 'right order' unfortunately fell foul of Joseph Bingham's learned analysis of the eighth Canon of I Nicaea, which allowed for lay baptism *in extremis*. Laurence was out of synchrony with the Fathers on this matter, but his mistake was understandable because none of the sacrileges committed against individual bishops by other bishops or by the imperial power in the early Church (and there were many) matched the long-term implications for Anglican episcopacy understood, as 'Catholic order', arising out of the Revolution of 1688. Not surprisingly, Dodwell's classical education gave him one comfort in this terrible

situation – Philo's reminder to his fellow Jews in face of imperial perfidy that one had the greatest ground for hoping in God
when most deserted by men. Those who deserted would
unquestionably include those who, through weakness of the
flesh, sought respectability by being seen attending the
'Williamite' Church but at the same time attempted to salve
their consciences by presenting themselves for communion at
a Nonjuring Eucharist, notwithstanding caution about
performing 'an Unlawful thing' by consorting with a 'distinct
and opposite Communion'. Communion was communion and
could not be parcelled out. The early Church judged all
prayer, 'especially Public and Solemn' prayers, to be 'Acts of
Communion'. What had 'Primitive Rules and Practices' to say
to this existential dilemma, a dilemma already faced by
'Church Papists' in the reigns of Elizabeth and James I?
People were, by the standards of the Primitive Church clearly
cutting themselves off from the integrity of communion
'without any Solemnity of Sentence' and needed to acknowledge the status of penitent.[9]

Such thoughts slowly led the majority of Nonjurors – albeit in
some instances reluctantly – to consider abandoning all links
with the state. After all, if they acknowledged a royal
supremacy in their post-Revolution condition it could no longer
be because they were required to do so by the coercive power of
the state, because the only sovereigns they could acknowledge
were the exiled and powerless James II and James III. They put
off the moment of final decision by intermediate expedients such
as choosing suffragans for the deprived bishops under the Act of
1534 (26 Hen. 8, c. 14) but still submitting their choice to James
II, with the embarrassment of being told by the King that he was
consulting the Archbishop of Paris and the Bishop of Meaux
before granting the *congé d'elire*, then using Hooker's *Of the
Laws of Ecclesiastical Polity*, Book VII, Chapter ii, 3, in order
to justify consecrating bishops-at-large, and then finally, in the
1730s, obtaining a *sui generis* consent from James III as if the
exiled King was a landlord settling a lease. But the reasoning
impelling a total abandonment of the state was already clearly
set out in an exchange of letters between Thomas Smith and

Henry Dodwell in 1699 in which Dodwell began from the premiss that the Ante-Nicene bishops had supreme authority in their own 'districts' and without appeal. He allowed that the fourth canon of Nicaea allowed appeals to 'higher sees', but he knew of no instances in which the bishops of 'higher Sees' presumed to judge an appeal except synodically. In the post-papal world it was clear that since God was the 'Author of all lawfull Government', it followed that all subjects were obliged 'to pay their due deference to their several governments, so long as civil society lasted.' But in Britain after the Revolution if the present 'Possessors' of government took acts which were inconsistent with the 'antient Constitution' of the Church, God would not countenance such acts because they would 'dissolve the present Church as a body and Communion'.[10]

Part of the later English Nonjuring community, under Thomas Deacon, was to resolve itself into the 'Orthodox British Church', absolutely convinced of their superiority to any other Christian body in purity and integrity, even if they conceded a partial affinity to the sadly corrupted Orthodox East.[11] This purism led to some waspish categorizing of the entire Scottish Church as a 'secret Society', a charge bitterly resented by the Scottish Episcopalians as it effectively cut them off from the intellectual mainstream of Anglicanism as surely as their Jacobitism did from political and social privilege.[12] The intellectually freewheeling Bishop Herbert Hensley Henson was later to write of them in characteristic fashion: 'Their repudiation of the national authority threw them back on their sacerdotal principles, and compelled them to develop their ecclesiastical theory apart from the grand limiting conditions which governed the sacerdotalism of Laud and his followers.'[13]

The providentialism of the Remnant inevitably found its locus in the survival at all costs of the Anglican liturgy as it had been received, even though they found the form of the 1662 Prayer Book somewhat less than satisfactory. Almost all the Nonjurors in England to some degree hankered after the First Edwardine Prayer Book of 1549. Jeremy Collier thought that it was 'formed by divine assistance and discharged by human infirmity'. By comparison, the Second Prayer Book, thought the saintly Bishop Thomas Wilson of Sodor and Man, was a 'deformed, disordered Cranmerian changeling', and Edward Stephens dismissed it as 'the pest of the nation'. The fact that a post-1688 establishment bishop like Wilson could align himself with the most out-and-out Nonjurors on this sensitive issue shows just how isolated was Sodor and Man. (At the Elizabethan Settlement Bishop Stanley ran the diocese for more than a decade by completely ignoring royal Injunctions and the Prayer Book!)[14]

The question of whether the 1552–1662 Prayer Book was an 'anti-liturgy' was never agreed in so many words. Stephens doubted the validity of its eucharistic consecration because of its lack of an *epiclesis* (it was, he said with lawyer's caution, 'at least doubtful'); but for most High Churchmen, whether Juring or Nonjuring, the role of the established Book involved the very survival of Anglicanism and gave to it a certain providence. Roger Laurence's Prayer Book legalism could be seen as just an extreme form of a reverence which permeated the whole Nonjuring (as indeed the whole High Church) body.[15] A certain sea change took place in the Scottish Remnant from the 1720s. Thomas Rattray, the greatest liturgical scholar writing in English in the eighteenth century, published in 1728 an *Essay on the Nature of the Church* based directly on patristic sources. This paved the way for the Canons of 1743 which finally freed the Scots Church from the idea of royal (even Stuart) supremacy because lay headship and parliamentary interference alike were seen to be in conflict with the synodal pattern of the early Church. Then, appropriately, in 1744 Rattray, now Bishop of Brechin and Primus, produced a critical edition of the Liturgy of St James. Although it was never much used in its entirety in the Scottish Church, it did help to free Scottish Episcopalians from 'PrayerBook-olatry'.

Unquestionably, it was in the field of worship (albeit mostly learned from books) that the Nonjurors were chiefly drawn to Orthodoxy. Edward Stephens paved the way before the Schism. Jardine Grisbrooke has likened him to John Mason Neale in his 'boundless and fearless zeal for what he believed to be the Catholic faith and practice' and in his 'eager longing for the reunion of Christendom'. Stephens – perhaps uniquely in Anglicanism at that time – wrote around 1704, 'The Greek Communion I take to be the only true Catholic communion in the World, and therefore preferable to any other.' 'The greatest Schism of all', he believed, was that between the Latins and the Greeks, in which the Latins were 'certainly guilty'.

Stephens, who, as we have already seen, grieved over the Greek laity's ignorance of their own doctrine, tried unsuccessfully with others, before the Gloucester Hall project, to start a Greek College in Oxford and continued throughout his life to see 'a restitution of Catholic Communion between the Greek Church and the Church of England' as 'Practicable', in spite of what in all conscience he had to regard as serious corruptions in practice on the Greek side. Possibly in 1703, he wrote a manuscript entitled 'A good and necessary proposal for the restitution of Catholic Communion between the Greek Churches and the Church of England.' For years he circulated in manuscript his own version of the Liturgy of St James. But it has to be said that his influence was limited because for the greater part of his life he was a layman. Even his significant works remained in manuscript – the fate of many a lay theologian in the West.[16]

Those among the Nonjurors and conforming High Churchmen who were at all knowledgeable of Eastern Christendom were so at this time largely through the study of the Fathers. Thomas Smith was the only one who had hands-on experience of the Greek Church. Characteristic of the first stage of Nonjury was Henry Dodwell, for years a lay theologian yet Camden Professor of History at Oxford until deprived of his chair in 1691 for refusing to take the oaths to William and Mary. Thomas Hearne, the antiquary, described him as the greatest scholar in Europe when Dodwell died in 1711. No fact was said to escape him and he always fearlessly spoke his mind. Between 1673 and 1676 he wrote vehemently against Romanism but also against Protestant Dissent in his *Book of Schism*, tangling with the Presbyterian Richard Baxter over the unprimitiveness of setting up altar against altar. By the

1680s he was an international authority on St Cyprian.[17] After the Revolution, while struggling in conscience with his own allegiance, he returned to Roman controversy with his *Dissertation on the Bishops of Rome* (1689). Thereafter his energies were largely devoted to justifying the Nonjuring position and also to controversial issues in patristics, such as his idea that the soul's immortality rested in baptism rather than in its created nature, an idea which he firmly based on the earliest Fathers.[18] The implications of the Revolution for his Church weighed on his mind as nothing previously had done in a life full of controversy. 'God look on our distressed deserted Church', he prayed. 'They who have power in their hands are not content to betray the Rights on which we must subsist as a Church and a Communion when the Prince is not our Friend'. They were not content 'to leave Baal to plead for himself, but themselves undertake to be his advocates. How can we expect in so bad a ferment of the Laity that they will even vouchsafe to examine the merits of the cause, when they have already so great a majority of those who are concerned for these Rights who disown them? They must be great Lovers of Truth and ingenuity and of Religion and our old Church of England who will do so.'[19]

In matters of detail Dodwell was as critical of the Orthodox as Stephens was, publishing in 1709 a treatise entitled *Incense no Apostolical Tradition*.

The conflict between Dodwell and Chishull already referred to is very instructive for our theme. Dodwell was a patristics scholar pure and simple: he was no traveller. Chishull had a more pedestrian scholarly equipment and a far more conventional mind, but he was for a long time chaplain at the Smyrna 'factory' and planned 'a large work' on the Greek Church which he had apparently still not started in 1729, two years before his death.[20] Whatever he may have originally felt about the Royal Supremacy, when it came to a question of conscience over the deprivation of devout bishops Dodwell was able to stand aside from the Supremacy. Not so Chishull, whose reverence for the Supremacy was extreme and not unaffected by his knowledge that the Greek Church had accorded to the Emperor the style of 'King of Consecrated Persons and of the whole Christian Assembly'. Although he drew the line at the Crown driving good churchmen out of the Church, he allowed it the right to deprive bishops or inhibit their jurisdiction. Also like Roger Laurence, he was a Prayer Book legalist. For him Anglicans were the stewards of the Prayer Book liturgy, the clergy especially so because of their ordination vow. The formularies of the Church *must* be affirmed in their 'plain literal meaning', which he assumed was given by the Church and should not be 'drawn to some private sentiment'. Assuming that Dodwell's doctrine of the soul was contrary to the plain literal meaning of the formularies, he invoked episcopal authority against it, even though Dodwell had withdrawn himself from the authority of the state bishops. Chishull claimed that the 'whole Fabric of Religion' was at stake in this matter.[21]

Dodwell and Chishull agreed in their rejection of transubstantiation, but that was about all they agreed on. Chishull was uncomfortable even with the patristic idea of baptism, as the 'Light of Immortality'.[22] Dodwell, in his conviction that the soul was capable of a 'Divine Pneuma' was closer than Chishull to the Orthodox mindset, despite his lack of the immediate experience which Chishull had. To Chishull's alarm, Dodwell identified his *theologoumenon* with a very tangible idea of the Church which made his opponent uncomfortable, a Church in strict apostolic succession of faith wherein baptism, as access to this *pneuma*, was administered 'in Communion with the true Bishop'.[23]

The controversy over the soul involved a minute examination of the Fathers and demonstrates how totally enclosed the Nonjurors were in their scholarly study. Their premiss was that if a doctrine was 'True and Catholic for the first Four Centuries, it is so still ...'[24] There, however, in Dodwell, as in Collier, Brett and Deacon, an implication that in the seclusion of their study and oratory they knew better the implications of the Greek Tradition than the Greeks knew themselves. This was probably noticed and resented in subsequent negotiations.

The Nonjurors' treasury of patristic learning had its great-est effect on the Scottish Canons of 1743 wherein the clergy were enjoined to instruct their people in the 'truly Catholic Principles' of the 'Fathers of the Apostolical and two next succeeding Ages'.[25] W. J. Sparrow Simpson thought the Nonjurors were theologians with 'independent knowledge of their Fathers' – i.e. they did not simply quote their Fathers from the Carolines.[26] This seems to be a fair judgement. Having turned their backs on Establishment, their whole lives had to be rooted in the pre-Constantinian Church, because the Constantinian Church was yet another Establishment. The minuteness of their scholarship can nowhere be better seen than in Rattray's revision of George Skene's text of the Liturgy of St James. Skene and Rattray compared surviving texts with St Cyril of Jerusalem's account of his Church's Liturgy in the fifth *Mystagogical Catechism* and with the Liturgies of Clement, Mark, John Chrysostom and Basil. At that date *James* was still regarded as 'unquestionably one of the most ancient and valuable now anywhere extant in the Christian Church'.[27] The Rattray edition was the fulfilment of that intuition which had led Archibald Campbell to wish that the Church of England at the Reformation had directly adopted 'one of the ancient Greek Liturgies'.[28]

The vast patristic knowledge employed on the 'soul' debate brought the Nonjurors to an awareness of the doctrine of *theosis*.[29] Hence the increasing concern for the restoration of a sound *epiclesis* in Anglican Liturgy. Collier argued that this was essential and patristic because our Lord offered himself to the Father 'through the Eternal Spirit', an oblation which was 'made, though not finished, at the Institution of the Holy Eucharist'.[30] Something of this conception spilled over to those few sound High Churchmen who remained in the Estab-lishment and who read Collier's published work. John Johnson of Cranbrook, for instance, knew his Eastern liturgies well enough to be satisfied that the early Church so honoured the Eucharistic Sacrifice that any bishop who 'depraved it would have been forced to give way to another.'[31] Thomas Brett as a Nonjuror, acknowledged the Establishment man alongside his own man Hicks for this insight, revealing in so doing that many Anglicans before him had illegally supplemented the Prayer Book in order to make it more patristic.[32]

One reason why divines like Rattray appealed so consistently to the Church of the first three centuries was their belief that in that period the creative work of the Spirit was experienced in 'extraordinary gifts'.[33] It may be for the same reason that Bishop Petrie, according to a parenthetic remark by Bishop Andrew Macfarlane, followed the practice of confirming infants, thereby implicity rejecting the view of Confirmation as the 'mere renewal of the Baptismal Vows.'[34]

Consistently with this charismatic outlook (an outlook curiously shared, according to J. M. Neale, by the Church of Utrecht, at that very time losing its link with Rome), the Nonjurors assured the Greeks that they believed with Gelasius that the elements in the Eucharist were 'changed into a Divine Thing' and obtained thereby a 'divine efficacy by the operations of the Holy Spirit'.[35] Similarly Rattray, in his preface to the Liturgy of St James, writes of the elements undergoing 'a mysterious Change, though not in their substance, yet at least in their qualities, that very Body and Blood in Energy and Life-Giving Power ...'[36] In this case it cannot be a coincidence that the Nonjuring Liturgies have an exuberance of tone precisely to the extent that they freed themselves from the Prayer Book text. William Cartwright's *The Divine Office, containing devotions for the Canonical Hours Lauds, Tierce, Sext, None and Compline* of 1761 is particularly noteworthy in this respect, especially considering that it was explicitly designed for use in 'the Houses of all the Clergy' and in private fraternities. For instance:

Priest: Behold the Bridegroom cometh in the middle of the night, let us watch and pray that we enter not into temptation.

Cartwright's antiphon for saints' days has:-

'Truly great is thy Majesty, O Lord, on whose Presence

Millions of Angels attend, and before whose Throne with humble prostrations the Elders lay down their crowns';

while on Sundays the antiphon reads:-

V. 'The Lord is risen indeed, and restored life to the dead, Halleluya.
R. He is risen, He hath broken the gates of Brass and smitten the bars of Iron in sunder. Halleluya!'

Much of these offices comes directly from the Byzantine *Horologion*. Traces of Greek prayers already translated by Cosin and Taylor can also be found. Gunter Thomann points to a deliberate attempt to link up the Offices with the Eucharist after the Byzantine pattern.[37] The very 'Victorian' Sparrow Simpson is conventionally dismissive of Thomas Deacon's 1734 Liturgy for having 'all the Eastern exuberance, which is so foreign to the English as it is to the Western use.'[38]

We see then that the preferred norm of worship among the Nonjurors was 'charismatic' in a decidedly patristic sense. They were aware that the modern age was lacking in spontaneous gifts of the Spirit and that liturgy had therefore hedged itself with objective norms. In no way did their view of liturgy depreciate the inherent authority of a sacramental ministry, even though that ministry must be free of state and social norms. James Walker, Bishop of Edinburgh, used this analysis to show that the clergy must hold a stewardship by divine appointment in the succession of local churches. Such an arrangement, thought Walker, demonstrated 'a very striking, intimate and interesting' mode of connection with the 'very age of miracles ...' Bishop Kilgour habitually commended the priests of his Diocese of Aberdeen 'to the Direction of the Holy Spirit' and all the Scottish bishops uniformly invoked 'the Holy and undivided Trinity' in all their official deeds and mandates at a time when this was not a common practice in the Church of England. Ordination in the Scottish Episcopal Church was seen as a 'separation' by the Holy Spirit to the charism of 'Watchman for our Souls' and the sacraments, including Holy Unction, were described as 'the Holy Mysteries'. There is evidence that even at the turn of the nineteenth century congregations were taught that 'bodily prostrations, reverential gestures ... lifting up hands or eyes to Heaven' were 'natural signs of Elevation of heart and soul' and evidence of a desire to do 'all that we can to give God the Honour due to his Holy Name' seeing that men and women received their whole being 'Soul and Body' from Him and as such were redeemed and made 'Partakers of his Mercies'; soul and body keeping pace together in their devotions. This 'awful Reverend Demeanour in the worship of God', Alexander Christie told his congregation in 1784, 'as it is most due to his infinite Majesty, so it is also useful to ourselves, as it helps to warm and increase our devotions to Him'.[39] Similarly with the English Nonjurors, William Law stressed the consecrating Spirit as the source of ministerial authority in his *Second Letter to the Bishop of Bangor* in 1718. All sacerdotal power, said Law, 'is derived from the Holy Ghost, as Christ was consecrated in the Spirit before He began his ministry'.[40]

The theological backdrop to English and Scottish Nonjuring charismatic attitudes of worship alike was a consistent Trinity centredness. This is found at its most systematic in the writings of John Skinner the elder, the closest to a *starets* that the eighteenth-century Scottish Episcopal Church had. Skinner, who like all his co-religionists, was excluded from the Scottish universities, had a 'sovereign contempt' for 'natural religion' as it was there taught. He was suspicious even of Platonism, which he blamed for the theological strife of the fourth century and his own. He despaired of the way in which socinianism was now spreading both in England and Scotland. Philosophy when applied to Christianity, he said, was 'only a politer name for infidelity', and could do no more than busy itself with the 'mechanics of grace', making man a 'passive machine in the hands of nature. I think it no scorn to own myself, as a Christian, to be an active, a rational machine, in the hands of grace, working in me, in one sense, what nature worketh in another'. He was concerned to refute the mechanistic deistical model of divine intervention, which in his view amounted to no intervention at all. For him, Christianity was not 'a random accidental stroke, a sudden display only, some hundreds of years ago, of Divine power, but a preconcerted, well-ordered, constantly and uniformly carried on plan of wisdom and love, hid in a great measure from the sons of men, but opened up by degrees, and revealed unto the Church'.[41]

Skinner's affinity to the Greek Fathers was shown in his anti-Roman polemic. He confessed a simple and long tried method: wherever in doctrine or discipline his Church agreed with Rome it was always on 'names' of Greek derivation such as apostle, catholic, canon, anathema, ecclesiastical, episcopacy, presbyter, deacon, baptism, eucharist and such like. Where he differed from Rome, it was always over names of Latin derivation, such as indulgences, purgatory, supremacy, infallibility, sacraments, extreme unction, merits and transubstantiation. He located the Trinity primarily in Greek discourse and believed it to be essential to the 'right apprehension of every other Christian doctrine, and necessarily to be maintained, to the right discharge of every Christian duty'. The Church of the Old Dispensation 'had her shakar, her morning, twilight, greyness', and the Church of the New Dispensation 'now longs for, and expresses her faith of and in, that meridian brightness of light and illumination which she expected from her shepherd ...' That illumination was the life of the Trinity. In it the Church rested 'literally in brightness, in an everlasting noon, kept up by that true source and Father of lights, with whom is no parallax nor topic shadow.' Much influenced, like several High Church Anglicans of the day, by the writings of the Hebraist John Hutchinson and his preoccupation with typology, Skinner found the *shechinah* in the Church chiefly in the Eucharist wherein mankind was uniquely revealed in the image of God. He saw the Trinity prefigured in the Old Testament term *aleim* – 'engagers' that entered into a covenant for man's redemption. He writes of the 'seals of the covenant', citing Paul in 2 Corinthians 1:22 and Ephesians 1:13 on the 'earnest of the Spirit in our hearts' and St John on the servants of God 'sealed in their foreheads', finding here a clear indication of Chrismation of which western confirmation was in his view a degradation. Skinner's commonplace book makes it clear that his understanding of the procession of the Holy Spirit was Orthodox; he rejected the western tendency to accord the Spirit a subordinate role, although he declined to stand in judgement on the western Creed. To the Spirit the believer owed the regeneration of his nature and the sanctification of his soul. Through him the believer was empowered to every good work and to run the race with joy. Thus the Lord of hosts was not simply 'on our side' but 'one of us'. The Spirit was identified with the mixed chalice. Skinner declined to speculate further on the Eucharist. He simply believed that the words of the Saviour had to have a 'fixed and determinate meaning', albeit in 'incomprehensible words', words with which the Church had never dared to tamper. He was satisfied with the aphorism that it was the work of the Institutor, 'powerfully blessing', the work of the administrator, 'regularly dispensing' and the work of the partaker, 'nothing doubting'. In his *Dissertation of the Shechinah, or Divine Presence with the Church or People of God* (1753), Skinner stressed the importance of the *Urim* and *Thummin* of the Aaronic priesthood in the first Temple and the 'voice from heaven' or *Bathcol* in the second, noting Joel's prophecy, all pointing forward to Pentecost and the eucharistic sacrifice. The gifts of the Spirit, he admitted, had not always been present in the Church 'in such an eminent measure' as Joel's prophecy promised would be so, and yet they *had* been given 'in such measure as is useful for preserving the Church and warranting all its other spiritual administrations'. Outside the Eucharist the gifts would be given as occasion demanded, just as they had been under the Old Dispensation. The Scottish bishops asked Skinner to produce a plan for the training of ordinands. He responded by writing a *Dissertation on the Trinity*. The Rector of Wanstead in Essex, G. H. Glasse, having read it, wrote: 'I declare solemnly, that considering the circumstances in which it was written, the age of the venerable Author, his remoteness from the ordinary materials of information which access to public libraries may procure [Skinner lived in an isolated cottage in the midst of an uncultivated heath], the abstruse, and awful nature of his subject, and the ingenuity and specious sophistries of his opponents, ... that I believe the Manuscript in question, viewed in these lights, to be one of the most extraordinary efforts of the human mind which ever fell within my knowledge.' Skinner himself would have had a simple explanation in which his mental efforts played but a small part![42]

Such, then, was the background to the extraordinary Nonjuring approach to the Greek Church through its patriarchs.[43] We may now return to Archibald's extraordinary buttonholing of Archbishop Arsenios on his brief stopover in London in 1716.

Not discouraged by Arsenios's mercenary intent, Bishops Campbell, Collier and Spincks drew up a Concordat, dated 18 August 1716. It was signed by Campbell and Collier together with Bishop James Gadderar, another Scot. Spincks translated it into Greek but did not sign it himself because the other three wanted to adopt the Liturgy of St James and he was reluctant to abandon the Prayer Book.[44]

The senior Scottish bishop, Alexander Rose of Edinburgh, did not stand in the way of the negotiation although he made it clear that he did not think strict conformity in rites and usages was the best way of achieving true communion, especially when so many Orthodox rites were now associated in people's minds with Popery. Moreover, he thought the whole matter had been brought on too hastily.[45]

As already stated, Campbell thought union not 'impracticable'.[46] Neither he nor his fellow signatories disagreed entirely with Bishop Rose, for they wanted the Greeks to make liturgical allowances for the 'different Circumstances and Customs of Nations'.[47] But within days of the signing of the Protocol serious differences emerged among the signatories themselves, suggesting that Rose had been right in suggesting that the whole matter had been pushed too fast. Of course there had been a reason for the haste: Campbell, Gadderar and Collier had wanted a document in Arsenios's hands before he moved on. Arsenios obliged. He not only forwarded the document to the Greek patriarchs but he also took a copy with him to Russia and showed it to Peter the Great who was impressed and directed his senior clergy to send an encouraging provisional response, for which the Nonjurors thanked him.

The Greek response, although dated 12 April 1718, did not reach England until 1721 or 1722. The document states that it was determined 'in council assembled' of the clergy of Constantinople, yet it was signed by Samuel of Alexandria and Chryanthos of Jerusalem, which presumably means they were both in Constantinople when the British Protocol arrived. Who then was the moving force in the reply? To judge by the syntax it must have been Samuel (Capasoulis) because of the highly emotional first person singular in the response to Proposition 4 'on the eucharistic presence'. Samuel was highly politicized, as we have already had cause to see, and it is thought that at some stage in his career he made a secret submission to Rome. This might explain a certain degree of acidity in the response to the eucharistic question. A response, perhaps, of a cynic who knew which side his bread was buttered.[48]

Considering the uncompromising nature of parts of that response, the Nonjurors were remarkably upbeat in their rejoinder, in which they confidently averred that some agreement must eventually come because both the 'Catholic Remainder in Britain' and the 'Oriental Churches' both professed the authority ('determining rule') of the 'inspired Writings of the Old and New Testaments, as interpreted by the Primitive Fathers . . .'[49] Having said that, they boldly tackled the question of the Seven Ecumenical Councils in a way that only the 'purist' mentality which we have already seen the Nonjurors to possess could ever have contemplated. They took the Greek's insistence 'somewhat in abatement of regard', accepting the first six Councils in their declaration of faith, not seeing them, however, as having the level of 'Inspiration' of the Prophets, Evangelists and Apostles. They desired 'not to lye under any restraint imposed by the disciplinary Canons of those Councils'. As to the Seventh (II Nicaea), they could not assent to giving *dulia* 'to Angels or departed Saints', saying that the Jews did not worship angels even though it was angels who led them through the wilderness. Campbell and his colleagues had no difficulty in affirming that prayers of the living, together with the Eucharistic Sacrifice, were 'serviceable to the dead', for the improvement of their happiness during the interval 'between Death and the Resurrection', but they were uneasy about being forced into any more detailed statement about how this 'worked'. They wanted the patriarchs to produce a public exposition of the ninth article of II Nicaea in order to preclude all possibility of the 'Vulgar' being 'carried to symbolize too much with the custom of idolaters, without designing it, when venerating ikons'. Otherwise in Orthodox communion they might feel themselves less safe than the 'wise' among the present Orthodox.[50]

Such caution would have been unintelligible to the Greeks, as would the request that they declare 'by an express Article' that bishops as Christ's 'proper representatives and Vice-regents' were 'subject in Spirituals to no temporal Power on on Earth'. Here again we see the Nonjuring neurosis with Establishment raising its head: it came headlong into conflict with Orthodox prescriptivism. The Proposers seemed to have expected a simple response from the patriarchs. In fact the patriarchs neither agreed *simpliciter* nor disagreed, describing this particular request as 'obscure' and adding rather vaguely that 'all such things shall be settled, if the Union should be accomplished'.[51] The Orthodox had entirely failed to see the point which the Nonjurors were making.

Even less were they likely to see the point in the request the Church of Jerusalem be acknowledged 'the true Mother Church and Principal (sic) of ecclesiastical unity, whence all the other Churches have been derived, and to which, therefore, they owe a special regard'. The patriarchs took umbrage at such a disturbance of the 'the order of the five Patriarchal Thrones' as established by 'Orthodox Princes, and confirmed by Divine and Holy Synods'. For good measure they added – almost inconsequentially – that it would not be of 'any advantage or detriment to Religion' and was theologically indifferent. The Nonjurors innocently appended to their request about Jerusalem a scriptural quotation: 'but out of Zion shall go forth the law, and the word of the Lord from Jerusalem'. This was like a red rag to a bull. How arrogant, said the Greeks, for these barbarians, by quoting Scripture, to arrogate to themselves more wisdom and foresight than those who 'placed the thrones in their present order', almost as if these hierarchs had acted 'rashly and unadvisedly' – which God forbid, for they were 'divine men' who had the Spirit of the Lord. What the Nonjurors proposed for Jerusalem had, in the view of the Greeks, 'the face of an innovation'. The patriarchs hinted that it tended to the same effect as has been sought by the Bishop of Rome, namely to degrade them as a body. The only concession they could make was that, *if there was a union*, Jerusalem might have primacy over the Church in Britain. This did not please the Nonjurors as they had not wished so close a subservience![52]

Altogether, the Nonjurors had failed to allow for the immoveability of a prescriptive system of centuries' duration. They themselves had narrowly escaped the threat of extinction and renewed themselves by a re-examination of the Church of the Fathers. They believed therefore that all things were possible. But all things were *not* possible with the Greeks. In fact very little was possible which was not already in place.

The most potentially explosive issue remained that of the Eucharist. Confusion over whether the Greeks taught transubstantiation had, as we have seen, been sown by the diffuse and inconsistent reports of Basire, Rycaut and Smith, with Covel no doubt adding further to the confusion by word of mouth and epistolary comments of a cynical character. We have seen how delicate a matter it became during the Popish Plot controversy and how the Greek statement of 1691 could hardly have clarified matters in that atmosphere. This put the Nonjurors at a distinct disadvantage, although not on this specific matter. The patriarchs tried to warn them of baseless hidden fears with their own biblical aphorism: 'they were in great fear where no fear was', suggesting that they were entrapped in prickly fears bred in the Protestant North which clung to them 'like ivy to a tree'. The patriarchs were suspicious of the Nonjurors 'minimalism' for fear of what might lay behind it, so they themselves were not responding from a state of tranquillity. For them *adiaphora* in matters so close to the spiritual bone were unthinkable and almost verged on the blasphemous. They might well have had in mind the dictum of Eulogios of Alexandria: '. . . there is no room for condescension in matters of Orthodox Faith; economy can only rightly be displayed where dogma is not jeopardised'.[53] Unfortunately for the Nonjurors the patriarchs at that time were inclined to include under 'dogma' what their successors of the twentieth and twenty-first centuries might not. It was a bad time to expect the Orthodox to make fine distinctions.

What was actually at issue in this exchange had been confused by different readings. Lathbury adds to the confusion by only paraphrasing the patriarch's reply, thereby falling into the danger of accommodating it to his own nineteenth-century preoccupations. Williams is more helpful, giving the Nonjurors' own translation of the reply. In this version it runs as follows:

For to be against worshipping the Bread, which is consecrated and changed into the Body of Christ, is to be against worshipping our Lord Jesus Christ Himself, our Maker and Saviour. For what else is the sacrificial Bread after it is consecrated and transsubstantiated by the access of the Holy Spirit? Truly nothing less than the real Body of our Lord . . . Our Lord did not say, My Body is *in, or under, or with* this; but, *This is My Body*, shewing them the bread which lay in His hand. And, since the Shewbread of the Altar of the new Dispensation is changed into the Body of Christ, by the invocation and access of the Holy Spirit, and by the Prayer and blessing of the Priest in secret, the accidents only remaining immutable, which yet partake of the consecration; and the Bread after it is changed into, and made one with, the Body of Christ in Heaven, no longer subsisting under those accidents, that being then the property of the Lord's real Body; . . . therefore, when we draw near the

> Bread that is changed into the Body of Christ, and is so called upon the account of the visible accidents, we should say with Peter, I believe Lord, and confess that thou art truly the Christ, the Son of the Living God . . .

It is after this passage that the Shew-Bread of the New Dispensation is said to be 'changed, transformed, converted and transsubstantiated into the very precious and unspotted Body of our Lord'. The Bread becomes 'that which it was not before consecration'.[54]

The document cites Cyril of Jerusalem's First and Fifth *Catecheses* and Meletios Syrigus' *Treatise against the Luthero-Calvinists*, printed at Bucharest in 1690. It therefore itself becomes part of the theological confusion arising from the confessions of Peter Moghila and Dositheos. A crucial expression in this response which the Nonjurors with their purely textual knowledge of Orthodox liturgy could not evaluate, is 'and by the Prayer and blessing of the Priest in secret . . .' Generations of *sotto voce* recitation of key parts of the *anaphora* at considerable speed had created a pseudo-theatrical mystique which partially concealed the meaning of the text from the Orthodox themselves and confused an outsider for whom the whole text presented itself on the same level. Orthodox liturgical renewal in the twentieth century, especially the work of Father Alexander Schmemann on 'liturgical realism', has shown us how the Nonjurors and their Greek contemporaries were fated to be at cross-purposes. The sad fact was that seventeenth-century Greeks were not sufficiently familiar with their core of their own liturgical tradition. Parts of it had become detached and taken on a pseudo-life of their own. Anglicans like Stephens, Hickes and Collier, who steeped themselves in the textual tradition, were therefore in some sense more faithful to historic Orthodoxy than the patriarchs whose favour they sought. Yet neither they nor the patriarchs were able to stand back and see this in perspective.

There remain some important outstanding questions about this transaction. Firstly there is the question of whether all the terms were properly translated. But more importantly there is the position of the Patriarch Samuel. It had been noted that there were contemporary rumours that he had made a secret submission to Rome in order to cover himself against all eventualities in a state of things where all patriarchs were vulnerable to degradation by the Turks. He would not have been the first patriarch of his or immediately preceding generations to have an ambiguous relation with Rome. Like several of his predecessors, he had close contacts with the Jesuits who supplied him with literature from their Moldavian and Wallachian presses. It should be remembered that Thomas Smith had expressed grave doubts as to whether Orthodox statements based on such sources sufficiently expressed the *consensus fidelium* of Orthodoxy. In this Smith can now be seen to have been the most perceptive of the Anglican observers. Smith was no fanatic anti-Papist because he had an overpowering desire for the restoration of full Catholic communion and with it 'the blessings of true Christian Catholic peace . . .' He continued to the end of his life to have a keen interest in the life of the Roman Church, including the debate between the Archbishop of Cambrai (Fénelon) and the Bishop of Meaux (Bossuet) on 'mental devotion' and that between the Dominicans and the Jesuits over honours paid by the Chinese to Confucius. He happily translated the life of the Carmelite St Maria Magdalena Pazzi. At the same time he translated Orthodox hymns replete with traditional doctrine. He was familiar with that passage in Cyril of Jerusalem's twenty-third Lecture where he states: 'whatever the Holy Ghost has touched, is sanctified and changed'. Smith knew this to reflect the *epiclesis* of the Jerusalem Church in Cyril's own day. So we may safely regard his reservations as objectively intended.[55]

This is the appropriate moment to consider why Archibald Campbell and his colleagues won a more sympathetic hearing in St Petersburg than they did at Constantinople, so much so that one may reasonably speculate about the possible outcome in that quarter had Peter the Great not died at a crucial moment leaving his country and administration in huge confusion. Peter had first-hand experience of the Church of England from his time in England studying the science of shipbuilding. He rented the house of John Evelyn, a committed High Churchman. Professor James Cracraft sees significance also in the interest shown by Peter in Christian reunion while visiting Paris in 1717. On 14 June he paid a visit to the Sorbonne where he was pressed very hard by Gallican churchmen at odds with Rome to consider union between the French and Russian Churches. At first he seems to have been at a loss to know how to reply without making rash commitments. He made a self-deprecating remark about his being a 'mere soldier'. When pressed further he could not disguise his interest and said 'Ah, well, draw up a memoir for me on this matter, and hurry, for I am leaving soon. I promise that I will give it to the bishops of my country and will oblige them to reply to you.' It is clear that Peter was privately briefed by a priest while on his visit to the Sorbonne on the intermittent debate in the French Church over the authority of Pope Clement XI's bull *Unigenitus* condemning the so-called Jansenist theses found in Pasquier Quesnel's *Le Nouveau Testament, avec des reflexions morales*. The debate was most strongly pressed by the bishops who had signed the Gallican Articles of 1682. Cardinal Noailles in particular was opposed to the bull's reception in France and there was talk of schism. The memoir which was immediately drawn up on Peter's request had only one signatory who was not a known Gallican. In the event the issue was sidestepped. Two versions of a reply to the Memoir were prepared. Both made it clear that it would not be possible for the Russian Church to negotiate union unilaterally without the concurrence of the rest of the Orthodox Church; otherwise there might be a danger of breaking an existing union for the sake of forming a new one. But whereas the version sent immediately to Paris conceded the value of ongoing private conversations between theologians, a modified text, later published, forcefully insisted on the rightness of the Orthodox Tradition and argued that the Russian bishops were holding back not out of fear but out of humility, a humility which required the keeping of silence while there was no patriarch (or while the Greek patriarchs had not spoken – the text is unclear). It was as if the second text was being held in reserve in case the Gallicans tried to compromise the Tsar by publishing the exchange. It is likely also to have been linked with the mysterious appearance of an pseudonymous Latin treatise in Jena two years later, which argued that the French (read the Roman) and Russian Churches were irreconcilable. The probable author of this treatise was Stefan Yavorsky, the senior Russian Metropolitan, whom Peter made 'Guardian' of the vacant patriarchal throne on the death of Patriarch Adrian in 1700. Peter's closest confident on ecclesiastical affairs, Feofan Prokopovich, was of a different caste of mind from Yavorsky, but the most senior Metropolitan could not easily be sidelined. Hence a deliberate 'fudge', allowing the rigorist position to be published without attribution, thereby leaving the door open for any future negotiation while keeping the anti-ecumenists quiet. Yavorsky, a churchman not altogether untouched by that covert Romanism which stemmed from the publishing activities of Peter Moghila (Patriarch Dositheos was implacably hostile to him on this account but could not engineer his removal) might have felt the Jena treatise to be a sufficient shot across the bows of any attempt at a union with a Gallican schism and thereby a means of keeping his copybook clean with Rome, while Prokopovich could have felt that by this ruse future discussions were in no way compromised.[56]

If Feofan Prokopovich, Bishop of Pskov and Procurator of the Holy Synod in the prologued vacancy of the Patriarchate of Moscow, had such influence in the delicate relations between the Russian and French Churches, and if his signature appears on the reply of the Holy Synod to the Nonjurors' proposals, then it must be assumed that his understanding of what the Nonjurors were about was crucial to the general tenor of that reply. What then is known about him which might throw light on this question? It must be said that Feofan has had a very bad press from modern Russian Orthodox scholars, who with the wisdom of hindsight blame him for producing a rigid state control of the Church which led to widespread disillusionment among the nineteenth century-intelligentsia and so contributed to the Church's humiliation at the Revolution. Romantic images of the heroic, free and ill-fated Sobor of 1917–18 after the fall of the Tsar add to the feeling that something very evil was done to the Church under Peter the Great, and since Peter did not know any better a more ecclesiastical scapegoat must be found. Nicolas Zernov in 1962 and Dimitry Pospielovsky in 1998 both blame Feofan's crypto-Lutheranism. Pospielovsky claims in defence of this thesis that three quarters of the Bishop's library of 3,000 volumes consisted of 'Lutheran works' and that 'all his publications' amounting to seventy volumes were 'based on Lutheran works and concentrated on glorifying the power of the monarch, stressing the mystical powers of the monarchy, while denigrating and demystifying the episcopate.' It is known that after Peter's death there was a strong reaction against Feofan among the higher clergy and that even earlier 'the Kievan professors at the Moscow Academy, Archiman-drites Feofilakt Lopatinksii and Gedeon Vishnevskii, together with Metropolitan Yavorskii submitted a written protest to Peter which delayed the consecration of Prokopovich for two years'. Pospielovsky concedes that Feofan did not himself wish to be advanced to the episcopate but contrives within his framework to make even this appear suspect by adding that in a letter to a friend at the Kiev Academy Feofan confessed that he disliked the vestments, rituals and ceremonies associated with the episcopate.[57]

It may appear rash for a British Orthodox church historian specialized in Anglicanism and without access to Russian church archives, to question the judgement of Russian scholars, but this particular English church historian finds something very simplistic in the Zernov-Pospielovsky under-standing of Lutheranism which leads to a suspicion that more is being read into Feofan's possession and use of Lutheran works than is justified. In any case, whether those who resented him properly understood Feofan's role with the Tsar may be open to question. Although on the surface the Bishop appears responsible with Peter for the *Ecclesiastical Regula-tion* of 1721 which proved in due course to preclude the election of any future patriarch (although the abandonment of the patriarchate was not even hinted at the time), the facts equally alow the supposition that Feofan used his position of trust to moderate the state centralism of Peter as it already impinged in practice on the Church and which Peter clearly intended to set in stone after the model of the English Royal Supremacy but with a heavier hand. Feofan's own rough drafts for the *Regulation* are suggestive of this where he proposes a view of episcopal authority in a pastoral rather than a juridical mode which would have earned the full approval of the most purist of the Nonjurors: 'Every bishop should be aware of the measure of his dignity and should not think too highly of it. For the work is indeed great; but in Scripture no high honour is ascribed to this dignity: thus the Apostle, demolishing the Corinthians' inflated opinion of their pastors, states that the pastoral work owes the whole of its success and its fruits to God himself working in the hearts of men ("I planted, Apollos watered, but God gave the growth") . . . In the same place, pastors are called merely the stewards of God and stewards of his mysteries, which they will be if they faithfully abide in that work . . . God commands that good presbyters be considered worthy of double honour, especially those who labour in teaching and preaching (1 Timothy 5). Yet such honour is to be moderate, and not excessive and considered equal to the Tsar's . . .'[58] Here we see a great deal of subtlety; he is stating the irreducible doctrine of Christian *episkope* while doing honour to an Emperor who might be tempted to model himself more on Prussian or Swedish monarchy than on the age-old concept of the consecrated Byzantine *basileus*. Orthodox bishops throughout the history of the Church have not been immune to delusions of grandeur. There were indeed those like Archpriest Avakkum who thus accused Patriarch Nikon of recent memory. Priest Feofan would not have been the first, and is certainly not likely to be the last, to wonder if the Byzantine ceremonial attached to the bishop might obscure rather than enhance the essential nature of *episkope* as the pre-Constantinian Fathers understood it.

To have that degree of subtlety in so traditional a society as

seventeenth-century Muscovy required an unusual background, one more akin to that of contemporary Anglican
divines. Feofan was born into one of the small but indepen-
dent-minded mercantile families. He therefore had access to
the best available education. Initially this meant the Theological Academy at Kiev. Kiev and its Academy (founded by
Peter Moghila) was in the Polish sphere of influence until the
end of the Polish-Russian war in 1667. Its incorporation into
Russian territory had the effect of intruding a crypto-Latin
virus into the Russian Church which was not there before.
Prior to Moghila, Kiev had been a centre of resistance to
Uniatism and Roman thinking. In Feofan's day it provided a
broad boarding-school education leading up to the licentiate or
baccalaureate level. Moghila's decision to make Latin the
medium of instruction was fraught with problems. Ostensibly
it was because the old Slavic-Greek medium of teaching
lacked sophistication and subtlety. But imperceptibly it undermined Orthodox morale and the reading which was made
possible in the writings of the opponents of Orthodoxy led to
a weakening of the nuances of Orthodox Tradition for all but
the strongest-minded student.[59] That said, the Kiev Academy
turned out better educated graduates than other schools and it
is scarcely surprising that when Peter the Great decided to
leave the Patriarchate vacant and control the Church through
a Holy Governing Synod, he packed that synod with Ukraini-
ans, among whom was Feofan Prokopovich.

Moghila's princely scholasticism owed as much to his residence in Paris as to either Italy or nearby Jesuit Poland.[60] So
Prokopovich may have had his first taste of Western literature
and culture while at the Academy and this may have spurred
him on to self-directed studies in Italy. Cartesian philosophy
was in fact widely taught in the French-staffed Jesuit colleges
in the Balkans, so the western mindset might not have been all
that easy to avoid if one had his enquiring mind. In due course
Feofan returned from his studies in Italy no more convinced
of Roman scholasticism than before but with a mind wide
open to a radical new curriculum (not exclusively theological)
for the Academy whose staff he now joined. He left to

posterity a vast number of manuscripts. Pending a full scholarly appraisal, one can only speculate about quite how
comprehensive was his western learning. We know of his
interests in western mathematics, science and philosophy. But
did he have a firm view on western styles in church music
deriving from Giovanni Gabrieli, Monteverdi, Rigatta and
Rovetta which were slowly seeping through Eastern Europe
via Kaspar Forster, Adam Jarzebsky, Mikolaj Zielinski,
Martin Mielczewski and Barttomeij Pekiel? Nikolai Diletsky
was cultivating such music at Kiev and it was to be found in
other centres including Moscow wherever members of the
aristocracy had the money to pay for it. Foreign forms of
church music and the psychology that went with them were
not widely popular among the Russian clergy for whom Diletsky's idea of free composition as the fancy took one, without
reference to the ancient modes, was an example of dangerous
self-will which not only produced naive and shallow music,
impoverished beside the treasury of Slavo-Byzantine chant,
but introduced even in some of the churches of Moscow
according to one critic a 'Latin' habit of arm-waving and foot-
tapping to the rhythm of the organ accompaniment which was
alien to the spirit of Orthodox *ascesis*.[61] If Feofan had in any
way discovered, even at second hand from a sympathetic
advocate, the 'purer' style of Anglican cathedral music, his
sympathies could have been propelled in the Nonjurors' direction on a rebound against the 'popish' superficiality and 'idolatry' which he saw infiltrating the Church through the medium
of music, especially since the Gallican wing of the French
Church at that time was also complaining bitterly that the new
'Italian' style of church music was transforming 'into an entertainment that which has been created for no other purpose than
to produce in the Christian soul a holy and salutary sadness'.
The Parisian priest who made this comment objected to the
prostitution of even the 'Leçons de Tenèbres' which in his
view should only be sung on the Gregorian lamentation tone
and not by singers used to operatic arias and 'airs de cour'.[62]

This is enough of attractive but as yet unconfirmed specu-
lation. There are more substantive factors which also point to

a possible bias in favour of the Nonjurors on the part of the Procurator. Feofan belonged to the first generation of clergy after the liturgical reforms of Patriarch Nikon which included the abandonment of a rigid requirement for Christian converts to Orthodoxy to be rebaptized.[63] This marked a significant difference within the Orthodox family for the Greeks continued to insist on rebaptism. The Nonjurors are unlikely to have known of this difference, but for Feofan it could have been an incentive for him to treat the Nonjurors' proposal in an encouraging manner and to suggest to Thomas Brett that the Holy Synod might allow some latitude on canonical matters so long as the Nonjurors did not insist on rejecting Russian usage on principle.[64] This was particularly relevant in the matter of their wish to see Jerusalem as the prime patriarchate. In his ecclesiastical reforms Nikon had tried to follow the custom of the Church of Jerusalem.[65] An English translation by J. T. Philipps, of a 'Russian Catechism' was published in London in 1725. The timing was critical, although Bishop Kallistos is inclined to attribute the authorship to Yavorsky rather than Prokopovich.

One tantalizing question remains for Feofan researchers to elucidate. Did he read the Latin version of Thomas Smith's book on the Greek Church? If so, did he realize that Smith was after 1688 a Nonjuror and advising his brethren on matters Orthodox? Further, is there any record in Feofan's hand of his reaction to their proposal of a two-stage reunion: first a concordat allowing margins of variance in usage; then, in the fullness of time, 'A firm and perfect union'? The Nonjurors recognized that such an arrangement would be testing: they were not naive. It would require 'some limitations and indulgences on both sides', the drawing up of a new Liturgy 'compiled out of the Greek Liturgies' but with a few 'passages and rites' omitted. Though this might give offence to rigorists on both sides, those truly concerned for unity should find it 'unexceptionable' and even the Orthodox living in Britain might be persuaded to adapt the new rite for the healing of Christendom. Words of this sort, which would have been either meaningless or offensive to Greeks, might have found a lodging in a mind such as Feofan's which had seen considerable liturgical reform already.

How far could Feofan have gone without coming up against Greek intransigence? The historical record of the seventeenth century does not suggest that there was a set pattern of exchange between the two Churches. There was, of course, a stream of individual churchmen from the Orthodox East to Moscow, often bearing with them gifts. Monks from the Iviron Monastery on Mount Athos visited in the 1640s with a precious ikon: in return the monastery obtained special status in Moscow. In 1651 a particle of the Holy Wood was sent by Protosynkellos Gabriel of Jerusalem who two years later travelled in person to Moscow with the miracle-working ikon of Our Lady of Blachernae and a letter from Patriarch Paisios and his synod on its history and efficacy. In this way, incrementally, an impressive collection of ikons, sacramental vessels and vestments translated from Greek lands to Russian. But these courtesies were not without a political justification. Gabriel, who was well known to the Tsar's administration, acted as the Tsar's representative in Constantinople. Many Greek visitors to Moscow were there to persuade the Russian Empire to overthrow the Ottoman, especially during the long Venetian-Turkish war when it really did seem that Constantinople might at last be redeemable in a huge Greco-Russian Empire. Established Patriarchs, Cyril Lucaris and Athanasius Patelaros, gave their names to this appeal. The diplomatic correspondence is enormous, most of it addressed to the 'Prikaz' or Ministry of Embassies though written by ecclesiastics. Tsar Mikail and Patriarch Filaret were bombarded with details of the condition of the Porte. In November 1653 Athanasios Patelaros presented an 'urgent oration' to Tsar Alexei on the need to take immediate advantage of the Turkish 'decay' and occupy the throne of Constantine the Great. Christians, he said, must be relieved from the 'yoke of the Hagerons'. A clear connection was drawn between this appeal and the presentation of the ikon of Our Lady of Blachernae. A similar appeal was made in 1656 by Gerasimos Vlachos, leader of the Greek community in Venice. But these are extraordinary occurrences. The Greek church leadership had the respect and veneration of ordinary Russians – Cyril Lucaris especially. But after Patriarch Theophanes of Jerusalem played a hands-on role in restoring church order following the 'Time of Tumults' on behalf of Lucaris, the Greek Hierarchs for the most part left the Russian Church to itself. But when they *did* intervene, untypically, during Nikon's patriarchate, their intervention had destructive repercussions. Paisios Ligarides, who arrived either with Dositheos's authority or with his connivance, ostensibly to help Nikon with the revision of the service books, dazzled the Tsar with his 'prophetic gifts', obtained leave to invite Macarios of Antioch and Paisios of Alexandria to Moscow and after Nikon had followed Macarios' advice, contrived to get the Russian Patriarch deprived and deposed by a Church Council, only to be himself subsequently excommunicated by Dositheos, who deeply disapproved of Nikon's disposition and Ligarides' part in it.

The maverick role of John Sakutis, secretary to Patriarch Macarios, and of Archbishop Cyril Vestarchos of the New Monastery of Chios undermined Dositheos irenic efforts. Father Paul Meyendorff detects a certain cynical humouring of Nikon on the part of Macarios, perhaps because he did not take the implications of the reforms seriously enough. Neither he nor Patriarch Paisios offered Nikon anything like a liturgical blueprint, assuring him that *complete* unity was necessary only in matters of faith. While Macarios was impressed by what the Russian Patriarch said about the superiority of 'all things Greek' and the way he constantly spoke of his brother patriarch as 'our teacher', Paisios seems to have held back for fear that if he did anything which might fan unintelligible Russian divisions, he might not later be able to cool them down at a distance. After this, the Greek Hierarchs prudently kept their distance, and, impotent to do anything about Peter's abolition of the Moscow Patriarchate, endured the humiliation of having to address the new Holy Governing Synod as 'Beloved Brother in Christ', for the depressingly usual reason that they needed Russian cash to fend off the Turks. (Was this perhaps the reason why Macarios agreed to go to Moscow in the first place?)[66]

If a concordat had been reached with the Nonjurors, the Holy Synod would have needed to inform Constantinople: this much is clear from the reply sent to the Sorbonne in 1717. But after the depressing effects of the Nikon affair, the Greeks would not have been expected, nor indeed wanted, to take part in the preliminary discussions, nor would the Holy Synod have necessarily asked the Patriarch of Constantinople whether he had written to the Nonjurors and if so in what terms. Union could easily have been a *fait accomplis* on the Russian side with the Nonjurors pressurized to greater conformity after the event, with the easy concurrence of the Greeks.

How much the Nonjurors knew of the schism which followed Nikon's liturgical reforms it is difficult to say. Their main sources on Orthodoxy were Greek. But the way in which they stressed in their proposals that 'truth and right do not depend on numbers' may have been a coded way of saying that they knew the Russian Church faced the same dangers which had almost destroyed the Church of England.

Promising though the Russian contact may have seemed for a while, once Peter the Great had left the scene and Feofan's enemies had 'ganged up' on him, the interest shown became purely speculative, although the publication of the Feofan Confession in England in 1725 may suggest that it took some time for the truth to sink in.[67]

From the standpoint of today, after half a century of accommodation of rites, including even 'Western Rite' Orthodox Liturgies as a concession to those converts who, like Sparrow Simpson and some in the Anglo-Orthodox Society, found Eastern prayer too 'fulsome', the Nonjurors' project might seem reasonable. But it was too close to the Reformation and too suggestive of 'Jesuit' blandishments to give the Greeks of that time any degree of assurance. A comparison between their long-drawn-out negotiations and the Concordat between the Coptic Patriarchate and the British Orthodox Church in 1994 – the fruit of a mere six months of negotiation by letter, e-mail, telephone and flying visits – prompts feelings of some sadness, especially when it is considered that the 1994 union was achieved on the basis of the Liturgy of St James for which many of the Nonjurors fought in vain. The 1994 Concordat was not without its deficiencies both in the negotiations themselves and in the aftermath. Even in the twentieth century it was possible to conceal both facts and intentions on both sides of a negotiation, and language and culture remained a barrier to full and open exchange. Nevertheless, had the means of rapid communication of the last century been available to the Nonjurors, what might they not have achieved with a clear conscience?

The Nonjurors' efforts were probably already dead in the water before Archbishop Wake added the *coup de grace.* Smarting from their successful public exposure of Bishop Hoadley's heresies, Wake determined to act against them and wrote to the Orthodox patriarchs denouncing them as imposters and schismatics. Wake's intervention not only put the final dampener on the project but also, albeit indirectly, in the opinion of Bishop Kallistos, destroyed what little interest in Orthodox that remained in the main Anglican body, so that throughout the eighteenth century, in spite of the conversion of Lord Guilford and the curiously isolated study of the Slavonic service books by John Glen King in the 1770s, there was little impetus to reviving it until the Napoleonic Wars threw the Eastern Mediterranean open to a wider English public and the Romantic movement (notably in the person of Lord Byron) made the fate of Greece a matter of public interest for English readers. In that newly fertilized soil John Mason Neale was to strike his plough.[68]

All, however, was not lost entirely in the meantime. The affair did have a salutory effect on the devotional life of English Nonjurors right up to their extinction at the turn of the nineteenth century, and there was a longer-term effect on the Scottish Episcopal Church which was not dissipated until the latter half of the twentieth century when the 'Piskies' finally lost their distinctive identity in World Anglicanism.

On the Orthodox side also there was a little gain. The patriarchs were not impressed by Nonjuror references to the First

Edwardine Prayer Book as the 'most-ancient English Liturgy
. . . approaching the manner of the Oriental Church'; but they
were pleased by the willingness shown by Anglicans to read
translations of the Fathers and their Liturgies and even quote
them in the original Greek.[69]

Even before the reply of the patriarchs was received,
Campbell and Gadderar pressed on with the preparation of a
new Liturgy and secured compromises with other Scottish
bishops which allowed the informal use of the mixed chalice.
The patriarchs' response if anything speeded up this process
and the desire to vindicate the Nonjuring position by the adop-
tion of the Liturgy of St James as the Liturgy of the Mother
Church of Christendom. The Nonjurors were too scholarly not
to know that the patriarchs' identification of the Jerusalem
Liturgy with the Apostle James was simplistic. Nevertheless,
they used St James hereafter as a yardstick as well as a more
manageable form of worship than St John Chrysostom and St
Basil in the straightened circumstances of the Scottish Church.
Although the Scottish Church could not hold on to that
Liturgy, even as a permissive form, in the long term, their
struggle for it and their own efforts at vindication as the
surviving legitimate representative of the 'Orthodox Church of
Britain' in the northern Kingdom did ensure through historical memory that into the twenty-first century the Liturgy of St
James would be used somewhere in Britain and have its effect
in mediating Orthodox values.

Notes

1. George Williams, *The Orthodox Church of the East in the Eighteenth Century, Being the Correspondence between the Eastern
   Patriarchs and the Nonjuring Bishops* (London, Oxford and
   Cambridge, 1868), p. 6.
2. Thomas Lathbury, *A History of the Nonjurors* (London, 1843),
   pp. 323–6; Timothy Ware, (Bishop Kallistos of Diokleia), *The
   Orthodox Church* (London, 1963), p. 109.
3. Lathbury, ibid.
4. 'The Jolly Kist', Scottish Episcopal Archives, Edinburgh.
5. Harleian MS 3778, f.111, Bodleian Library, Oxford; Wanley to
   Covel, 21 December 1714, Add. MS 22911, f.163, BL. This is

what was known or imagined by the Anglican leadership: 'Garisimos, Patriarch of Alexandria, being between 80 & 90 years old, resigns his Patriarchate into the hands of his People, that he might go to Monte-Santo [Athos], and there end his days. The People thereupon Elect Samuel Archbishop of Libya in his Room, but Cosmos Archbishop of Mount Sinai by Money obtaining the Favor of the present Grand Vizir, the Church of Alexandria is so much oppressed, they send hither Arsenius, Metropolite of Thebais, with Gennadios a Cypriot & Archimandrite & Kathegumenos at Alexandria . . . to crave the Relief and Assistance of good Christians' Add. MS 22911, f.163v. One can only conclude from Wanley's supercilious tone that the Bishop of London had reason to doubt Arsenios' motives.

6. Laurence was an extreme Prayer Book legalist. He insisted on his own rebaptism because his original baptism was 'lay' and therefore in his eyes 'illegal' if not invalid. Not all his colleagues appreciated this stance. He proved to be a bitter controversialist, giving no quarter. Later he refused to adopt the phil-Orthodox Usages simply because they were not 'permitted' by the 'Established Liturgy'. See Lathbury, op. cit., p. 310, citing Thomas Brett's memorandum, 30 March 1728, also Henry Broxap, *The Later Nonjurors* (Cambridge, 1924), p. 27. Broxap characterizes Laurence as wanting in restraint and good taste.

7. For an illustration of the constant threat of violence against Nonjuring meetings for worship, see Thomas Wagstaffe the Younger to Thomas Brett, 20 October 1716, Brett MSS, II, f.305, Bodleian Library, concerning a raid on a service in Scroop's Court. See also Smith to the Earl of Yarmouth, 6 June 1689, Smith MS 66, f.119.

8. For George Hickes' comment, see his tract *The Constitution of the Catholic Church and the Nature and Consequences of Schism* (n. p., 1716), pp. 32–33.

9. Edmund Chishull, *A Charge of Heresy, Maintained against Mr Dodwell's late Epistolary Discourse concerning the Mortality of the Soul* (London, 1706, pp. 3, 15, 19, 23; Smith to Hickes, especially 7 November 1695 and 27 June 1696, Smith MS 63, ff.112–14; Smith to the Earl of Yarmouth, 6 June 1689, Smith MS 66, f.119; Edmund Elys to Smith, 12 May 1702, Smith MS 49, f.233; James Eckershall to Smith, 10 October 1693, Smith MS 49, ff.197–8.

10. Middleton, op. cit., p. 152, citing Henry Hammond's *Of the Power of the Keys; or Of Binding and Loosing* (1647); Smith MS 49, f.233; Dodwell to Smith, 30 August and 8 November 1697; ibid., f.153; Edmund Elys to Smith, 18 June 1690, ibid.,

f.213; also Roger Turner, 'Bonds of Discord Alternative Episcopal Oversight Examined in the Light of the Nonjuring Consecrations', *Ecclesiastical Law Journal*, 3 (1995), 403.

11. W. Jardine Grisbrooke, *Anglican Liturgies of the Seventeenth
and Eighteenth Centuries*, Alcuin Club, *XI* (London, 1958),
p. 134.

12. See, for instance, Norman Sievewright's *A Preservative against
Innovations in Politics and Society* (London, 1767), passim;
William Jones, 'The Life of Dr Horne' in Jones, *Collected
Works*, XII; also Bishop Gordon to Bishop Kilgour, 6 March
1777 (copy), Ep. MS 1146, Scottish Episcopal Archives.

13. H. H. Henson, *The Relation of the Church of England to the
Other Reformed Churches* (Edinburgh, 1911), p. 77.

14. Jeremy Collier, *Reasons for Restoring Some of the Prayers and
Directions as they stand in the Communion Service of the First
English Reformed Liturgy* (London, 1717), p. 37; W. J.
Sparrow Simpson, *The Prayer of Consecration* (London and
Milwaukee, 1917), pp. 92–95, citing Thomas Wilson's *Sacra
Privata*.

15. Ibid., pp. 92–95, citing Stephens's *Collection of Tracts and
Papers* (1702).

16. Grisbrooke, op. cit., pp. 37, 54; Sparrow Simpson, ibid., pp.
92–94; Rawlinson MS 564 (23), Bodleian Library.

17. Cf. his *Dissertations upon St Cyprian* (1682).

18. Cf. 'The Doctrine of the Church of England concerning the
Independence of the Clergy' in *Spirituals and Paraenesis
concerning the late English Schism* (1704). See the article on
Dodwell by J. H. Overton in the *Dictionary of National Biography*. Dodwell's work on the mortality of the soul took the
form of a commentary on Justin Martyr, buttressed with later
Fathers.

19. Dodwell to Smith, 30 August 1697, Smith MS 46.

20. Smith was on good terms with Chishull and is likely to have
advised him when Chishull went to Smyrna as chaplain. Cf.
Smith to Thomas Hudson, Smith MS 63, f.36v.

21. Broxap, op. cit., p. 33; Edmund Chishull, *A Charge of Heresy*,
op. cit., p. [iii] and passim; also his *The Orthodoxy of an
English Clergy-Man* (London, 1711), pp. 9, 13, 18–19.

22. *A Charge of Heresy*, op. cit., p. [ii].

23. Ibid., pp. 17–18. The 'soul' controversy was therefore compli-
cated by the High Church-Latitudinarian battle over episcopacy.
Thus Chishull, *A Charge*, p. [vi]. For a curious Victorian
commentary on Dodwell and the lay baptism controversy which
totally fails to see the trinitarian and pneumatological dimen-
sion, see Thomas Debary, *A History of the Church of England*

from the Accession of James II to the Rise of the Bangorian Controversy in 1717 (London, 1860), pp. 426–9.

24. Dodwell, *Immortality Preternatural to Human Souls, The Gift of Jesus Christ, Collated by the Holy Spirit in Baptism ... by a Presbyter of the Church of England* (London, 1708), p. 2.

25. Cf. George Grub, *An Ecclesiastical History of Scotland* (Edinburgh, 1861), pp. iv, 16.

26. Sparrow Simpson, op. cit., p. 62.

27. *The Ancient Liturgy of the Church of Jerusalem. Being the Liturgy of St James, Freed from all the Later Additions and Interpolations of whatsoever kind, and so restored to its Original Purity* (London, 1744).

28. Archibald Campbell, *The Middle State* (1721), cited by Sparrow Simpson, op. cit., pp. 70–71. Campbell specifically wished this because it would have allowed for 'a proper and propitiatory Sacrifice'.

29. See especially J. Pitts, *The Holy Spirit the Author of Immortality. By a Presbyter of the Church of England* (London, 1708), pp. 112–19, citing Athanasios, Cyril of Alexandria, Gregory Nazianzen, John Chrysostom, Theodoret of Cyrus and the *Macarian Homilies*.

30. Collier, *Reasons*, op. cit., pp. 25–26; also *Defence of the Reasons*, p. 103. Cf. Sparrow Simpson's comments, op. cit., pp. 71, 74.

31. John Johnson, 'On Sacrifice' in his *Works*, I (Library of Anglo-Catholic Theology, Oxford, 1847), p. 17.

32. Thomas Brett, *Dissertation on Liturgies*, cited by Sparrow Simpson, op. cit., pp. 65–66.

33. Rattray, *Some Remarks on the Circular Letter of the Edinburgh Bishops* (1723), cited by Thomas Stephen, *The History of the Church of Scotland from the Reformation to the Present Time*, IV (London, 1845), p. 192.

34. Cf. J. M. Neale, *The Life and Times of Patrick Torry, D.D.* (London, 1856), pp. 34–35.

35. Williams, op. cit., p. 98. Cf. C. W. Dugmore, *Eucharistic Doctrine in the Church of England from Hooker to Waterland* (London, 1942), p. 148.

36. *The Ancient Liturgy of the Church of Jerusalem*, op. cit., p. xi.

37. Gunter Thomann, *Studies in English Church History* (2nd edn., Stoke-on-Trent, 1993), p. 134.

38. Sparrow Simpson, op. cit., p. 98.

39. James Walker, *The Conditions and Duties of a Tolerated Church* (Edinburgh, 1806), pp. 28–29; address of Bishop Kilgour to the presbyters of the Diocese of Aberdeen, 29 August 1782, Episcopal MS 26, Scottish Record Office; example of deed of elec-

tion – that of Alexander Jolly 1798, Episcopal MS 2190; James Christie to John Dowden, 20 December 1886, Dowden Papers, 171/3, National Library of Scotland; Petition to the Reverend James Taylor of Thurso, 5 August 1733, *Craven Papers*, Episcopal MS 2174; Joint Letter of the Scottish bishops to Bishop Robert Gordon, 17 April 1777 (copy), Episcopal MS 1142; Alexander Christie, MS sermon for the 11th Sunday after Trinity 1784 (given again by Christie on the 13th Sunday after Trinity 1802), Episcopal MS 2167.

40. Cited by A. Keith Walker, *William Law, His Life and Thought* (London, 1973), p. 23.

41. *The Theological Works of the Late Rev John Skinner*, I (Aberdeen, 1809), pp. 91, 96–97, 101–2, 105–7, 113, 132, 135, 198–9, 345–6, 383, 409–10; II, 297.

42. Ibid., I, pp. cxliv–v, cl, 20–21, 28–29, 36–37, 52–54, 74–75, 137–42, 154, 157ff, 227, 230, 233, 248–9, 250–1, 327; II, 13–14, 18–20, 71ff, 105, 108–14, 176–7, 204, 243, 246–7, 397–400.

43. Readers are warned that the cursory treatment of these negotiations by Archbishop Methodios Fouyas in his book *Orthodoxy, Roman Catholicism and Anglicanism* (London, 1972), p. 37, shows little sign of familiarity with the texts or the context and that his conclusions are therefore inevitably simplistic. The same may be said of Nicolas Zernov's characterization of the negotiations in his *Eastern Christendom* (London, 1961), p. 159.

44. Cf. W. Walker, *The Life of the Right Reverend Alexander Jolly and the Right Reverend George Gleig*, (Edinburgh, 1806), p. 270. Cf. Rowan Strong, *Alexander Forbes of Brechin* (Oxford, 1995), p. 90.

45. Rose doubted if 'the people' would ever accept prayers for the dead.

46. Quoted by Thomas Brett in a letter to Bishop George Smith, 30 April 1730, Scottish Episcopal Archives. Cf. Broxap, op. cit., p. 31.

47. Lathbury, op. cit., p. 312.

48. Ibid., p. 235; Runciman, *The Great Church in Captivity*, op. cit., pp. 310, 381n.

49. Williams, op. cit., p. 84.

50. Reply of 29 May 1722, Lathbury, op. cit., pp. 316–17, 327.

51. Ibid., pp. 314, 322.

52. Ibid., pp. 219–33, 311, 327.

53. *Patrologia Graeca*, 103, 953.

54. Williams, op. cit., pp. 57–58.

55. Cf. Thomas Smith, *An Account*, op. cit., p. 159; Smith to George Hickes, 21 June 1704, Smith MS 63, f.28; Smith to

Archbishop Narcissus Marsh of Dublin, 14 February 1698–99 and 23 January 1700–01, Smith MS64, ff.182, 194.

56. James Cracraft, *The Church Reform of Peter the Great* (London, 1971), pp. 37–49; Cf. Marc Szeftel, 'Church and State in Imperial Russia' in Robert L. Nichols and Theofanis George Stavrou (eds), *Russian Orthodoxy under the Old Regime* (Minneapolis, 1978), p. 130. For Dositheos's hostility to Stefan Yavorsky, see George A. Maloney, SJ, *A History of Orthodox Theology Since 1453*, op. cit., p. 152.

57. James W. Cunningham, 'Reform Projects of the Russian Orthodox Church at the Beginning of the XXth Century' in J. Breck, J. Meyendorff and E. Silk (eds), *The Legacy of St Vladimir* (Crestwood NY, 1970), p. 156; Dimitry V. Pospielovsky, *The Orthodox Church in the History of Russia* (Crestwood NY, 1998), pp. 16, 109ff.

58. Cracraft, op. cit., pp. 227–8.

59. Cf. Hugh F. Graham, 'Peter Moghila – Metropolitan of Kiev', *The Russian Review* (1955), pp. 345–6; George W. Simpson, 'Peter Mohyla: Ecclesiastic and Educator', *Ukrainian Quarterly*, 3 (1946–47), 242ff. Cf. Zernov, *Eastern Christendom*, op. cit., pp. 148–9.

60. Cf. William H. McNeill, *Venice*, op. cit., p. 233. The reason why Moghila was able to spend so much time in Paris is that he was the son of a Moldavian prince and so had no problem of financing himself.

61. See Vladimir Morosan, 'Liturgical Singing or Sacred Music? Understanding the Aesthetic of the New Russian Choral Music', in Breck, Meyendorff and Silk, op. cit., pp. 72–73, citing Antonin Preobrazhensky.

62. See Jury Serach, 'On Teofan Prokopovich as Writer and Preacher in his Kiev period', *Harvard Slavic Studies*, II (1954), pp. 211–23. The anonymous priest, like some seventeenth-century John Tavener, objected to turning lamentation into importunity. Tavener criticizes Beethoven's *Missa Solemnis* for the same thing. Cf. René Jacobs's notes to his Concerto Vocale recording of Marc Antoine Charpentier's 'Leçons de Ténèbres du Jeudi Saint' (Arles, 1978). Lyons was probably not alone among French cities at that time in having its parish churches denied the use of an organ so that the Gregorian chant might stand in its purity.

63. Paul Meyendorff, *Russia, Ritual and Reform. The Liturgical Reforms of Nikon in the 17th Century* (Crestwood NY, 1991), pp. 62–63.

64. Note by Brett in Brett MS XVIII, f.85, Bodleian Eng. Theol. C.MSS, cited in Broxap, op. cit., p. 33.

65. McNeill, op. cit., p. 236.
66. Paul Meyendorff, op. cit., pp. 47–62; G. V. Popov (ed.), *Greek Documents and Manuscripts, Icons and Applied Art Objects from Moscow Depositories* (International Conference 'Crete, East Mediterranean and Russia in 17th c.', Moscow 1995), passim. The Greeks failed to grasp the class system in Russia or to understand that both Nikon and Archpriest Avvacum represented a popular reform movement but were divided on the proper mode of renewal which would embrace both the monarchy and the boyars. Dositheos, who as secretary to Patriarch Nectarios and Exarch in Romania had long-term interests in Russia and understood the situation best among the Greek patriarchs, acceded to Tsar Feodor's plea that the anathemas against Nikon be lifted. He continued throughout his patriarchate to promote a printing house in Moscow run by expatriate Greeks as a means of combatting Roman polemic and in the 1680s sent two Greek scholars familiar with the schools of Venice and Padua, the brothers Ionnikios and Sophronios Likhoudes, to further the work, building on the earlier work of Gabriel Vlasios. It was not only Dositheos who repudiated Paisios Ligarides after the damage which he did to the Moscow Patriarchate. Patriarch Methodios III of Constantinople condemned Ligarides' history of the Jerusalem Patriarchate.
67. Thomas Consett also edited a set of documents which appeared in print in 1729 under the title *The Present State of the Church in Russia*. It would be interesting to discover how many subscribers made this publication possible. The odds are it was a very select company.
68. Cf. Derek Baker (ed.), *The Orthodox Churches and the West* (Oxford, 1976), pp. 247–8. Neale could have been influenced to turn to Orthodox studies by reading Lathbury. The timing certainly suggests this as a possibility. The revival of patristic learning at the end of the eighteenth century, pioneered by Martin Routh, which paved the way for Neale's work, is well covered by Arthur Middleton in Part Four of his *Fathers and Anglicans*, op. cit. It is worth nothing that Baker's volume contains Bishop Kallistos's earliest thoughts on the Earl of Guilford. Lathbury, op. cit., pp. 312, 323.
69. Ibid., pp. 322–3. Cf. Henry Sefton, 'The Scottish Bishops and Archbishop Arsenius' in Baker, op. cit., pp. 239–46, also Thomas Stephen, op. cit., IV, pp. 225–8 for a more naïve view. The text of the Concordat between Coptic Pope Shenouda III and the British Orthodox Church authorizing the Liturgy of St James in England may be found in *The Glastonbury Bulletin*, VII (1994), 87.

CHAPTER SIX

THIS OUR SENSELESS AGE

'Reason and nature, apostrophised and praised ...'
(John Redwood)

The 'screening' of Anglicanism from Orthodoxy after the failure of the Nonjuring attempt at communion was as abrupt as it was mysterious. It was not as if the 'High Church' then ceased to exist and the Church of England changed into an altogether different animal. The Church of England remained externally the same as it had been. Despite the high concentration of patristic learning in the separated body of Nonjurors, there were still comparable churchmen who settled for the Revolution settlement in Church and State, among them clergy retaining their preferments with at least a theoretical chance of attaining to the highest office. True, the Whig caucus for long chose to prefer 'latitudinarians' for the episcopate, but in the following years men like Edmund Gibson and Thomas Wilson bucked the trend.

The reason for the cut-off – like the reason for the failure of 'organic unity' as an objective of the Ecumenical movement in the latter part of the twentieth century – must be sought in a wider change in mental climate rather than in personalities and structures, a change which brought about a loss of nerve in the High Church party, creating a spiritual vacuum ultimately filled by the Evangelical revival and the Methodist movement. The spiritual dilemma of the High Church Wesley brothers epitomizes much that was disoriented beneath a surface calm. The 'Holy Club' at Oxford which they tried to make a framework for their spiritual lives, proved inadequate to the task and they were thrown against their will into a whirlpool of incompatible objectives. Older cultural rigidities which the Carolines and the Orthodox had shared because of a selective adherence to patristic texts became inadequate to withstand the shifting quicksands of a new popular culture which thrived on a radical scepticism about what had once been common values. High Churchmen might be still convinced – as indeed their early nineteenth-century successors like Hugh James Rose were – that they knew the exact 'extent of the shore' and that the important thing was to 'bring the Apostolic and Primitive Catholic Church' into the life of the Church of England rather than accommodate Dissent, but an unfamiliar ocean was now encroaching on the shore.[1]

Fundamental to the sea change now in progress, later to be given classic English expression in Matthew Arnold's poem of disillusionment, *Dover Beach*, was a shaking of confidence in the objectivity of transmissions from the past. A modern French cultural historian Paul Hazard has detected even among Roman Catholics of the period a tendency for the 'very notion of historicity' to dissolve, and Keith Walker – the biographer of William Law – has expanded on this within the English context:

> Men sensed the difficulty of accurately estimating past events; they knew of the variety of interpretations and they were coming to think that the present should concern them more.[2]

In this climate, never fully grasped in all its dimensions at the time, churchmen like Edmund Chishull saw 'socinianism' (the buzzword for heterodoxy in the late seventeenth century) as 'contagious'. Chishull regretted that religion, like politics, had become a matter of mere 'party opinion'. The great William Beveridge bewailed this too at the time when all classes of people were lemming-like succumbing to the fabrications of the 'Popish plot' and politicians in the emerging party groupings were manipulating the hysteria for their own short-term advantage. A secular mentality which simply ignored history as the medium of salvation was reaching a stage where it could no longer see the past as an unbroken continuum bearing 'inner power' to give meaning to the present. The believer was increasingly faced with the raw 'specificity of events' and perhaps a consequent 'desolation of reality'.[3]

'To such a degree of temerity has this our senseless age advanced, that there is scarcely anything in Christianity itself which is not either called into doubt in private, or made matter of controversy in public. So much so, that even those doctrines and rites, which many ages back, and from the very beginning of the Church, have everywhere been received, at last in these our days come into hazard and are assailed, just as if we were the first Christians, and all our ancestors had assumed and borne the mere name of Christ, and nothing more ... Forsooth in these full late times, it seems new lights are boasted of, new and greater gifts of the Holy Spirit are pretended; and therefore new forms in the use of all ecclesiastical administrations are daily framed and commonly adopted ... Hence these tears, hence so many horrible schisms in the Church.'[4]

Arthur Middleton describes Beveridge as a 'mind weary of controversy' and seeking spiritual solace in 'primitive doctrine and practice'. It could be that a less constructive mind like that of the church historian William Cave might deserve such a description, but it is misleading for a modern reader as a description of Beveridge because it suggests (no doubt unintentionally on Middleton's part) a degree of superficiality and naivety which was not there. Some in this period whose orthodoxy was challenged by the prevailing milieu undoubtedly had an insecure obsession with what the Dominican scholar Père Christian Duquoc has memorably called a 'nostalgic elsewhere'. Biblical imagery, says Duquoc, can be 'elevated too hastily to a conceptual level', especially under the pressure of a siege mentality. But Beveridge was genuinely concerned with the obfuscation of the 'marks of the Church' and, as

Duquoc himself says, the presence of those marks in the Church's very brokenness constitutes 'imperatives of transformation' in the *eschaton* which a Churchman like Beveridge knew must be honoured in faith.[5]

Each generation does have some tendency to exaggerate the contrast between present experience and what went before and this can sometimes lead to a calling in aid of a 'golden age'. But Beveridge's *cri de coeur* is surely not in this category. It raises questions of epistemology. What does it mean to derive one's faith from past event; what substance does the idea of a diachronous communion of saints have if the past events of sanctity are called in question? Churchmen like Beveridge had already passed through fire in defence of their Church tradition in time of war and revolution: they now faced the threat of spiritual death by a thousand cuts in a society superficially at peace. Churchmen were divided on how to combat creeping historical scepticism which reached even to the conciliar proclamation of the Incarnation and the Trinity. Thomas Smith thought that dialogue with socinians verged on the scandalous, but his friend Henry Dodwell felt that his own 'present condition as a Laick' enabled him to take 'advantage of promiscuous conversation' in an attempt to bring the fight to the enemy before they carried all before them and the 'Genius of this Age' was fixed in scepticism.[6]

Ironically, the movement of historical scepticism gained some fortuitous impetus from the work of the Jesuit Dionysius Petavius (1583–1652), who, in a treatise on the Trinity demeaned the authority of the Ante-Nicene Fathers, on the ground that they did not sufficiently understand the 'principal article of the Christian Faith concerning the Divinity of Christ'. George Bull, in an effort to mitigate the effect of citations of Petavius by deists and socinians in his own day, argued that the Jesuit's real motive had been to invalidate the Ante-Nicene witness to the primitive constitution of the Church, which the Church of England espoused, in the interests of a Papal Supremacy which began after Nicaea. John Pearson was similarly anxious about Petavius in his *Vindiciae Epistolarum S. Ignatii*. But it was not only the Ante-Nicene

Fathers who came under fire. In addition to Jean Daillé, the Dutchman Episcopius [Simon Bischop] attempted to demolish the Council of Nicaea itself on the ground that its Creed was 'precipitately framed from excitement if not fury' in a 'maddening and unblessed party spirit, on the part of the bishops who were wrangling and contending with one another from excessive rivalry, rather than as what issued from composed minds.'

Episcopius's argument was taken up by Arthur Bury, Rector of Exeter College, Oxford, as we shall see, and in turn Bury was answered – not to universal High Church satisfaction because of the writer's connections with the Cambridge Platonists – by Thomas Sherlock in his *Vindication of the Doctrine of the Holy and Ever-Blessed Trinity*.[7] Much High Church scholarly energy between the 1670s and the second decade of the eighteenth century was diverted into upholding the Fathers against this creeping erosion of their authority, even when they felt that their ingenious and fanciful opponents had in fact but a 'meane knowledge of the Fathers'. Whether in the hands of a controversial Protestant like Daillé or Episcopius or in the hands of socinians or deists of a home-grown variety like Toland, Whiston, Collins, Tindal and Clarke, the thrust of the anti-Fathers argument was to raise profound questions about historical verifiability. The criticisms might be text-specific, but as the defenders of the Fathers had to point out time and time again the principle of scepticism thus applied would have the effect of rendering all the ancient texts unreliable in a *primary* sense, especially as the records of the early Church were relatively few in number and the surviving writings of the early heretics in many instances known only in fragmentary quotations in the writings of the Fathers. The critics were claiming in effect that if a Father was to be treated as reliable it was necessary first to know not only *what* he believed or did not believe, but also *how* he believed or did not believe – something which, at this distance of time, it was assumed to be unlikely, if not impossible, to ascertain.[8]

It was probably for this reason that western apologetics at this time became increasingly fragmented into appeal to

Scripture, appeal to 'primitive observance' and appeal to reason. We see this hinted already in Basire and Rycaut and fully blown in Covel. Covel was among those who brought a purely linear historicist perspective to his observations on unfamiliar religious practice. He admired the Catholic proto-biblical critic Richard Simon and the Bollandists' critical edition of the lives of the saints because they seemed to stand aside from Tradition and great religious literature in the context of the time in which it was written, like any other literature. Caught between an age of juridical prescription and an age of subtle form-criticism, his sceptic mind, honed in classical scholarship and the natural sciences, could not see in its own terms a religious culture in which perception came through a mixture of ikons and words, not arranged in a linear pattern and not subject to the rules of logical consistency. He lacked the sense of what is now called 'contextual theology' in which you address the whole context of a religious system and not just its dissected parts. Hence his distortion of Ortho-dox eucharistic belief, a belief which the Orthodox them-selves, harassed as they were by Romanist polemic, were not always able to express consistently in answer to persistent sceptical questioning. Covel gleefully forced logical equations between eucharistic and baptismal imagery, failing to see that Orthodox belief statements, because doxological in nature, were logically non-reversible except in a scholastic framework which itself does damage to their delicate balance in worship.[9] Such a caste of mind, which in a less extreme form than in Covel, was widespread in the eighteenth-century Churches of England and Ireland, could explain a falling-off of Anglican interest in the sacraments (Sancret, Bingham and Waterland being notable exceptions) and therefore of interest in such an essentially sacramental system as the Orthodox Church.

It will therefore scarcely surprise the reader to find that the present writer is not seduced by the idea recently propounded by J. C. D. Clark that the eighteenth-century Church of England inherited from the preceding century a culture and sense of unity which made for stability. Post-Revolution English politics certainly worked through inherited institutions. But that kind of conservatism had little to do with Tradition in the theological sense. In eighteenth-century Anglican writings, prior to Alexander Knox and Jones of Nayland on the cusp of the following century, the Fathers at best appeared like icing on the Establishment cake, quoted from time to time for immediate forensic purposes, mostly to deter internal efforts at reform, such as those of the Feathers Tavern petitioners in 1772 and 1774 aimed at securing parliamentary modifications to the Prayer Book of a doctrinal nature. Those efforts were similarly resisted by parliamentary means and an examination of the parliamentary debates does not reveal any deep respect for Tradition in the Caroline sense. By that stage, individual clergy won respect for personal qualities but were rarely reverenced for their solemn office. Sermon-sampling was as widespread in the Church of England as it was among Dissenters – most notably in the proprietory chapels, built on subscription and independent of all diocesan jurisdiction. The road to that denouement was via a steady solvent of popular satire aimed at the institutions of the Church.[10]

Before turning from scholarship and a Fellowship of All Souls to politics, John Redwood gave us a penetrating if theologically limited study of scepticism in the period covered by this book.[11] Redwood finds in the last four decades of the seventeenth century and the first three of the eighteenth a slide into 'liberality' – theological, philosophical and moral. It was fed by the development of satirical literature, the coffee house and journalism. It was, at least for a time, resisted vigorously. Redwood thinks the reaction 'almost puritanical', but this is stretching a theological point. A similar mistake is made, more incongruously, by David Self in a *Church Times* article on Jeremy Collier and the stage.[12] The High Churchmen were not 'puritans' obsessed with filth but serious men defending a whole cosmology which they felt to be under threat.

Redwood, perhaps unconsciously, locates the true seriousness of the issue with his linguistic coinage 'social deism'.[13] The ribald verse of men like Rochester, read aloud in coffee houses had a deeper and more pervasive effect than learned treatises.[14] Edmund Gibson as Bishop of London in a pastoral letter of 1728 linked the decline in reverence for sacred things with a general mood of levity in what our own age has called the 'chattering classes'. The sickness of society, he said, was moral, not intellectual.[15]

Redwood sees the change in *Weltanschauung* as an intellectually logical extension of the Protestant Reformation, starting with the rejection of indulgences and the breaking of images. It is certainly true that pamphleteers, like the one in 1676 called for the repression of the 'Growing boldness of Atheism', almost invariably brought popery into the picture, as if by reflex.[16] But the current conviction was that popery and atheism were bedfellows, not that one had given birth to the other. In 1680, for instance, shortly after the putative Popish Plot, one author claimed to be betraying a plot hatched between Rome, the Turks and the 'Hobbists' (i.e. the disciples of Thomas Hobbes, the notorious author of *Leviathan*) to 'introduce Atheism into England'.[17] Ever since the plots against Elizabeth there had been those who had been convinced that Rome had a permanent strategy in place to subvert the kingdom with its information constantly updated by assiduous agents. Thus, for instance, an anonymous publisher of a translation into English of Count d'Elci's *Lives of the Cardinals* in 1706 wrote in his Preface:

> Here in England, since by our happy Reformation we have shaken off the yoke of the Papal Tyranny, we seem to be altogether unconcern'd at what passes in the Court of Rome, and not to mind their Counsels and Deliberations. But I am sure they are not quite so unmindful of our Concerns. There is nothing transacted here but what they are fully inform'd of by their Emissaries; and they will never be wanting to contribute their Endeavours for pulling down of Church and Constitution.[18]

While Popery was thus seen as an ever-present menace, there were other things in High Church minds to blame for the weakening of faith and morals. First and foremost there was the revival of literary interest in Lucretius and Epicureanism which reached its peak in 1700 with the publication of Thomas Creach's translation of the Roman poet. Many traced the interest back to Hobbes. There was an accompanying interest among natural scientists in the materialism of Democritus. The idea of material necessity, it was feared by High Churchmen, would make retributive justice seem a nonsense in the absence of a controlling God saying 'I will repay' ...[19]

A deeper High Church fear was that of hysteria. Hysteria was found not only on the streets of the metropolis; it was in danger of invading the universities. At Exeter College Oxford in 1690 the fellows were thrown into confusion when the Rector Arthur Bury published his book *The Naked Gospel*, over whether it was to be read as an attack on the Trinity. But it was not confined to theological discourse. In true 'tabloid journalism' fashion, that issue became entangled with the question of whether college fellows had been sexually active with female college servants, indeed to the extent of spawning two bastards. Such was the heat raised that the college visitor, the Bishop of Exeter, was refused entry. Convocation eventually condemned the book and forced Bury to make a limp recantation which convinced no-one.[20] In the meantime, by a conjunction which was High Churchmen's worst nightmare, the history of christology in the early Church was being publically rehearsed in Oxford. Redwood comments: 'The controversy generated by the whole [Bury] enquiry shows well the way in which seventeenth-century debates such as these managed to mix the personal and the trivial with the general and important ...' 'The scandal', he adds, 'was national, although the concerns ... were parochial ...' He also draws our attention to the way in which Bury, when put on the defensive, wanted to distinguish between the 'usefulness' of some beliefs which had lead to Christianity's early successes and the 'inutility' of certain dogmas and disputes over them which worked against the further spread of Christianity in the years leading up to the emergence and spread of Islam. Archbishop Tillotson may well have held views very similar to these. In Redwood's view, Bury was bound to be condemned for 'wishing to undress the Church of all the Councils, decrees and dogmas in his search for purity and style.'

The Exeter College controversy brought the great High Church polymath Dr George Bull once again to the defence of orthodoxy, a defence which he had begun in 1670 with his massive *Harmonia Apostolica* and continued in 1685 with his *Defensio Fidei Nicaenae*. His new *Judicium Ecclesiae Catholicae* was no less weighty – and equally inaccessible to those without the classical languages. Perhaps for that reason alone the psychological drift was against Bull and his fellow churchmen. Theological debate was fated to be held in future in the English tongue. The drift can be clearly seen in retrospect in a sudden spate of reprints of older socinian works by tract writers who were not afraid of denigrating Athanasios on the ground that he had been condemned by no less than six councils – an *ad hominem* argument if ever there was one.

The grand debate was beginning to scrape the bottom of the barrel. The *Apostolic Constitutions* rediscovered in the sixteenth century but never previously a matter of controversy, were now dragged in, buttressed by quotations from Tertullian and Cyprian, to 'demonstrate' trinitarian 'silences' which were deemed to be fatal to the Cappadocian Fathers and the teaching of the first four general councils, the bedrock of Caroline Anglicanism. This was no rigorous historicism: texts were used as seemed convenient to a *parti pris*. In the process there was a danger of any semblance of spiritual authoritative Tradition going out of the window. People began accusing each other quite liberally of misapplying texts. Herein our old friend Edmund Chishull played a part but did not come away from the business wholly unscathed by William Whiston. In the end there was a sort of stalemate, where 'whenever a cleric wrote on the Trinity, even with the best of intentions, there would be those who saw in his unfortunate choice of words too great a leaning towards tri-theism or alternatively to anti-trinitarianism'. The Church of England might remain formally trinitarian, but havoc was being played with lives and beliefs, with this scholar passed over for promotion, another expelled from his university, yet another deposed from the headship of his college. There is some truth in Voltaire's quip

that Samuel Clarke was turned down for Canterbury because
he was 'not a Christian', albeit he was the most 'learned' and
'respected' man in the kingdom. Even with the greatest latitude, there were some men now who were just too hot to
handle.[21]

In the background there was the strangely unsettling figure
of John Locke – philosopher, political apologist for the Revolution and amateur scientist – who in addition to floating an
idea of the 'social contract' at a time when High Churchmen
were feeling sore about whether or not to 'take the oaths', was
known to have been collecting scriptural texts under the
heading of *Non Trinitas*, a preoccupation probably due to his
closeness to the deist John Toland.

The most alarming aspect of the current climate for High
Churchmen was the way in which their old preoccupation with
transubstantiation was now being turned inside out by the freethinkers in an effort to throw doubt on the Trinity. Redwood
rightly perceives that attacks on William Sherlock (a Nonjuror
returned to the Establishment) in the context of the Trinitarian
debate was driving a wedge between 'real' and 'nominal' trini-
tarians in a way that was deeply demoralizing.[22]

Redwood is surely right on the evidence that he has given
us to say that 'Reason and nature, apostrophized and praised,
eulogised if not worshipped, were in many respects more
fundamental bones of contention than were the issues they
attempted to analyse ...' If there was one issue, however, that
was almost destructive of morale, Redwood thinks it was the
irony and ridicule which could be heaped on the biblical
record of creation. 'The kind of social irresponsibility apparent in many a playhouse jest or many a chance remark in a
tavern, reflected the unguarded thoughts of later seventeenth-
century gentlemen who were willing in their hearts to doubt a
God in order to savour a joke.' Many of the 'atheist-hunters',
as Redwood calls them, were aware of this in their correspondence. A new sort of mental climate had come about in
which the association of reason with ridicule put the whole
traditional Christian enterprise on roller skates. Redwood cites
the phil-Orthodox Edward Stephens as writing on this danger

in 1704. It led directly to the Sacheverell crisis of 1707 in which hysteria about 'the Church in danger' played a major part. High Churchmen became so unsettled that even the stiffness of Quakers in not taking off their hats took on apocalyptic proportions. More reasonably, a fall in church attendance and communion and an increasing neglect of the rites of passage, which were sensed though not statistically proven to be worse than before, made the ground feel unstable under many a High Churchman's feet.[23] Fears on this score were more than justified in 1736 with Lord Hardwick's Judgement in *Middleton v Crofts* which held that the canons did not bind the laity *proprio vigore* but were merely declaratory of what has been the case. Archbishop Bancroft at the time of the 1604 Canons had assumed them binding, although in some cases requiring the Common Law to enforce them. But by the early eighteenth century the authority of church courts was in any case undermined by acts of general pardon which annulled the canonical penalties. At a time (1717) when the Church of England lost effectively its deliberative Convocation the implications were horrifying for High Churchmen. For wherein lay the defence of orthodoxy in future save in the uncertain will of Parliament?[24]

A sea change had taken place within two generations – between Ralph Cudworth, the Cambridge Platonist writing in the 1670s and the generation of George Berkeley. It was not due to a change in the use of the English language, although Redwood concedes that this was also at work. What Redwood in secular fashion calls 'old fashioned spiritualism' was giving way in public circles to a novel concept of reason which simply ignored what an older generation had seen as the necessary consequence of scriptural texts. An object lesson is found in the way serious efforts were made (quite unsuccessfully) to persuade the classicist Richard Bentley not to exclude 1 John 5:7 from his edition of the Greek New Testament on the ground that it was an 'essential part of the Church's case against the Arians'. Bentley was scornful of such a measure of judgement, asserting that he was guided solely by his scholarly comparison of early texts. William Whiston took a similar approach to the study of early liturgical texts and in due course argued for their greater christological authenticity in comparison with the later views of the Cappadocians and the Councils. On purely textual grounds he accused Athanasios of forgery.[25]

When such procedures are taken to their logical conclusion they lead to a drastically new idea of causation which seemed to High Churchmen to rob the Creator of all his honour and deny entirely the reality of Providence. This comes out in Francis Gastrell's Boyle Lecture for 1697 where an atheist is defined as one who says 'there is no God that *governs the world, and judgeth the earth*' or one who says there is no God who *'appoints laws and rules for men to act by'*. Samuel Butler saw an atheist as he who draws a 'map of nature by his own fancy'.[26] Bentley tried to save the concept of gravity for a providential system by calling it a 'personal force used by God to keep the world in being and the planetary system in revolution', which suggests he was well aware of the depth of the problem which Enlightenment thinking was uncovering.[27]

The Establishment High Churchmen, though they had a more comfortable time than the Nonjurors in their garrets, were increasingly isolated psychologically. The Cambridge philosopher Henry Moore wrote to Lady Conway of the 'orthodox men':

They push hard at the Latitude men as they call them, some in their pulpitts call them sons of Belial.[28]

They were as men roused to prophetic anger but they could not regain lost ground. Redwood shows that at least some of the High Church clergy were aware that Christianity was under threat from 'social and economic events'. There was no more space for the spiritual composure of Andrewes, Taylor and Cosin. These clergy had uneasy consciences about the Revolution even after they had effectively accepted it. A theory of 'providential right' was coined by men like John Sharp, William Lloyd, Francis Atterbury, William Sherlock and Edmund Bohun to justify accepting the *fait accompli*. It was even claimed that such a concept was 'a fundamental feature of historical Anglican doctrine'. Some of those exercised by growing irreligion gratefully resigned themselves to this revisionist interpretation as a vindication (hopefully) of a 'personal intervening God'. It was a risky strategy. The Nonjuror Edmund Elys was disgusted that Sherlock, who had once deplored a 'wirligig Conscience' had proved it true of himself.[29] This slippage left the unreconciled Nonjurors as more of a rump than would otherwise have been the case and so liable to the internal strife which nearly always seems to afflict numerically small Christian bodies of the 'Catholic' type.[30] Those High Churchmen who accepted the compromise for what they convinced themselves were higher theological interests found themselves thrown together with some odd bedfellows – William Stillingfleet, Thomas Tenison, Henry Compton, Gilbert Burnet. Their original theology was thereby considerably compromised, as Henry Sacheverell found when he was impeached by Parliament in 1710.[31] Notwithstanding the theories of J. C. D. Clark and William Gibson, concerning a continuity in the Church of England between the seventeenth and eighteenth centuries, no Georgian bishops, with the exception of Atterbury and Wilson (and possibly Gibson) were in the mould of the Carolines. To describe them as such is to import a very sociological element into the definition. The vision which opened Anglicans to the world of Orthodoxy in the seventeenth century had lost clarity: it required historical convulsions on an unprecedented scale to open the door once again.

Notes

1. Cf. Thomas Brett, *Dissertation on Liturgies*, cited by Sparrow Simpson, op. cit., p. 68.
2. Paul Hazard, *The European Mind* (London, 1935), p. 47; A. Keith Walker, *William Law, His Life and Thought* (London, 1973), p. 17.
3. For a modern Orthodox comment on this phenomenon see Nikos Nissiotis and Philip Sherrard in A. J. Philippou (ed.), *Orthodoxy: Life And Freedom* (Oxford, 1973), pp. 56–57, 60–63.
4. Edmund Chishull, *The Orthodoxy of an English Clergy-Man*

(London, 1711), pp. 2, 11–12; William Beveridge, Preface to his *Codex Canonum Ecclesiae Primitivae vindicatus ac illustratus* (London, 1678), quoted in the 1848 Oxford reprint of Vicentius of Lerins' *Against Heresy*, pp. ix–x.

5. Middleton, *Fathers and Anglicans*, op. cit., p. 192, citing Cave's *Lives of the Apostles and the Two Evangelists St Mark and St Luke* (reprint, Oxford, 1840), pp. vii–viii; Christian Duquoc OP, *Provisional Churches*, op. cit., p. 75; see also ibid., pp. 21, 25–26, 66.
6. Cf. Edward Bernard to Thomas Smith, 8 January 1693–4, Smith MS 47, d. 132, Bodleian MS 15654; Dodwell to Smith, 3 July 1675, ibid., 49, f.121. See also Smith MS 49, ff.205–19. High Church scholars of this eminence were aware, as previous chapters have shown, of the difficulty of using defective texts. Cf. S. L. Greenslade, *The Reformers and the Fathers of the Church* (Oxford, 1960), p. 3, and also Middleton's comments, op. cit., pp. 18–19, 21.
7. Cf. Middleton, op. cit., pp. 244–5.
8. Ibid., p. 222 and Chapters 11 and 12, passim; also Bernard to Smith, 23 March 1694–5, Smith MS 47, f.161.
9. Cf. Covel, *An Account*, op. cit., pp. 54–56, 60–61.
10. For a definitive account of the late eighteenth-century High Church, see Peter B. Nockles, *The Oxford Movement in Context. Anglican High Churchmanship 1760–1857* (Cambridge, 1994).
11. John Redwood, *Reason, Ridicule and Religion. The Age of the Enlightenment in England 1660–1750* (London, 1976, 2nd edn., 1996).
12. David Self, 'The single source of all filth', *Church Times*, No. 7179, 22 September 2000.
13. Redwood, op. cit., p. 174.
14. Ibid., pp. 15, 41–42, 45.
15. Ibid., p. 27.
16. Ibid., p. 154.
17. Ibid., p. 47, citing *The Counter-Plot: or The Close Conspiracy of Atheism and Schism Opened, and, so Defeated.*
18. *The Present State of the Court of Rome: or, The Lives of the Present Pope Clement XI and of the Present College of Cardinals. With a Preface by the Publisher* (London, 1706), p. xi.
19. Redwood, op. cit., pp. 40–41, 111, citing Ralph Cudworth, *The True Intellectual System of the Universe of 1677*.
20. See contemporary High Church comment on the Bury affair in Smith MS 47, ff.69–70, 73–75, Bod. MS 15645.
21. Redwood, op. cit., pp. 156–9, 160–3, 165–6. In John Henley's *Oration on Grave Conundrums, and Serious Buffoons* of 1729

fun was made of philosophy, theology and aesthetics, including the 'Clementine' Liturgy in the *Apostolic Constitutions*. The Earl of Shaftesbury produced the most polished and influential work of this kind, *Characteristicks of Men, Manners, Opinions, Times* (London, 1711), published previously under the heavily ironic title *Sensus Communis: An Essay on the Freedom of Wit and Humour*. For further comment on the Bury case, see William Gibson, op. cit. p. 54.

22. Redwood, op. cit., pp. 162–3.
23. Ibid., pp. 14–19.
24. Gordon Crosse in S. L. Ollard, Gordon Crosse and Maurice F. Bond (eds), *A Dictionary of English Church History* (3rd edition revised, London, Oxford and New York, 1948), p. 90.
25. Redwood, op. cit., pp. 178, 199, 201–3, 210.
26. Thus John Turner, *A Vindication of the Rights and Privileges of the Christian Church* (London, 1707), cited by Redwood, p. 26. Gastrell's lecture was published in 1697 under the title *The Certainty and Necessity of Religion in General*. See also Redwood, p. 31.
27. Redwood, op. cit., p. 104.
28. Cited by Redwood, p. 60 from British Library Add. MS 23216, f.275.
29. Elys to Smith, 2 December 1690, Smith MS 49, f.220.
30. Cf. Roger Turner, op. cit.
31. Cf. Gibson, op. cit., pp. 41–45.

EPILOGUE:

SOME ORTHODOX AND ECUMENICAL REFLECTIONS

> 'Great structures of sensibility and of conceptuality, be they Semitic, Greek or Latin, have been allowed [by God] to collapse, but the rocks struck by the thunderbolt have become precious stones in the foundation of the heavenly Jerusalem.'
>
> Olivier Clément in A. J. Philippou (ed.),
> *Orthodoxy: Life and Freedom*, op. cit., p. 87

Readers will have noticed from the outset that there is no intention here of idealizing the Orthodox Church, even though the author belongs to its tradition. All religious traditions are dilapidated, impoverished, broken, more or less, no matter what divine charge is laid upon them; and those adherents who claim otherwise would do well to heed the words of the Lord of Life: 'Blind? If you were you would not be guilty, but since you say "we see", your guilt remains.' (John 9:41) The Ulster Churchman Nicholas Armstrong whom some at the time of the Oxford revival recognized as an apostle of the Catholic Apostolic Church with responsibility for Greece, spoke movingly of the Greek Church:

> '... before it magnify itself, let it study its history. Why has God permitted two terrible captivities to overtake it, the oppression of the Byzantine emperors and the wasting tyranny of the false prophet? Her hope at this day, which she even builds upon prophecy, and visions, and revelations, is

that, such as she is, she may become the teacher of the whole world, the fountain of pure worship and holiness for all the nations of the earth ... Has she found out the sins which the Roman emperors fostered and Mahomet was commissioned to chastise?' There is love implied in grieving that a acceptance of bondage 'under the powers of this world' and 'dependence on them in all their vicissitudes' had put at risk the Church's 'heavenly hope' by a 'quenching of the Spirit', a love which recognized that in spite of its weakness that Church had not opposed with violence but endured patiently, 'abiding God's time for retribution ..., satisfied with the orthodoxy of her opinions'.[1]

The problem for the Caroline Anglicans and their Nonjuring successors was that they encountered Orthodoxy at a particularly 'broken' stage of its pilgrimage, – and, fighting as it were, to escape from the brokenness of their own 'establishment' – they made demands on their Orthodox brethren which they were unable to grasp. By the seventeenth century, the Greek Church had fallen into the mode of *phyletism*, an attitude which associated the Orthodox faith almost entirely with Greek language and culture. It had once been what Rudolf Sohm termed a *Gesamtgemeinde* or 'universal spiritual totality'. After the Turkish conquest it declined into an *Ortsgemeinde* ('legal entity') and from thence, as it became physically weaker, into *phyletism*. It would be fair to say, using the words of William Laud and Herbert Thorndike, that since 1454 much had 'slipped by' the Greek Orthodox and that because they were largely unaware of it, they had suffered especially badly from the 'injury of time'. As time passed, worse was to follow. At the very moment when the Nonjurors were receiving the Response of the Greek patriarchs, a sizeable part of the Patriarchate of Antioch was determining to form the Melkite Schism by adhering to the distant Patriarch of Rome, unable any longer, as a largely Arab body, to bear Greek hegemony. Christos Yannaras has shown how Greek Orthodox intellectuals in the period after this book – Vikentios Damodos, Nikiphoros Theotokis, Evgenios Voulgaris,

Neophytos Vamvas – tried to revive spiritual life in the Greek Church by introducing elements of western pietism, Enlightenment natural theology, the 'religion of feeling', and 'Christianity as Culture', which last only reinforced *phyletism*. *Phyletism* became an obstacle to receiving any sort of renewal, especially from the grassroots upwards, even though in principle, as the patriarchs' reply to Pius IX indicated, the body of the Faithful were the custodians of living Tradition. Movements like God's Army in Romania and the Logos Foundation for Orthodox Renewal in the United States were proscribed by hierarchs. In March 1989 the Bulgarian hierarchy demanded of their considerably weakened and shortly to collapse Communist government that it disavow a committee of laity and lower clergy set up for 'Religious Rights, Freedom of Conscience and Spiritual Values', claiming that it was totally inconsistent with the Canons and Church Tradition and its members ipso facto not part of the Church 'structure'. In 1977 Greek newspapers made extraordinary attacks on Archbishop Philip Saliba of the Syro-Antiochene Church in North America (and by implication Archbishop Iakovos, head of the Greek Church in North America) for daring to suggest a single Orthodox Church in the United States. Archbishop Philip was even addressed as 'Mr Saliba' and Archbishop Iakovos accused of something close to apostasy.[2]

It is now widely accepted among Orthodox theologians that this virus needs to be purged. The corrosive effect of such exclusivity is well expressed in a poem by the Serb Miodrag Pavlovic in which he speaks bitterly in the persona of a medieval Serb making his pilgrimage to Constantinople.

> I set off for the immortal city
> In search of icons and psalters of ritual joy
> and to sing in the choir beneath the golden arches.
> At the gates the Varangian guard would barely let me pass.
> In the Hagia Sophia they denied me Communion
> and I walked the streets thirsting ...
> I had no alms to give the beggars,
> Nor yet was I myself a beggar

In that city full of ships and flowers.
I knew no one save the Lord God himself.[3]

One can see in these lines much that may explain the frustrated bloodletting by Serbs during the 1990s. Their historic animus is of longer standing even than that of the Irish.

Indeed one can find in modern Orthodox writing, both Slavic and Greek (but more so Slavic) startling evidences of a frustration with the Church in its historical context. Towards the end of his life Nicolas Zernov wrote of it as a 'perplexing body', at one and the same time 'intensely alive and partially paralysed' with 'mental sectarianism'. Also at the end of his life of service to the Orthodox Church, Paul Evdokimov wrote:

> Orthodoxy has sunk back into the soporific comfort of static forms ... The length of services, an eloquence no longer appropriate for the temper of the day, indifference towards witness, the atrophy of the universal priesthood are no longer justified when seen beside the anguish of a questioning world. Its dynamism has taken refuge in national and juridical provincialism, the aestheticism of the elite and the folk superstition of the masses. As soon as Orthodoxy hinders the forward move of Tradition, it degenerates into an immobile traditionalism and betrays its vocation.

Evdokimov thought the Church needed to be reminded of its eschatology, for true Orthodoxy placed its feet in the prints of living eschatological Tradition which bestowed an 'adult freedom' as a gift. If it had a mind to, Orthodoxy could always transcend its 'historical type', for its whole past was but an initiation and it had access to power which could waken 'living sleepers'.[4]

Evdokimov is not alone in this view. Emmanuel Clapsis suggests that Orthodoxy derives its living understanding of the Gospel not from history but from an experience of the future sacramentally realized in the Eucharist, moving from eschatological experience to history, not *vice versa*. In similar vein,

Metropolitan John Zizioulas of Pergamon argues that the *eschaton* respects history not by copying but by transforming it, 'transcending especially the antinomies and limitations of history' in the word of God coming to us from the end. There is a degree of agreement on this from the Anglican theologian Bishop Stephen Sykes who recognizes that there must be an immediacy in the reception of Tradition (*anamnesis*) if the distortions caused by human 'pattern building' are to be avoided. There must be, says Bishop Stephen, a way of hearing 'the sheer particularity of the human experience' of the divine.[5]

The theological renewal in Orthodoxy in the twentieth century is difficult to fully evaluate in either Orthodox or ecumenical perspective. Much of it derives from a recovery of the thought of St Gregory Palamas, which was lost in the period of this study. Different scholars take different views on it, so that it would be simplistic to present a wholly Palamite vision as *the* way through to Orthodox reintegration. The present writer is grateful to Professor David Melling for a warning on this at a late stage of preparing the book for publication. The fact remains that the Palamite vision has given hope to Orthodox scholars weighed down by the weight of history and ethnicity. Thirty years ago Christos Yannaras foresaw the recovery of a 'communion of persons', the 'reality of salvation', in the disintegration of tight ethnic communities and the cramping of the human spirit in the artificial parish systems of large connurbations. He yearned for the recovery of the Gifts of the Spirit – prophecy, true theological teaching, loving kindness. 'Embodied in individual persons', every such gift would serve as a sign of the Church's path. 'Outside and all around these individual gifts there would exist only desert, the 'triumph of the irrational in history', 'the lordship of the powers of this age ...' '... and blessed is he who will not be scandalised waiting for the new revelation of the Spirit, that is, the final Pentecost of the Church.' Olivier Clément has sensed the same outcome, writing of the fulfilment of the 'other scriptures', i.e. 'those liturgical, doctrinal commentaries through which Christ the

Spirit (in the sense of Paul's "Lord, the Spirit") does seek to actualise His Word. Clément too speaks of 'charismatics' who realize the promises made by Christ in the closing passage of St Mark's Gospel.[6]

Neo-Palamism is welcomed by Clément 'for its admirable balance of the transcendental and the omnipresent, of christology and pneumatology, of personality and eucharistic grounding, of unknowability and divine presence in the very experience of self. The same feeling is expressed by the Roman Catholic scholar Gerry Russo in a study comparing St Gregory with Karl Rahner. Russo is impressed by the way in which Palamas rejected the analogy of being in favour of 'true contemplation, transcendent to all creatures.'[7]

This line of reasoning presupposes a distinction between 'spiritual intellect' and 'natural reason', the former grasping meaning not from sensible data but 'divine intelligence'. It is antipathetic to abstraction and even to analogy drawn from objects by the natural reason. Divine ideas are seen as the Divine Energy manifested in visible form. Thus Maximus the Confessor said long before Palamas: 'The immediate experience of a thing suppresses the concept which represents the thing'. Evdokimov calls this 'communion knowledge', even 'nuptual' knowledge, a perception by the whole of one's being, direct participation and grasp, the 'conviction of things not seen' (Hebrews 11:1).[8] In patristic discourse it has been known – perhaps misleadingly for modern Western minds – as *theoria*.[9] It is far from theoretical.

One could argue from this that Caroline Anglicans, and more especially their eighteenth-century successors, for all their patristic learning, were trapped in a western epistemology which made them dependent on purely logical and psychological models of authority, faced with a God who confronted them with 'shattering magnitudes' but 'only symbols' to express them, with a consequent pressure to 'dematerialise' the symbols (Yannaras finds this equally in Catholicism and Protestantism). At the same time the loosening of the sense of the past as a vehicle of Tradition, discussed in Chapter 6, tended more and more to a model of reality in which one could 'no longer present the past as an unbroken continuity bearing inner power'. Any attempts to re-establish links led to breaks in the fabric, unexplained contradictions, based on rational ideas of constancy and regularity which do not in fact interpret but radically disentangle the specificity of events. This is Philip Sherrard's 'desolation of reality', the 'husks of knowledge' rather than knowledge itself. Forty years ago when the present writer set out to do initial research in the Anglican literature of the period from 1760 to 1832, a period since brilliantly traversed by Dr Peter Nockles, such an impression formed in the mind, albeit not in a systematic fashion. The High Churchmen of the period were serious men, seeking after holiness, but they seemed beset on all sides by what Sherrard calls 'hostile attachments and persuasions'. Apart from the Scottish Episcopalians, who had remained outside the university intellectual system, these churchmen seemed unable to break through to a spirit of liberty in the Divine Presence. Sherrard says well that 'no amount of taking thought, no amount of scheming and deliberation, discussion and conference, is of the slightest use while the fundamental categories with which the mind itself operates remain unchanged.'[10]

One crucial lack in Anglicanism in the seventeenth and eighteenth centuries was that of monasticism. Monasteries are critical as places where reintegration of vision can take place when parishes, cathedrals and university divinity faculties have been infiltrated by social and intellectual fashion. By the time the Nonjurors attempted their 'British Orthodox' *ecclesiola in ecclesia* (of stark necessity in the form of house-churches), the Anglican psyche had become precariously fragmented despite all appearances on the institutional level. Prayer Book legalism was set against philosophical latitudinarianism and pietism. By this stage the tendency for Anglican liturgy to be constantly challenged on intellectual grounds made impossible any 'integrist' sense of Holy Tradition.[11]

We can see the dilemma acted out in the Preface to the American Prayer Book of 1789, which reviews the objections of the Restoration Settlement of 1662 and the abortive review

of it in 1689 through the lens of eighteenth-century colonial
rationalism. The Church of England's general aim in these
reviews, argues the Preface, was:

> to do that which according to her best understanding might
> most tend to the preservation of peace and unity in the
> Church, the procuring of reverence, and the exciting of
> piety and devotion in the worship of God, and finally, the
> cutting off of occasion, from them that seek occasion, of
> cavill or quarrel against her Liturgy.

It was hoped that this could be achieved so that nothing in the
Prayer Book was contrary to the Word of God or sound
doctrine . . .

> which a godly man may not with a good conscience use and
> submit to, or which is not fairly defensible, if allowed such
> just and favourable construction as in common equity ought
> to be allowed to all human writings . . .

Even so, it was conceded that this text could not be the end of
the matter, further alterations would in time be 'found expe-
dient'. The logical implications of such provisionality have
been spelled out in recent decades in reactions to the American Prayer Book of 1979. In an article 'The Gnostic Book of
Common Prayer', Father Robert Politzer, pointing to modern
research on the gnosticism of the first three centuries, argues
that a theological analysis of the 1979 book would reveal a
penetration of gnostic doctrine into the worship of the Episcopal Church, in respect of Original Sin, a dualist concept of
the world controlled by evil powers, the divinity of Christ, the
doctrine of the Atonement and the 'elevation of knowledge to
the level of dogma'. Writing in the *Seabury Journal* in 1986,
Father Robert Crouse said that the integrity and authority of
the Anglican tradition, already showing signs of fragmentation, 'will not well sustain a too radical revision or rejection
of the Prayer Book.'[12]
What was lost in this intellectual fragmentation was very

significant. We have seen evidences that our seventeenth-century Anglican observers of the Greek scene felt some spiritual superiority towards their Greek brethren. Some of it was cultural, especially in Covel. But a great deal related to deep roots in Caroline Anglicanism. We have already seen that the heirs of the Carolines could on occasion be accused of hypocritical purism. The truth is somewhat more honourable. Jeremy Taylor, whose shadow fell over all the late Carolines, argued that since the sacraments were *mysteries*, they must be handled by 'mystic persons'. By this he did not simply mean 'consecrated' persons whose sacramental acts brought grace *ex opere operato*. He *did* expect at the very least some sign of holiness in the person outwardly called. Archbishop McAdoo has shown from Taylor's most intimate writings on eucharistic devotion that he was very much against indulgence in scruples and incessant self-reproach because he believed that the Incarnate Christ presented himself eucharistically 'in a way that was nearest to our capacity', albeit one that was surrounded in a 'mystery of light', 'circles of glorious and eternal fire'. He knew that the proclamation at the Eastern altar – 'Holy things for holy persons' was immediately followed by the responsory 'One is holy, one is Lord, Jesus Christ to the glory of God the Father.' While both Andrewes and Taylor maintained an attitude of 'reverent unknowing', they were not absent-minded professors but pastors deeply committed to the salvation of their people and involved in their lives. What their disciples found in Greek lands could not help but horrify them with its often crudity and pig-ignorance. Covel, of course, being Covel, a fastidious man, condemned the Greek clergy for a fairly global ignorance of their own mysteries, but even humbler observers in our study still found large numbers of Greek clergy disingenuous and unworthy.[13]

What was at stake here was an expectation just as strong among the Carolines as it was among the *devotio moderna*, the Methodists and the Moravians, of a 'heart truly turned to God' and an intelligent awareness of what was involved – a heart crucified with Christ and born again of the Spirit. They found it difficult to imagine this state of mind amid the slovenliness which they encountered in Greek worship.[14]

What the Orthodox who had dealings with our Carolines could never have realized because it could only be known from the inside of Caroline spiritual practice and even then only in hindsight, is that the most profound and abiding effect of the sixteenth-century Reformation on Anglicanism lay not on the field of dogmatic theology but in that of 'spiritual discipline'. The locus of tradition in Caroline theology has been said to consist in 'dynamic expectation' through the sacraments rather than in anything more formal. It had, of course, theological implications, but these lay in the realm of Orthodox mystical theology rather than anything in the western dogmatic tradition – Andrewes' notion of 'recapitulation of all in Christ in the holy Sacrament – a kind of hypostatic union of the sign and the thing signified' – and Laud's daring suggestion in a sermon of 1637 to the Lords of the Garter that the 'greatest place of God's residence on earth' was not the pulpit but the altar because a greater reverence was due to the Body of the Lord than to his word. Bishop Geoffrey Rowell has recently formulated it in the course of assembling an 'Anglican *Philokalia*'. He identifies a conviction that the hidden givenness of sacramental life takes precedence over short-term assessment of success and satisfaction in the spiritual life.[15] But by the eighteenth century this instinct had been largely buried under massive historical detritus so that it seemed that English Christianity and Orthodoxy were a universe apart. By the middle of the twentieth century there were phil-Orthodox Anglicans like Derwas Chitty whose outlook was well-nigh apocalyptic, in spite of the renewed Anglican interest in Orthodoxy starting with John Mason Neale. Chitty in his famous address to the Fellowship of St Alban and St Sergius in 1947 while feeling that Orthodoxy was then capable of giving Anglicanism the kiss of life, feared that the kiss might come too late because within as little as fifty years he suspected that the 'great successful Church of Anti-Christ will be claiming to build the Kingdom of Christ on earth' and the Church of the faithful remnant might be 'scattered in small numbers ... feeble and sorely smitten', with its unity not fully perceptible, even though with her 'will be the Fellowship of the Holies, Heaven on Earth, the Image of God'.[16]

There are those – cynics or realists – who would say that when such a disjunction has taken place as we have seen in the last two chapters no recomposition is possible. After all, seventeenth-century Anglicans had observed the Greeks tending to their timepieces and trimming their lamps in the midst of an infidel state simply because their elders had taught them to do so, yet failing either to warn of danger or to urge greater and greater prayer. This seemed to say that the Orthodox had kept a glimmer of light on the frontiers of sacred time and space but had failed, through nervelessness, to advance the unity of the Household of God or even to stem the relentless tread of the death watch beetle across the fabric of their Church. Surely this was a system gone wrong beyond recall. Yet history has a habit of making fools of those with such glib preconceptions. We have seen in these pages evidences of a renewal of Orthodox mystical theology in the twentieth century which is truly astounding. In Russia, even in the worst last days of the Soviet regime, laymen like Alexander Ogorodnikov seeded bible study groups. Irina Ratushinskaya in a Moldovan labour camp could extend the Orthodox humanism of Anna Akhmatova in her poetry, and a prophetic priest, Alexander Men, addressed the evil of the political system and the weakness of his church hierarchy at the cost of his own life. In the American Greek Church the spiritual gifts were sought afresh and received, including the gifts of healing and evangelism, while in the Orthodox Church in America (the former Russian Metropolia) liturgical renewal was both taught in seminary and achieved in the parishes. Throughout the Orthodox world new concepts of iconography developed, renewing without distorting the traditional models and a new creativity emerged in musical settings of the Liturgy, leading to a flourishing of para-liturgical expressions of great potency – in the musical settings of Arvo Pärt, Sofia Gubaidulina, John Tavener and Ivan

Moody, which have the power to move even unchurched aesthetes. Although the old viruses of phyletism, nationalism and anti-semitism are still there – and wrought havoc in the Balkans throughout the 1990s – Orthodox have begun to recover that stillness and watchfulness which the Carolines (and the Quakers!) so much prized. For centuries Orthodox episcopal governance may seem to have been weak; but Bishop Kallistos has helpfully pointed out by reference to the difference between western and eastern shepherds, that a bishop may lead from 'the front' without exerting punitive power from 'behind'. An anonymous monk on Mount Athos is quoted by Olivier Clément as saying:

> The supernatural force of Orthodoxy ... comes precisely from its weakness; it is projected at the end of history and has no hold on the course of the world. She seems doomed to humiliation. She is called to repent and be zealous in the stead of all.[17]

Modern Orthodoxy can present one with what one is least expecting from its outer characteristics. Some years ago a Canadian Lutheran bishop, Robert Jacobson, chronicled a drastic transformation in his own outlook on Orthodoxy. He recalled his undergraduate condescension in terms very reminiscent of John Covel. He had felt then a fascination with the 'popular' character of Orthodoxy but at the same time he had a refined horror at 'how woefully ignorant the clergy were of even the basic elements of biblical and historical criticism which we western students took as the main fare of theology'. Years of subsequent ministry in what he described as a dry land of the spirit eventually brought him to a realization that perhaps – all this notwithstanding – the Orthodox were better able than his brand of Protestantism to integrate 'what happens to them below and around their ears to what is happening to them through and above their ears'. He now regretted the way in which many church buildings of the Reformation traditions almost dared the passer-by to 'figure out how to get in here' and rather gave them impression when you entered them that

'Heaven is collapsing on you'. This he did not find with Orthodox churches.[18]

The Orthodox paradox perceived by Bishop Jacobson may be due to most observers of Orthodoxy having been taught for some considerable time to 'walk on one leg', namely the leg of intellectual argument. Bishop Nikolai Velimirovic of Zika told his Anglican friend George Bell in 1921 that in approaching the Tree of Life he felt the need to walk on three legs – brain, heart and soul. He was intimidated by the Anglican theologian Oliver Quick because he seemed only to walk on one leg.[19]

Nevertheless, the obstacles to real as distinct from notional rapprochement between modern Anglicanism and modern Orthodoxy remain considerable. The late Professor S. L. Greenslade noted that at meetings of Anglican-Orthodox dialogue the Anglican delegates will always want to argue about the context of Orthodox dogmatic tradition and expect Orthodox to listen to criticism of it in terms of the 'human element in the Church'. Also they will want Orthodox to discuss the content of ideas like justification and grace which have never been the issue for Orthodox that they have in the West. This model of Anglicanism is not without some counterpart in Caroline Anglicanism but it is now almost caricatured. Thus there is a heavy pressure on the Orthodox to say something new. It sits uneasily with Vladimir Lossky's idea that truth has no external criteria but is 'manifest of itself' and 'made inwardly plain' to the Church. It threatens Orthodoxy with what Mother Thekla of Normanby once described as 'a regressive infinity of terminal points lost between yesterday and tomorrow'. From the Orthodox standpoint it can be an offence to the 'unequal and particular nature' of many truths. This would explain why documents issuing from Anglican-Orthodox Dialogue look very much like documents produced by other bilateral dialogues – anodyne and abstract. And behind it all there lurks a 'temperamental limitation' which makes the 'spirit of the West fret' at Eastern habits of thought and modes of action.[20]

The successors of the Carolines found themselves trapped

in a hostile debate with freethinkers in which each patristic document in their armoury was minutely analyzed as if a slide under a microscope. Archimandrite Vasileios of Iveron has warned of a similar danger to Orthodox of receiving back from Western scholars the texts of their Fathers in just such a way and ending up with a 'malignant growth or a fixation with antiquity' such as an archaeologist might have. This, he says, would fail to do justice to the 'ancients' themselves and would cause 'sickness' to Orthodox, because in Holy Tradition 'God is known unknowably, seen invisibly', not in a series of documents. 'The person is saved, the ancient beauty is restored ... each person sums up the whole ... All find their rhythm of life, and glorify God with their whole being ...'[21]

A specialist ecumenical language at the present day is likely to be a 'mere commodity, passively received, manufactured elsewhere'. To achieve true reconciliation between Anglican and Orthodox in the twenty-first century may therefore be too delicate a task for human endeavour, unless it is raised to the level of the Spirit groaning in a manner altogether beyond human words (Romans 8:22). Olivier Clément has said that 'the time of theology as speculative science has gone and the time of theology as prayer has come'.[22] If this is so then maybe we should revisit urgently the concept of the holy, i.e. that which is set apart and raised above the conventional forms of being into the realm of the Spirit. It is central to the Nonjuring Communion Office of 1718. At the beginning of its eucharistic prayer, it declared, 'holiness is thy nature and thy gift' and it proclaimed the object of the Incarnation to be 'to strengthen our nature, and renew thine image within us'. For that 'glorious end', it said, 'thine eternal word came down from heaven'. Elsewhere the service prayed that at the day of the general resurrection 'we, and all they who are of the mystical body of thy Son, may altogether be set on his right hand and hear that his most joyful voice. Come ye blessed of my Father, inherit the Kingdom prepared for you from the foundation of the world.'[23] Thus did the social and intellectually sidelined Nonjurors lay claim to words in their daily worship of which the natural mind knows nothing. Today too much of our ecumenism (and one might also add of our worship), says Archbishop Rowan Williams, is 'naturalistic' and static. It is menaced all the time from 'the outside' and anything it achieves looks strangely like death – the 'ultimate stable condition', the 'privacy of Satan'.[24] What is missing for authenticity is the power of the Spirit. Bishop Anders Nygren of Lund once complained that there were too many ecumenists in his day who were inclined to 'shake down the fruit before it has matured'. The desire to 'cut corners' is usually a sign of unquietness. If we concentrate on cutting out too much of a gut in an urgent desire to stop a cancer, we may be over-looking new metastases which have spread far beyond the original site. In the Lord's Work prayer in the Spirit is the sure antidote to that all too human disaster.

Perhaps the fault of all current ecumenism (and here the most isolationist among the Orthodox would heartily agree) is that living prayer has not kept pace with intellectual endeav-our and diplomatic engineering. Just a few Western Christian communities seem to have grasped this and sought to act on it. One could specify Taizé, the Evangelical Sisters of Mary, and the Benedictines of Chevetogne. The inspirer of Cheve-togne, Dom Lambert Beauduin, along with the Abbé Paul Couturier, advocated a spiritual ecumenism which sought convergence of traditions through an ever deeper penetration of worshippers into the heart of Christ within their own tradi-tions. Couturier believed in the need for *assainissement* – cleansing, decontamination – before true unity was achieved.[25] If we are Christian, we know that in the last analy-sis divisions among us are the poisoned fruit of sin, even though the immediate factors sustaining this or that division may be somewhat remote from personal sin. Sin, as St Basil the Great said, reduces humanity to mere particles struggling in competition and repelling each other. The only antidote is constancy in prayer and *metanoia*, an attitude, as one English ecumenist aptly put it, of standing or kneeling and not simply sitting or 'lounging forward'.[26] Olivier Clément thinks that 'historical Orthodoxy' can only 'receive and penetrate' 'spiri-tual Orthodoxy' (by which he presumably means the realm of

Divine Energy) by way of repentance, and Nikos Nissiotis, writing alongside Clément, argued for a 'purification of Tradition for the sake of a better continuity of Tradition'.[27]

What form then, should constancy in prayer for unity essentially take? Confession alone would lead to weakness, petition alone would be self-regarding. Intercession presents neither of those problems because in itself it is disinterested. We may find some help here from an unexpected source. Throughout his mature life, from his doctoral thesis on the communion of saints to his *Letters and Papers from Prison*, Dietrich Bonhoeffer showed a consistent awareness not only of the need to root all 'scientific' theology in corporate prayer (one remembers his disgust as a graduate student at finding that his professors saw no such need and his later conviction that 'God waits for sincere prayers and responsible actions') but more specifically of the importance of intercession. This he felt necessary for any dialogue with 'the Pilot of the world'.[28] For him theological thinking of necessity must always be a 'continued hearing [of] his voice'.[29] Bonhoeffer came to believe that God could be 'in the facts in just such a way that, through the indwelling in us of Christ who has overcome the world, he can cause us to stand fast by them.'[30] So the 'primary manner of God's indwelling in the facts and his ruling in history is *reconciliation*'.[31]

Bonhoeffer defines intercession as an essential moment in the self-realization of the Church, the 'last possible action . . ., the final human commitment'. It has the nature of 'endurance' and surrender of action to God, where we are able to do no more, where our commitment to action lives on in the form of intercession.[32] But this is no mere multiplicity of personal crises. For Bonhoeffer, while moral duty can never be taken away from the individual, it is not individuals but the 'collective person' who *in* the individuals, hears, repents, believes. The centre of action lies in this collective person, the communion of saints. The reality of the collective person is not to be thought of as separate from that of individual persons but 'as one of them'.[33] In *The Cost of Discipleship* Bonhoeffer says: 'there are no direct relationships, not even between soul and

soul. Christ stands between us, and we can only get into touch
with our neighbours [presumably he means *creatively*] through
him. That is why intercession is the most promising way to
reach our neighbours, and corporate prayer, offered in the
name of Christ, the purest form of fellowship'.[34] 'Even when
my hearing of the word is intermittent, that of the community
is still not so.'[35] The communion of saints (here and hereafter)
is therefore for Bonhoeffer a 'horizon' of personality.[36]
Participation in it is 'not so simply personal to myself as is the
colour of my eyes or the abilities of my intellect. It is given
to me and laid upon me as a constant claim, that I should
know myself and regard myself as in solidarity with the
collective person, because and in so far as I begin my being
in such solidarity'.[37] Essentially for Bonhoeffer the community of intercession is 'from God to God', i.e. consists in the
life of the Trinity and so cannot dissolve into the fate of the
many or the few.[38] God is patiently standing with us as
Church and waiting for us to do what he asks of us – in intercession.[39] It is not for the Church to declare all aspects of the
truth committed to it just when it wishes, but rather it must
maintain a 'reverent silence' in prayer, for it is not master
over its subject but is 'contained with it in history'.[40]

For Bonhoeffer, the primacy of intercession derives from
his conviction that there were two 'uniquely fundamental
doctrines' – The Two Natures and the 'Threefold Office' – of
prophet, priest and king. These represented the *'pleroma* of
God'.[41] In intercession we are united in intent with the
indwelling Christ as High Priest of the new covenant.

This could well be the only way to prepare for the outcome
prophesied by Derwas Chitty and preserve something of
historic unity between the Anglican and Orthodox traditions
for which many have sacrificed their ministry and endured
much pain. Bishop Sarapion of Thmuis, friend of St Antony
and scourge of the Manichaeans, knew that the Lord of Life
altered, changed and transformed his creatures, being alone
'incorruptible, unalterable and eternal' and that whatever he
changed was into the 'franchise (*empolitenomenoi*) of faith and
full knowledge of the truth . . .' 'We beseech thee to make us

living men. Give us a spirit of light, that we may know thee the true God and him thou didst send, even Jesus Christ.' Central to this experience had to be the Eucharist, the living sacrifice 'scattered on the top of the mountains' but 'gathered together' to become 'one' through the 'God of truth', the image of the 'holy and only Catholic Church'.[42] The Communion of Saints is central to the eucharistic reality, as may be seen in the way in which in the Clementine Liturgy Andrew, the brother of Peter, and James the son of Zebedee are vocalized as commanding the liturgical acts.[43] And the Communion of Saints is sustained by the angelic hosts, besought by the Primitive Church 'for the bringing to nought of the evil one and for the establishment of the Church'.[44]

But the power of intercession is not confined to the eucharistic *event* because the Church itself is a eucharistic *reality*. The Kelham Father David Jenks grasped this when he said that through the fellowship and power of intercession, liberally combined with thanksgiving, we are 'meant to enter into the joy of heaven'.[45] In the Clementine Liturgy worshippers were exhorted to commemorate the holy martyrs so that they might be 'counted worthy to be partakers of their conflicts' – a lifetime and not merely a ritual vocation.[46] What is the 'single fundamental intention' pulling everything in the bewildering life of the Church around itself 'as it were by a magnet', asked Hans Urs von Balthasar, 'unless it is the power of intercession?'[47] And that intercession must be, in order to have potency, 'in Christ' and his love. As Balthasar has said, love, the *semper magis*, should lead unambiguously to the unifying of different perspectives. There must be 'full human transparence to the Word, a holding ready of the heart, in order to find the pure harmony between word and response in the act of praise ...' Only thus can reality conform to the Pauline vision: 'justified in the Spirit, seen by the angels, proclaimed to the peoples, believed on in the world, exalted in glory'. (1 Timothy 3:16) Christ, says Balthasar, 'nowhere controls his own glorification' but he entrusts himself 'in what concerns his glorification in prayer to the Father, from whom the Spirit goes forth into the Church and world to accomplish conviction, vindication and glorification.'[48]

In this transaction, as Bonhoeffer and Dumitru Staniloae also noted, the Spirit is the mid point between persons fulfilling, in Christ, a longing for communion. He 'stirs us through our knowledge of life, turning all our experience Godwards.' We are not thus to be reduced to *abject* silence (this is not what Bonhoeffer meant) but rather empowered to a reticent activity beyond 'any capacity of our own working'. Glorification thus becomes, as Balthasar puts it, the correlative of truth.[49] That truth is essentially rooted in the Church as the Body of Christ and in the Church we must for ever contemplate it so that we grow ever more in desire to pray for the Church 'as the glory of God upon earth and as the witness of Christ's life to the world . . .' Such contemplation must reproduce in us, 'in however faint degree in most of us, the priestly life of the divine Victim', never in chance events but in the constant will of God. This will be the 'present illumination of the future, the fellowship now of heaven's denizens . . .'[50]

The unitive call is to the 'Angelic Life', a life in truth not confined to monasticism where it is usually invoked. At a very early date Egyptian Christians saw Gabriel and Uriel making a 'pillar of light' whereby they led the Hebrews into the Holy Land.[51] 'What is the assembling of the Church to learn, asked Hooker, 'but the receiving of Angels descending from above? What to pray, but the sending of Angels upward?' Hooker believed, with Orthodox Tradition, the angels 'unweariable and even insatiable in their longing to do by all means all manner good unto all the creatures of God, but especially unto the children of men . . .' He saw the common prayer of the Church, the prayer of intercession, as 'common unto men *with* Angels'.[52]

Derwas Chitty understood the saints in heaven to enjoy a special angelic privilege as unemotional (*apatheis*) sacraments whose life was not their own but Him, and through whom 'something more of the central secret of His Kingdom' is expressed. That secret is the power of the Resurrection resting upon them. Church unity therefore, thought Chitty, depended not on identity of moral teaching or on historical origins, or on sacramental forms or on theological language or on an 'abstract theory of holiness' but on the 'actual Holiness of God which is the Communion of Saints.'[53] As shares in that Communion, says Balthasar, our fervent intercession can 'ravel' us back from our discontinuous 'inner circles' and reunite us through God's *debarim* (word-deeds) 'as they fall vertically and unforeseen into the horizontal existence in time ...'[54]

In the midst of the First World War carnage, David Jenks warned of a tendency in the English clergy not to commend such exalted aims in prayer 'lest we should discourage some who are not strong'. It was an understandable concern on their part, for they knew their people. But in this way, thought Jenks, 'the power of the Church is not felt in the land' because 'the supernatural power of the collective life of the Church' is not understood.[55] The Ethiopian *Church Order* placed 'integrity of heart' at the centre of worship, or perhaps rather integrity of *hearts*.[56] Maisie Ward in her remarkable and iconic book *Receive the Joyfulness of your Glory*, reminds us that God's call to us to share his eternal glory is absolutely continuous, so that we can never 'escape the demandingness of this summons' and that what he expects of us is simply a perpetual readiness to 'receive all from Him so that we may offer back to Him this *all* in order that all flesh together may see the glory of God ...' Otherwise, she says, we 'starve in the midst of plenty.' 'The vision of God's glory cometh not by human effort' but neither can it be divorced from human silence, tribulation or endurance 'for the word of God and for the testimony of Jesus Christ'. Unfortunately, she adds, the very specialized nature of the information which we have today about material things has made the task of giving glory and attaining wholeness more difficult for us. The more knowledge we have, so also the more pulverized and depersonalized it is. We enter into an 'abyss of loneliness' and acquire a 'universal nervousness' which is in danger of becoming a corporate incapacity such as the clergy of the First World War suspected to be true of their people. Miss Ward comes close here to the intuition of Archbishop Williams already quoted. Paradoxically, she says, the disease of being incapable of prayer can only be cured by prayer, pre-eminently the prayer and absolution of penitence. Central to her book is the experience of the Transfiguration. From this she concludes that 'until we begin to move mountains' we are spiritually dead and cannot receive glory. We must hold up our cupped hands, she says, like St John in Sister Joanna Reitlinger's ikon of the Transfiguration, 'beggarwise to Glory ...' The smallness of those hands may then receive God's infinity 'to overflowing on the world's behalf ...'[57]

What, then, is needed for the restoration of organic unity is not schemes and devices, even less endless theological reports, but an 'ecumenism of litany' – 'for the peace of the whole world, for the good estate of the holy churches of God, and for the union of all'. We would do well to remind ourselves of the emphasis in the Liturgy of St James, taken up by those Nonjurors who adopted it, on boldness to enter the holy place – boldness and compunction of heart, knowing that the Father has already glorified our places of worship with the Theophany of His Christ and the visitation of His Spirit and that he has said 'be ye holy as I am holy', so that we may proceed 'from glory to glory advancing'.[58]

In this present context the litany of an early British monk, Angus the Culdee, springs to mind as an example. It throws a vivid light on the 'Dark Ages' with shafts of light not only from Byzantium but also from that 'stygian Coptic darkness' which John Covel did not even wish to face. The litany is remarkably similar indeed to one in the Coptic Raising of Incense:[59]

> The kinsfolk I have encountered; close is our friendship
> after reckoning their feasts, I will number their troops.
> The troops of heaven's archangels, around Michael, noble
> and holy ...
> The troop of ancestors around Noah, over ranges of main-
> seas ...
> The troops of Apostles round Peter, with the disciples of
> Jesus ...

The troops of holy bishops of Rome, round Peter the splen-
did ...
The bishops of Jerusalem with James of the dignities ...
The bishops of Alexandria with Mark, red-fiery and royal
...
The monks round Antony, whose courses are mysterious
...
The troops of noble saints of Erin, with Patrick who is
highest ...
Columcille, who sets up with the troops of the saints of
Alba ...
Every saint who has been, is and shall be, up to Doom ...

Against the incitement of the world – for great is its might
...
I appeal by every offering wherewith thy Body
Has been offered up in showers
below the clouds upon the holy altars.

There is something of this in the *Preces Privatae* of Lancelot
Andrewes and in the Nonjuring devotions of Thomas Deacon
and William Cartwright. An ecumenism of litany – this,
perhaps, is the only way left open to us to gather together the
fragments of devotion which fired the Caroline divines to
'look to the East' and apply them to the present hopeful state
of Orthodoxy in the twenty-first century.[60]

Notes

1. Nicholas Armstrong, *Sermons on Various Subjects, Preached in
   Different Congregations of the Church in England and Ireland*
   (2nd series, London, 1879), pp. 85ff; Thomas Dowglass, *The
   Book of Job, An Allegorical History of the Christian Church*
   (London, 1853), p. 17. Cf. within the same tradition, however,
   the more censorious comments of J. T. A. Bohm, *Lights and
   Shadows in the Present Condition of the Church* (3rd English
   edn., Glasgow and London, 1887), p. 35 and [W. J. Bramley
   Moore], *The Church's Forgotten Hope*, 3rd edition, Glasgow
   and London, 1905, p. 205.

2. William Laud, *Works* (Library of Anglo-Catholic Theology, 6th edn., Oxford, 1849), II, xv; Herbert Thorndike, *Works* (LACT, Oxford, 1844), I, I, 591; Cf. quotations from the Fathers in an article by Constantine Scoutaris in *Sobornost*, Ser. 2, no. 2 (Winter 1975), 115; *Tsurkoven Vestnik* for 30 March 1989; articles by Charles B. Ashanin in *The Logos*, passim, 1969–1973, including 'Orthodox Non-Persons. A Manifesto' (V, 1972). Cf. Philippou, op. cit., p. 138. For the Melkite schism, see Philip A. Khairallah, 'Crusades, Missionaries and Printing Presses', *Eastern Churches Journal*, 1:2 (1994), 112–20. Those Arabs who stayed under Greek authority did not acquire an Arab Patriarch until 1899.
3. Miodrag Pavlovic, *The Slavs Beneath Parnassus*, tr. Bernard Johnson (London and Saint Paul, 1985), p. 52.
4. Philippou, op. cit., pp. 39, 106–7.
5. Emmanuel Clapsis, *Orthodoxy in Conversation, Orthodox Ecumenical Engagement* (Geneva and Brookline Mass., 2000), pp. 31, 33; John Zizioulas, 'Eschatology and History' in Thomas Wieser (ed.), *Whither Ecumenism?* (Geneva, 1986), p. 68; Stephen Sykes, 'The Grammar of Narration and Making Sense of Life', *Anglican Theological Review*, LXVII (1985), 124, 135.
6. Philippou, op. cit., pp. 88–89, 144–7.
7. Gerry Russo, 'Rahner and Palamas: A Unity of Grace', *St Vladimir's Theological Quarterly*, 32 (2) (1988), 157.
8. Philippou, op. cit., pp. 39, 53.
9. Cf. Bishop Hierotheos of Nafpaktos, *Orthodox Spirituality: a brief introduction* (Levadia, 1992, English tr. 1994), pp. 26–30, passim. Bishop Hierotheos is a noted Palamist. For him Palamas has reinvested the notion of Divine Glory with vibrant meaning. He criticizes western scholastic philosophy for being able to conceive the degradation of the intellect only, not that of the soul.
10. Nikos Nissiotis in Philippou, op. cit., pp. 60–65; Sherrard in ibid., pp. 53, 56–57; Yannaras in ibid., p. 133.
11. Cf. a perceptive comment by Barry Spurr in *The Word in the Desert. Anglican and Roman Catholic Reactions to Liturgical Reform* (Cambridge, 1995), pp. 87–104, passim.
12. Ibid., pp. 93–94, 103–4.
13. Henry McAdoo, *The Eucharistic Theology of Jeremy Taylor Today*, op. cit., pp. 178–9, 183–5, 188.
14. Covel, *Preface*, pp. xiii–xiv. For a late flowering of the Taylor outlook, see William Law, *Treatise on Christian Perfection*, in *The Works of William Law*, ed. G. B. Moreton (London, 1892–3); Cf. J. H. F. New, *Anglican and Puritan. The Basis of*

their Opposition (London, 1964), p. 100.

15. Cf. Rowan Strong, *Alexander Forbes of Brechin*, op. cit., pp. 119–20. Bishop Kenneth Stevenson has reassessed the so-called virtualist concept of the eucharist presence on which it was said that this spirituality rested and has found it fundamentally Orthodox. See his *Covenant of Grace Renewed. A Vision of the Eucharist in the Seventeenth Century*, op. cit. See Bishop Rowell's introduction to Geoffrey Rowell, Rowan Williams and Kenneth Stevenson (eds), *Love's Redeeming Work. The Anglican Quest for Holiness* (Oxford, 2000) in *Church Times*, no. 7233 (5 October 2001), p. 17.

16. Derwas Chitty, *Orthodoxy and the Conversion of England* (reprinted by the Anglo-Orthodox Society, Colchester, 1990), p. 9. See also his 'The Communion of Saints' in W. H. Frere (ed.), *The Church of God. An Anglo-Russian Symposium* (London, 1934), p. 172.

17. Bishop Kallistos of Diokleia has noted that in the twentieth-century revival of monastic life on Mount Athos there has been a peculiar intensity of stillness and watchfulness – of *hesychia* and *nepsis*. He has described it from personal experience as a 'living silence'. See his foreword to Archimandrite Vasileios Gondikakis, *Hymn of Entrance. Liturgical Life in the Orthodox Church* (Crestwood, NY, 1984), p. 8. Ibid., pp. 88–89. Cf. Bishop Kallistos, 'Primacy, Collegiality and the People', in Philippou, op. cit., p. 129; also Philippou, p. 129.

18. Robert Jacobson in *The Eastern Churches Journal*, (Summer 1994), pp. 88–89, 93, 96–97, 99.

19. Velimirovic to Bell, 24 November 1921, cited in Muriel Heppell, *George Bell and Nikolai Velimirovic. The Story of a Friendship* (Birmingham, 2001), p. 22.

20. Methodios Fouyas, *Orthodoxy, Roman Catholicism and Anglicanism* (London, 1957), pp. 242–4; Rowan Williams, 'What is Catholic Orthodoxy?' in Kenneth Leech and Rowan Williams (eds), *Essays Catholic and Radical* (London, 1983), pp. 12–13; see also John Brownlie, *Hymns of the Russian Church* (London, 1920), p. vii.

21. Vasileios Gondikakis, *What is Unique about Orthodox Culture?* (Montreal, 2001), pp. 28, 33, 62.

22. Cf. Philippou, op. cit., p. 103; Rowan Williams, *The Truce of God* (London, 1983), p. 56.

23. John Dowden, *A Historical Account of the Scottish Communion Office*, op. cit., pp. 311–14.

24. Rowan Williams, op. cit.

25. Cf. Geoffrey Curtis, CR, *Paul Couturier and Unity in Christ* (London, 1964), p. 83 and passim.

238   *Anglicans and Orthodox*

26. Clement Rogers, *A Church Genuinely Catholic* (London, 1940), p. 109.
27. Clément in Philippou, op. cit., p. 101; Nissiotis, 'Our History: A Limitation or Creative Power?' in Philippou, pp. 59–72, passim.
28. Heinrich Ott, *Reality and Faith. The Theological Legacy of Dietrich Bonhoeffer* (London, 1971), p. 295.
29. Ibid., p. 448.
30. Ibid., p. 442.
31. Ibid., p. 306.
32. Ibid., p. 296. Cf. *Letters and Papers from Prison* (3rd English edition, London, 1969), p. 118.
33. Ibid., p. 209.
34. Bonhoeffer, *The Cost of Discipleship* (6th English edition, London, 1959), pp. 87ff.
35. Ott, op. cit., p. 228.
36. Ibid., pp. 244–5.
37. Ibid., p. 210.
38. Bonhoeffer, *Sanctorum Communio* (1930), cited by Ott, p. 206.
39. Ott, ibid., p. 216.
40. Ibid., p. 239.
41. Ibid., p. 449.
42. John Wordsworth (ed.), *Bishop Saraphion's Prayer Book* (2nd edition, London, 1923), pp. 61, 62–63, 65, 77, 79, 84,
43. R. H. Cresswell (ed.), *The Liturgy of the Eighth Book of the 'Apostolic Constitutions' Commonly Called the Clementine Liturgy* (2nd edition, London, 1924), pp. 38, 52.
44. Wordsworth, *Sarapion*, op. cit., p. 61.
45. David Jenks SSM, *A Study of Intercession* (London, 1917), p. 98.
46. Cresswell, op. cit., p. 68.
47. Hans Urs von Balthasar, *The Glory of the Lord. A Theological Aesthetics. Volume VII. Theology: The New Covenant* (Edinburgh, 1989), pp. 9, 100–1, 262. Cf. Henri de Lubac, SJ, *L'Eglise* (2nd German edition of 1968, cited by Balthasar, pp. 102–3).
48. Dumitru Staniloae, *Theology and the Church* (Crestwood, NY, 1980), pp. 62–63.
49. Balthasar, op. cit., p. 311, citing Heinrich Schleier in *Festschrist fur Romano Guardini* (1965).
50. Jenks, op. cit., pp. 21, 68, 104.
51. Cf. David Frankfurter, *Elijah in Upper Egypt. The Apocalypse of Elijah and Early Egyptian Christianity* (Minneapolis, 1992), p. 322.

52. Cited by A. M. Allchin in *A Taste of Liberty* (Oxford, 1982), p. 20.
53. Chitty in W. H. Frere, op. cit., pp. 160, 167–8.
54. Balthasar, op. cit., pp. 163–4.
55. Jenks, op. cit., p. viii.
56. Wordsworth, *Sarapion*, op. cit., p. 51.
57. Maisie Ward, *Receive the Joyfulness of Your Glory* (London, 1952), pp. 13, 15–16, 55, 57, 62, 68, 68, 83, 88, 95, 97, 100–1.
58. The translation used here is that of John Mason Neale and R. F. Littledale (2nd edition, London, 1869), adapted and corrected for modern worship in the Celtic Orthodox Church.
59. Whitley Stokes (ed.), *The Martyrology of Oengus the Culdee* (London, 1905), pp. 274–7. The litany in the Coptic Raising of Incense runs:

> Hail to the Church, the house of angels ...
> Hail to thee, O Mary, the Good Dove ...
> Hail to Michael the Archangel, hail to Gabriel
> who made the proclamation to Mary ...
> Hail to the great John the Forerunner, ...
> Hail to the Evangelist, hail to the Apostle Mark,
> The beholder of the Divine ...
> Hail to Stephen the first martyr ...
> Hail to the crusader, my master Saint George ...

60. Invitation of the Deacon in the Coptic Liturgy of St Basil.

INDEX

Reformation Church of England had adopted an Eastern Liturgy 167, 194; hoped for canonical and liturgical concessions in the event of union 173; affirmed that the prayers of the living were serviceable to the dead 175

Canopius, Nathaniel, Archbishop of Smyrna
studied at Balliol College, Oxford, introduced coffee-drinking to England, suffered at the hands of the Puritans 15

Carroll, Thomas
Roman Catholic assessment of Jeremy Taylor's patristic orthodoxy 28

Cartwright, William
his Nonjuror (qv) Offices charismatic in tone 168–9

Charles I, King of England and Scotland
injunction requiring the universities to teach the Fathers 17; compared to the martyred Cyril Lucaris 70, 77

Cheke, John, humanist lay theologian
lectured at Cambridge on Chrysostom and Maximus the Confessor 10

Chemnitz, Martin
assertion that the Greeks dissented from transubstantiation at the Council of Florence questioned by Dodwell (qv) 92

Cheney, Richard, Bishop of Gloucester
sustained debate with Puritans by placing Reformers in the context of Holy Tradition xvi

Child, William, Caroline composer
established high standard of music in Restoration Church 81

Chishull, Edmund, Chaplain at Aleppo
saw Cappadocian period as Church's 'meridian light' 37; clashed with Dodwell (qv) over the unbaptised soul's mortality 159; ambivalent to Nonjurors' taking oath to William and Mary but grieved that good men were driven out 166; saw socinianism as 'contageous' 199; in controversy with Whiston on Fathers and Councils 207

Chitty, Derwas
saw Orthodoxy as capable of giving Anglicanism the kiss of life 223; saw angels as sacraments of divine life, forming the Church as the Communion of Saints and conveying secret of the Kingdom 232

'Church in Danger' hysteria in early 18th century
had some foundation 209–10

Chryanthos, Patriarch of Jerusalem
signed reply to Nonjurors' letter 174

Clark, J. C. D.
on 18th-century Church of England 203–4, 211

Claude, Jean, Huguenot minister of Charenton
challenged the authenticity of Greek eucharistic testimonials collected through Nointel (qv) 113; regarded by Covel (qv) as mistaken in assuming Greek clergy learned in eucharistic controversy 137

Clement IX, Pope
in collusion with French to subvert Greek Church 115

Clément, Olivier
on actualisation of the Word in the Church through the Spirit,

254 *Anglicans and Orthodox*